RAIMUNDO PANIKKAR

A Pilgrim Across Worlds

Edited by

Kapila Vatsyayan

Côme Carpentier de Gourdon

NIYOGI BOOKS

Published in association with

INDIA INTERNATIONAL CENTRE

Published by
NIYOGI BOOKS
D-78, Okhla Industrial Area, Phase-I
New Delhi-110 020, INDIA
Tel: 91-11-26816301, 49327000
Fax: 91-11-26810483, 26813830
email: niyogibooks@gmail.com
website: www.niyogibooksindia.com

Editor: P.K. Jayanthan
Layout Design: Ganga Rai
Cover Design: Shashi Bhushan Prasad

ISBN: 978-93-85285-39-4

Publication: 2016

Printed at: Niyogi Offset Pvt. Ltd., New Delhi, India

Contents

Preface

Kapila Vatsyayan

Raimundo Panikkar was an extraordinary person—a philosopher, a theologian, and a scholar of comparative religions. He lived in India for many years. He taught at several universities in Europe and the USA. He explored the many dimensions of dialogue at the level of philosophical and religious discourse. More than that, he reflected deeply on the present predicament of humankind. He left behind vast literature spanning many decades and published in many languages.

This volume comprises the contributions by Raimundo Panikkar's contemporaries and some, I would say, his disciples and pupils, besides Madame Milena Carrara Pavan, who has worked tirelessly to compile his bibliography. Bettina Bạeumer has written an introduction to the volume. She has with great sensitivity spoken about the life of Raimundo Panikkar, specially in Varanasi, where she collaborated with him in the preparation of the Anthology *Mantramanjari: The Vedic Experience*. Her narration of Panikkar's journey from Roman Catholicism to delving into primary Vedic sources is as faithful as it is illuminating. Pertinently, Bauemer has commented on the contributions made by the participants at the seminar ranging from Anand Amaladass, Maciej Bielawski, Fred Dallmayr, George Gispert-Sauch, Grevel Lindop, Clemens Mendonca, Joseph Prabhu, Oscar Punjol, Francis d'Sa, and others. There is little that

I need to add to her introduction. The seminar was organised by the Asia Project, India International Centre, Instituto Cervantes, New Delhi, and the Kapur Surya Foundation.

Bettina Baeumer's introduction refers to two remarkable presentations made by Raimundo Panikkar, one in a major international seminar on The Concepts of Space, and the other in a seminar on The Concepts of Time. Also at a very different level Raimundo Panikkar had contributed an article for a special volume of World Affairs on 'Eternal India'. This article has also been included in this volume. While the essays on the Concepts of Space and Time deal with primary categories, the article 'The Dharma of India' focuses attention on the existential reality of India. Since these essays are perhaps not so well known internationally, it was considered appropriate to include them here.

Way back in 1984 an international seminar on The Concepts of Space was organised by the Indira Gandhi National Centre for the Arts in New Delhi. The participants ranged from scientists, philosophers, men of religion, archaeologists, anthropologists, art historians, sculptors, and artists. They came from all parts of the world—from far off Caribbean, Nigeria, Indonesia, Australia, Mexico, Canada, and USA; and closer from the USSR, France, Germany, Hungary, Poland, Spain, Czechoslovakia, and Italy, and still closer from Nepal, Sri Lanka, Thailand, and so on. Dr D.S. Kothari, who inaugurated the seminar, gave a historical view of the developments in modern science, specially the theory of relativity and the principles of waves and quantum mechanics, and observed that the philosophy of modern physics had a special relationship to Upanishadic and Buddhist thoughts. Dr Raja Ramanna drew attention to the division of all knowledge in the categories of *Citta, Acitta,* and *Isvara* and went on to identify some inconsistencies.

Thereafter Raimundo Panikkar, with an incomparable intensity, spoke about the concepts of space. He said that for all traditions, space was a fundamental symbol. 'The psychological experience of space origin probably rose with the awareness of external distance. Inner space and Outer space are two faces of one and the same space.' Quoting a vast number of primary sources of many philosophic traditions, he asserted:

'(1) it is characteristic of modern Western culture to have reduced space to a physical extension; (2) there is a primordial and universal experience of space which is more holistic and circumscribed to the Outer space, but of which Inner and Outer are aspects.' The presentation electrified the audience. Right through the seminar there were references to what Raimundo Panikkar had said.

A couple of years later a complementary international conference was held on The Concepts of Time. Once again this was a gathering of scientists, philosophers, poets, architects, sculptors, and others. Professor J.M. Malville, whose book *Time and Eternal Change* was released on the occasion, highlighted the fact that our varied experiences of time could be described in terms of arrows, cosmological, thermodynamics, biological, cultural, sociological, historical, spiritual memory and knowledge. Raimundo Panikkar raised fundamental questions on the concept and power of time from the viewpoint of a thinker and philosopher. In the earlier seminar on space, Raimundo Panikkar had asserted that there was 'no Outer without Inner space.' Here he asserted equally emphatically that the 'experience of time is intrinsically connected with the awareness of the life and of reality. It is pervious to any epistemological split between subject and object. … there is no possible phenomenology of time because its awareness cannot be encompassed in one single act of consciousness. Consciousness itself is temporal.' Panikkar's paper takes us through the journey of the introduction of calendar and chronological time, the quantitative and qualitative dimensions to time as the very revelation of the structure of reality and thus of our Being. He reminded, 'But reality is not exhausted in time alone. And we moderns can only with difficulty accept a non-dualistic relation with an inseparable and yet distinct dimension of reality: Time and Timelessness.'

For me, as the organiser of both the conferences, it was an experience to hear him with the intensity which he alone could bring to his intellectual reflections.

At another level, Raimundo Panikkar contributed an article for the 'Eternal India' issue. He asks whether there is 'a basic incompatibility between the *kosmology* of traditional India (including all *dharmas* which have flourished in the subcontinent) and the *kosmology* underlying technological civilisation.'And he cautions that 'modern techno-science is the Trojan horse which will destroy those cultures that uncritically introduce "modernity" into their midst.'

In the Epilogue to the volume, I had drawn attention to Raimundo Panikkar's concerns about the existential reality of India. This is a far cry, ranging from Cartesian idealism to a more holistic view of life known to India, but where India stands at a crossroads.

Finally, I cannot but help the temptation, rather an urge, to share three personal experiences, which have a bearing on the nature of communication with Raimundo Panikkar.

The first is when he was still in the robes of a Roman Catholic priest. It was winter. I was in Madras (now Chennai) with a Romanian dance ensemble. In the dead of night came 'knock, knock, knock'. And what do I find? Two priests. One a Roman Catholic priest, Raimundo Panikkar, and the other a priest of the Greek Orthodox Church, Father Andrei Scrima. Raimundo Panikkar in his typical style said, 'We have to meet Paramacharya (Sankaracharya of Kanchi Mutt).' I said, 'How do we meet Paramacharya? He is out on tour.' I had no direct contact with him. But I could, even at this late stage, bother Dr V. Raghavan. And I did just that. We travelled miles that night covering typical streets in the outskirts of Chennai (where grains are spread out on the road) where Paramacharya was giving a discourse under a huge pandal. A message was sent to him. He came out and sat on a hay-stack, while Panikkar and Scrima sat below. This was indeed a reversal of roles. I remember the many icons I have seen of Christ giving discourse. This time it was Paramacharya who was giving the discourse to two priests from Rome and Greece. What transpired does not matter. What was important was that this scene has left an indelible mark in my mind. Apart from this, what is important is that Raimundo Panikkar's quest for knowing religion and philosophy at the deepest and the purest was so intense that no matter whatever the opportunity, he never missed it. I thought that this narration would be of relevance in this volume, because it speaks of the nature of Raimundo Panikkar's quest.

The other memory is at another level. I had gone to Switzerland to attend an international seminar on The Dialogue of Religions under the auspices of Global Dialogue, where the participants included Raimundo Panikkar, Maulana Wahiduddin Khan, Samdhong Rinpoche, and Grevel Lindop. I cannot recall the weighty discussions on these dialogues of religions and civilisations, but most vividly recall a trip on a ropeway with Lindop and Panikkar. As we ascended, our conversation transcended the earthly to reach the spiritual. We shared the experience, yet we were making our own individual journeys. Panikkar reflected on life. The going up and coming down the ropeway was for him the levels of life in its ascension and descent. For Lindop it was poetry and painting. For me it was re-living the experience of the mountains, of the Himalayas.

The last meeting in Tavertet in Catalonia, where Raimundo Panikkar had settled, was most precious. We went for a long walk along the cliff. It appeared as if the Red Canyon of the USA has been turned upside down: the caverns below spoke of the depth of life as much as the travel by the ropeway reminded one of the callings of the mountains, of the heights above. Later, we sat at his dining table in the background of his huge library. We talked softly and gently. Few words were exchanged but there was a great communication in silence. Now, of course, Panikkar was no longer a Roman priest, nor a Hindu, nor a Buddhist. He had once talked about himself, 'I started as a Christian, I discovered I was a Hindu and returned a Buddhist, without ever having ceased to be a Christian.' Now Panikkar was a hermit, a hermit transcending all religious boundaries. In fact, the very last meeting was in his little room, where he had lit an incense stick. He sat down cross-legged, spoke a few verses. And then sat in silence. This was his meditation, but it was also a *satsang*. He told me that he held this daily or weekly meeting where people came in and sat silently and left as silently.

Raimundo Panikkar had travelled, travelled always. After having experienced the flint-like sharpness of the intellect and breadth of his ecumenical concerns and extensive communication skills, he says in the remarkable book *A Dwelling Place for Wisdom*:

> The oft-decried homelessness of the modern person results from the fact that scientific cosmology is not able to offer the person a human dwelling place. The scientific world is no dwelling place.… The person is homeless because the scientific worldview has lost the human dimension, and even more so because this worldview's dwelling place has not been erected by wisdom but by an extrapolating calculation.… Hence, the first dimension of a dwelling place is the world as our homeland. The world is a dwelling place for all—the homeless, the poor, the people. In a word the primary dwelling place of wisdom is our universe, or world, and still more concrete, our Mother Earth.

Understandably, he wrote in his last letter, 'It is now perhaps time to go.'

Introduction

Bettina Baeumer

It is time that the genius of Raimon (or Raimundo) Panikkar is rediscovered in India. Papers collected in this volume are the outcome of a seminar organised in his memory. They intend to bring him and his ideas back to his fatherland. After retiring from professorship in Santa Barbara, California, Panikkar chose to settle down in Spain, or rather Catalunya. This is the reason why he became more present, not only in Spain, but also in Italy and in other European countries. But leaving alone this biographical-historical circumstance, Panikkar's thought is essential and relevant in today's India. This publication is the first attempt to reflect on his contribution, with the hope that it will not remain isolated, but lead to a living dialogue on the themes contained in this volume.

In our multicultural world Panikkar is a bridge and a prophet. A bridge between cultures, between tradition and modernity, between religions, and between disciplines. A prophet, because long before intercultural and inter-religious dialogue became catch-words he elaborated the philosophical and practical bases which are still valid today. In his role as a bridge he defended Indian thought in a European context, and Western thought in an Indian context. Sometimes his was a lonely voice. For example, in philosophical and theological seminars in Europe at the highest level, he was the only Indian who asserted that India had a philosophy! His greatness was to pass through these walls of misunderstanding with the conviction that he had to pave the way for a real dialogue. He was the pioneer of preparing and living such a dialogue at all levels. Some of his most fundamental insights and concepts were the result of such a dialogue—his holistic vision, his advaitic or a-dualistic understanding, and his cosmotheandric insight. These concepts and ideas emerged from specific traditions. But he enlarged their scope so that they could encompass many traditions. One example is the expansion of the Christian concept of the trinity to a universal trinitarian paradigm. It was his intense work on the Vedas that kindled his vision of the relationship of Cosmos, Man, and the Divine—the cosmotheandric (or the anthropocosmic) insight, which again he applied to different cultures and religions.

His study of Buddhism convinced him that the theory of *pratityasamutpada*, or the interconnectedness of all things by dependent origination, has a universal validity, and can be 'homologised' with the Kashmir Saivism concept of *sarvam sarvatmakam,* 'all is connected with the totality', 'everything consists of everything else', 'all is in all', and so on. From these different traditions arose his holistic vision which encompasses several traditions, without negating differences.

Panikkar repeatedly stressed that his work is the result of his life and experience at the crossroads of cultures and religions.

I have been a witness to the development of his thought, having been associated with him as a pupil and collaborator right from 1961 practically till the end. Our most intense collaboration was on the Vedas, in preparation of the Anthology *Mantramanjari: The Vedic Experience*. I could closely observe his style of working. He would be inspired by a text of the Vedas, go deep into its meaning, and transform his inspiration into an introduction, in conformity with the translation which was a collective effort. His inspiration was contagious. We practically lived in the Vedic atmosphere. Out of that immersion arose insights of a more universal nature, the most important being the cosmotheandric vision.

Panikkar could create a bridge also between mysticism and the practical implications of his experience and thought which are very relevant in the present world—the questions of peace, human rights, ecology, all of which cannot be solved without an intercultural and inter-religious approach. The contribution on his concept of human rights in this volume is especially relevant as an example for the implications of such a dialogue.

The authors of this collection of essays reflect on some of the many facets of Panikkar's multi-disciplinary *oeuvre*. Milena Carrara introduces us to *Opera Omnia*, his complete works, which she has edited and published in 12 volumes arranged by topic as per the author's own autobiographical description of his lifelong inquiry. She concludes that his writings are like the proverbial finger that points us to the invisible goal of all spiritual journeys, the mystical, inaccessible Mount Kailash.

While Grevel Lindop movingly recollects his impressions of the hermit of Tavertet's scholarly, poetic and monastic personality, Maciej Bielawski attempts to pierce the mystery of his guiding spirit through his life story and literary output. Oscar Pujol evokes the intercultural adventure on which Panikkar embarked almost from the day of his birth as an Indo–Spanish *mestizo*, so to speak. He was seeking 'full communion with reality' by weaving a very Indian synthesis between East and West that stops short of syncretism or eclecticism but exposes the modern concern with historical truth as another materialist obsession that India shunned through most of her past.

Bettina Baeumer in her paper tries to sum up Panikkar's original critique of 'modern man' as a Western creation of a materialistic, technological (and in his words, *technocratic*) civilisation which needs to be tempered by returning to a 'pre-rational world' fed on symbol, ritual, and prayer. George Gispert-Sauch highlights the deeper unity hidden within the complex personality of the scientist, philosopher and theologian he was. He defines him as a pioneer of a new era, a 'missionary', although not in the conventional sense since he strove not to change anybody's outer religion but rather to help all discover the truth which leads us to the absolute Being by liberating or 'absolving' us from our limitations. The Spanish-born long-time resident of Varanasi personified *samanvaya,* the 'being together', which can be compared to a polyphony and which Côme Carpentier relates to the quest for 'the one that binds the many together' in the European tradition of Perennial Philosophy going back to the late Middle Age.

Exploring his 'revisioning of reality' Francis d'Sa points out that Panikkar sought to retrieve religions from their culturally determined strictures by finding harmony in their *mythos*, over and beyond their *logos*. He underlines that in that view every creed is incomparable and unique though it is interconnected with all others, through what he called *ecosophy*, the 'wisdom of the earth' and through the third and highest dimension of every religious tradition. Clemens Mendonca clarifies what symbols meant for him and how they are fundamental for trans-religious education since they alone can express the mystery of reality and give us an awareness deeper than reason opening us up to the understanding of the ontological reality. As universal symbols that transcend specific faiths, he indicated three—breath, bread, and *dharma* or the 'source', the divine law that keeps all things together. Anand Amaladass also discusses this fundamental notion when he refers to the Vedic *rtatattva*, the rhythm of being, to which Panikkar dedicated one of his most important writings. It alludes to the 'radical relativity of all that exists' and rests on a reality defined as a non-dualistic polarity which implies on everyone's part a 'mystical' tolerance rooted in the realisation of radical interdependence between all things.

Panikkar saw such an awareness not as the expression of a merely rational decision but rather as the consequence of an experience. It was the guiding principle to his approach to inter-religious dialogue, discussed by Joseph Prabhu, who sees him as a mediator between Spinoza's monism and Sankara's apophatism. There is no doubt that the precondition to a peaceful and fecund encounter between religious thinkers and leaders is to rise above egos in order to achieve a dialogical, and not merely dialectical, dialogue. To convert, argues Panikkar, is to be converted and inter-religious exchange implies an intra-religious, internal debate and reflection for contemplation as he said, is 'the very breath of life'.

In the context of the current and inevitable meeting between religions and civilisations, the issue and the concept of human rights is salient. Fred

Dallmayr analyses the contribution of the great Indo-Spanish philosopher to this vexed question. Although he defined the very notion of rights as a feature of a modern ego-centered society based on impersonal law and free contracts between individuals, as opposed to the traditional view of a cosmic web in which each person is only a knot connected to all others in the greater whole, Panikkar saw that in a mechanised, hyper-organised market world there is a need for rights to be protected but he highlighted the requirement for 'rightness' or 'rightfulness' if collective and individual rights are to be meaningfully negotiated and respected. 'Humane rights', which imply duties, may thus be a more apt definition.

What Panikkar pleads for is a radical transformation of Man and of society. If his ideas and his approach are taken seriously, many issues plaguing today's world, and India in particular, could be solved. As an appendix we have added a rare fictional story entitled 'The Tragedy of the Grand Inquisitor' first published in 2002 in the *Temenos* journal.

It is hoped that the contributions to this volume will serve as challenges and inspiration for the task ahead, that of bridging cultures and religions, as well as tradition and modernity.

Modernity and Tradition in Panikkar's Thought

Bettina Baeumer

Let me start with a powerful text of Panikkar describing the human condition today.

> Once "there was" a man. Different from "primitive" man, this man had consciously lived for millennia. He had survived the *avataras* of history, and he had all the riches of the world at his disposal, yet it seemed that he had no hope. He could not stand any longer to turn his gaze upwards. He remembered the scant success of any type of "progress" and the failure of all the humanisms in trying to liberate humans from their inhumanity. Wars, revolutions and violence had disturbed him, and they solved nothing. All the sophisticated inventions of the human genius had since long become boring and monotonous. And all the lofty conquests of the human spirit had not succeeded in satisfying even the most elementary of human needs. And while the man was "educated" and well-fed, millions died of hunger, victims of injustice. The man was unsettled and unhappy, he was shaken, and he doubted whether the future would be bearable. He found the present intolerable, and he knew that his past was lost for him beyond recovery. Besides, he was aware that he could not return to the past, and even if he could, he knew well that he would

> not have liked to remain there. He had constructed a whole vision of the world, a world-view that some would call an ideology. He had reflected on everything: he thought of all things that could be imagined and he discovered the powerlessness of reason alongside its justification. He could prove the existence of God, and equally could disprove every one of these "proofs"; he could discover life as full of meaning, but he could equally argue to prove its meaninglessness. He could conceive to solve all his problems with the help of technology and at the same time he could show that this very technology was the greatest scourge that had ever befallen human existence. He began to suspect that what had been called "freedom" and "democracy" was nothing but an expression of human despair to find the truth. His thoughts began to waver. He felt the fear which would overtake him while doing one thing or another; it was enough never to think about the ultimate consequences of anything. Thus he was exhausted. He went in search of an icon (a divine image); he began to sing and to dance, to gesticulate, and even something similar to a prayer, inarticulate, arose from his being. Soon he fell asleep, or he died, or he was destroyed by forces beyond his control. Nobody noticed his disappearance. And yet: something had happened. (*Culto* in *Opera Omnia*, V. IX.1: 355–56)

This is a powerful metaphor, and more than a metaphor, of the predicament of modern man conscious of the limitations of his reason, and of so-called technological progress. In the face of the hopelessness and meaninglessness of the human situation, the way to overcome the contradictions is a return to the pre-rational world of symbol and ritual, mantra and prayer, connecting the 'man' to another dimension that cannot be manipulated by human agency.

Panikkar's sharp criticism of modernity is hardly known in India, or is known only to a limited circle, but its relevance to the Indian situation cannot be overestimated.

'Modernity' is a very relative word; relative because it comes from *modus*, mode, which, in some languages like French and German, also means 'fashion', something that is temporal and passing. 'Modernity' has strong Western connotations, but Panikkar emphasises that the concept should also be extended to other cultures which have their own respective modernities. But instead of following the pressures of the Western push towards modernity,

> Other cultures should not modernise themselves, but they should perhaps return to their ancestors, transform themselves, deepen themselves or do something else. It is always the problem that, with the best of intentions, we use words like development, modernity, progress etc., as if every culture should strive towards these values which are so precious to the West. The aiming towards modernity is intrinsic to the West, and extrinsic to almost all other cultures. Therefore, I am critical regarding the trend stating "we should modernise!" This is a Western idea. "To modernise" means adapting to the present times. But which time? Which present?" (Das, *Abenteuer Wirklichkeit,* p. 94)

Panikkar describes modernity by three basic factors—technocracy, secularity, and history (in his usage of the term 'myth'—'the myth of history'). Let me just briefly summarise these factors. Ever since the 1960s Panikkar was deeply critical of what he calls technocracy. What would he say now, 50 years later, what with the tremendous changes (to avoid the word 'developments') of information technology, besides the other areas of technologies! He distinguishes between *techne,* which also includes art and handicrafts, and modern technology, which is the fruit of one civilisation, namely the Western. He consciously chose 'technocracy' to highlight the domination of technology over humanity. It is,

> … by reason of the evolutionistic and progressivistic mentality with which the modern West has attempted to justify, consciously and

> unconsciously, its world domination—all is evolutionary progress, from the Stone Age to our Western civilisation. From fire to electricity, arrows to nuclear missiles, a linear, homogeneous (with peaks and valleys, of course) evolution mounts to the sky. This progress can of course be used for good or evil—as if good and evil were values fallen from the sky independently of precisely the ideology that seeks to justify these values. (*Cultural Disarmament*, p. 47)

An essential factor that characterises modern technology is the different notion and experience of time,

> Technocracy has a time of its own, which is neither nature's, nor that of the temporality—the historicity—of culture. Technocracy's time is *technochrony*, and is based on acceleration. Human beings must adapt to this acceleration if they hope to survive in the technocratic world. The self-sufficiency of technocracy—which, of course, is more than applied natural science, inasmuch as it implies an entire civilisation—reaches its culmination in "nuclear energy," which is the unleashing—that is, the accelerated expansion—of the energy stored in the atom. This acceleration of energy creates the possibility—or even, some would say, the probability—of the extermination of the human species. (*Cultural Disarmament*, p. 48)

The factor of 'secularity' is quite clear, and it implies a separation from religion, the church, etc. 'The myth of history' belongs to Panikkar's specific criticism of the domination of the Western 'myth' over other cultures. One of his challenging theories is precisely 'the end of history'—but I am not going into this complex subject of his thought. 'History' again is a Western notion.

> Traditional Man, in most cultures, lives not in history, but in the cosmos. His life is reflected not exclusively, or even mainly, in

> human history, but rather in the totality of cosmic forces. Men know that they are children of nature, and that they share in nature's lot. They come and they go, they are born and they perish. They belong to the universe, and only a small part of that same universe constitutes the historical development of their human fellows. (*Cultural Disarmament*, p. 51)

Whatever may be its apparent power, a discerning eye, like that of Panikkar, can sense the lurking death instinct of modern technological civilisation,

> As a matter of fact, Western culture, spreading itself thin over the planet, seems to destroy itself, or fall prey of a death instinct. Yet other cultures appear somewhat powerless to contribute to solving, or at least easing, the human predicament of contemporary Man." (Foreword to: Jeanine Miller, *The Vision of Cosmic Order in the Vedas*, p. xi)

What colonialism has done to non-Western cultures, and what neo-colonialism is doing today in the name of globalisation, is to weaken, or even destroy, the self-confidence of traditional cultures. There is a constant attempt at self-justification in the face of this 'thin layer' of modern Western domination. But it is precisely the contribution of traditional cultures that could help in solving the present crisis—provided they are conscious of their values.

Let us first analyse the contrasting approaches of 'modernity' and 'tradition'. The concept of time has already been mentioned—the Western and modern idea of linear time, and hence of 'progress'. The traditional relation to time is embedded in cosmic and human rhythms—and 'rhythm' is one of Panikkar's favourite words, who even titled his last book *The Rhythm of Being*. From his long elaboration on 'rhythm' (pp. 38–50), let me just quote these lines, 'Rhythm is the marriage of space and time, in the tantric sense that the one is the other—time has become space and space, time. You can distinguish them, but cannot separate them.' (*The Rhythm of Being*, p. 48)

Traditional cultures live with the cosmic rhythms, and enact and re-enact them in their festivals and rituals. Human life is rhythmically celebrated with its personal and social sacraments. In other words, secularised and technological time is in contrast to sacred and rhythmic time. In the article on 'Time in Indian Culture' which I wrote in collaboration with Panikkar, I ended with the sentence, 'No one (in the Indian traditional culture) is afraid of "losing" time, precisely because "lost time" is being regained.' (*Cultures and Time*, UNESCO, p. 83).

The most important contrast in the basic assumptions underlying modernity on the one hand and traditional cultures on the other is between dualism and non-dualism. The Sanskrit word *bheda* would be most fitting to characterise the post-enlightenment and technological Western culture, more than *dvaita. Bheda,* from the root *bhid-,* to split, to cleave, to break, to cut or rend asunder, to pierce, and epistemologically to distinguish, implies a split, a separation, a difference, whether between man and nature, spirit and matter, body and soul, or between human beings and societies. Modern science depends on *bheda* distinction, analysis, dissection up to the splitting of the atom. 'In spite of his conquest of matter and of space, modern Man has lost his self-consciousness.' (*Der mittelalterliche Mensch*, p. 585)

The basic dualism of subject–object is at the root of one of the greatest dangers—not to say evils—of modern civilisation—making Man an 'object'. In *The Rhythm of Being* Panikkar analyses this attitude in terms of a devastating criticism of modern science,

> The traditional criticism of the scientific paradigm consists in saying that it leaves no place for God, to which the scientist responds that there is no need for one. In contrast, my criticism of the scientific paradigm maintains that it leaves no place for Man. The great absentee in the scientific *mythos* is Man. Gods there are aplenty, in the form of black holes, galaxies, and infinites great and small, limits, thresholds, and so forth. Devils are legion; biomolecular sciences provide a virology quite as imposing as any

> medieval demonology, and modern "medicated" Man proceeds in fear and trembling in a world of invisible germs and viruses of all sorts. Matter and especially energy are all-pervasive, as are time and space. Only man does not come into the picture. There is an observer there, of course, a so-called intelligent observer, who may even have programmed the computer, and who doubles from time to time as the onlooker agog at what can be observed. Man, however, cannot be located among the data. It would be considered suspicious if the observer were found to be manipulating the information too much for the sake of a particular experiment. On the contrary, Man is in a certain way *the obstacle* to pure information. One reckons with man mainly as a disturbing factor, a modifying parameter—necessary, to be sure, but somehow obscuring the purity of the measurements.
>
> Man as an object, of course, appertains also in the field of science. Everything Man *has*, including genes, may be conveniently digitised, homogenised, and fed into the latest supercomputer, but this does not tell us what Man is, or *who* Man is, much less *who I am*. Modern science has been as wary of anthropocentrism as classical theology was of anthropomorphism, so that anthropology now seems to be afraid of its own subject matter unless it is reduced to sociological or scientific parameters. (*The Rhythm of Being,* p. 400)

Traditional Indian culture, which expanded throughout Asia, is based on non-duality, *advaita, abheda.* Panikkar is equally critical of monisms as of dualisms, and he is against the common translation of *advaita* as 'monism'. 'Monism' carries the danger of all monoculturalisms, based on one religion, one culture, one language, one nation, etc. which is precisely the sin of Western civilisation. Non-dualism, or in his translation 'adualism'—I have to add, precisely in the form of the *paramadvaita* of Kashmir Shaivism, which does not exclude anything—is the only way to solving the crisis of today's world. Leaving the exclusive field of religion and philosophy, adualism must be applied to all fields, according to Panikkar. Again, more fitting to the Kashmir Shaiva concept than Saṅkara's *Advaita*, this adualism must have space for multiplicity, implying the interconnectedness of all things—in Buddhism *pratityasamutpada*, in Shaivism and other systems *sarvatmakatvam*, 'all is related to the whole', 'every part contains the Totality', etc. Panikkar goes into great length to substitute the current translation of *advaita* as non-dualism by adualism.

> Having translated *advaita* as non-duality has had deleterious consequences in the encounter of cultures. The dialectical method is based on the principle of non-contradiction. If *advaita* is "nondualism" and at the same time claims to be non-monism, then *advaita* is pure contradiction. Excluding any other plurality, we cannot escape the dilemma of either one or two without falling into contradiction. We cannot *deny* both one (not two) and two (not one) at the same time. It would amount to negating two and non-two. The only dialectical escape is simply monism, which is the great pitfall into which many interpreters have fallen when they interpret *advaita* rationally, that is, dialectically. *Advaita* cannot be reduced to a concept. (*The Rhythm of Being*, p. 216–17)

What is clear, however, is that since the Upanishads, *advaita* is not the conclusion of a syllogism, but the result of a mystical insight.

My criticism is that besides justifying this translation, it would have been more meaningful to go into the different connotations of *advaita* in the two systems, Vedanta and Pratyabhijna, which would have added to the clarity to which he was aspiring.

We have to see how Panikkar defines tradition. According to him,

> '(R)eflecting on tradition is itself traditional, but on the other hand it contradicts tradition. True tradition is different from education

> or even traditional training, and it is passed on in a living and spontaneous way, without being programmed. And by passing it on, it gets deepened.... Tradition cannot be manipulated. It is a process which belongs to the life of a culture.... Asking about the meaning of tradition implies that what one is asking for is no longer tradition, but spiritual and intellectual heritage, historical customs, etc. The meaning of tradition is precisely that it is so obvious that it makes any question possible. (*Die Zukunft kommt nicht spater*, p. 53)

I want to draw attention to a topic which, according to Panikkar, can bridge the East–West divide—the medieval understanding of Man. Frequently in academic discussions in India, the (mostly) superficial comparison between East and West is based on a diachronic imbalance, as if one could compare a 10th century Indian philosophy with 20th century Western thought. Tradition should be compared with tradition, and modernity with modernity. Panikkar takes the classic example of medieval thought in Europe and in India.

According to Panikkar, medieval Man is the link between modern Western and non-Western cultures.[1] 'Medieval Man' (*homo medietas*) means also Man as the intermediary, the connection between God and the world, between earth and heaven, as many cultures accept a *triloka* with their respective inhabitants. According to John Scotus, Man is '*tertius mundus*', a third world—between angels and animals, between the immortals and the mortals, and between spirit and matter. Thus Man has a mediatory role, between God and the world. This traditional medieval conception is very different from the dualistic model of understanding Man as an object. Rather, Man is a *murti*, an icon, an image of the Divine (*imago Dei*), with a divine origin and a divine destiny. The great mystic Nicholas of Cusa goes so far as to say that Man is 'in between God and nothing' (*intra Deum et nihil*). In non-dualist Kashmir Shaivism with its triadic structure of Siva (the Divine), Sakti (his Energy) and Nara (Man, creation), Man is actually a descent of the Divine, Siva in his own self-limitation. In medieval Christian theology, Man is a co-creator alongside God (*Bonavenatura*). In the Indian tradition, whether upanishadic or tantric, Man is a microcosm, containing the entire universe in himself.

All these conceptions of Man are embedded in a holistic world-view and self-understanding—what Panikkar has developed extensively as the cosmotheandric vision.

Modern views of Man are based on dualism, of Man and God, Man and nature, matter and consciousness, etc., opening the doors to alienation, manipulation and exploitation. According to Panikkar, it is only within a re-integration of the traditional and medieval image of Man, East and West, that a balance can be achieved. This would then be the basis for an inter-cultural dialogue which is not biased, and which would lead to a re-integration of the Cosmic and the Divine in human life. This integration of tradition has to be based also on symbolic, intuitive and archetypal ways of thinking. It opens the way to contemplation and mysticism. Contemplation, the greatest challenge to modernity, is in his words, 'the very breath of life', and mysticism is 'the fullness of life'.

There is another danger in the relationship between traditional and modern cultures, the exploitation of not only material but also spiritual resources.

> Without idealising archaic cultures, we should go against the inhuman aggressiveness of the industrial civilisation. We have so far exploited the material resources of the pre-industrial world, and now we also want to profit from their spiritual values. Industrial culture is a superstructure of human life, and it is not necessary for a perfect, happy, balanced and cultured life. These archaic cultures can help us to attain a simplification of life, and to return to what I call the cosmic rhythms of the world….

It is not a matter of learning some techniques which will help us to function better in the industrialised world. This could lead to a kind of prostitution of spiritual practices, utilising them for our material benefit. (*Das Abenteuer Wirklichkeit*, pp. 101 ff. Emanzipation von der Technologie)

However, such a re-integration is not possible without a radical transformation of consciousness, the necessary *metanoia*. The solution has to be as radical as the problem is—"radical" meaning "going to the roots".

Pluralism is an essential approach to the present situation, but it has 'to avoid the temptation of falling into a global alternative and into a "decaffeinated" pluralism.' 'Decaffeinated' is a nice expression for a pluralism in which the specific characters of each culture are lost.

> The great challenge of our days is a consciousness that is intellectually profound and that echoes the multi-secular experience of humanity, having also taken seriously the other cultures…and which recognises only those pluralistic solutions which do not tend to reduce everything to a common determinator…. This is precisely the failure of both monism and dualism—that they are easily understandable, but they are not adapted to reality as it is. (*Concordia e Armonia*, p. 121)

Endnote

1. R. Panikkar, "Der mittelalterliche Mensch – Bindeglied zwischen der Moderne und den nicht-westlichen Kulturen", in *Homo medietas*, Festschrift für Alois Haas, pp. 585–604.

Raimon Panikkar's Relevance in a Pluralistic World: Re-Visioning Reality

Francis X. D'Sa, SJ

Introduction

Raimon Panikkar, like Martin Heidegger, based himself on everyday language. One could even assert that his writings intended to bring out the originality of language.[1] The reason? Metaphors of such language tend over the course of time to be drained of their original insights. However, it is the original thinker who goes to everyday language to discern the wheat of insights within the chaff of clichés.[2] It is through language that one discovers the what, who, and why of life in this world. One of Panikkar's earliest students and closest collaborators told me how exasperating it was to work with Panikkar because he always had the 'feeling' that whatever he wrote was not exactly what he set out to write.[3] Such perhaps is the destiny of a great writer, thinker, poet.

In what follows I wish to discuss Panikkar's contribution and examine its relevance for our pluralistic world.

From my study of Panikkar's writings I have arrived at the conclusion that his contribution is to be located in his comprehensive understanding of and approach to reality. The subtitle above refers to this. In the first pages of his last, but undoubtedly major, book *The Rhythm of Being*, Panikkar writes,

> Speaking in the language of our times, we may say that we are at a cross-roads not only in human destiny but in the very history

> of reality. These are the 'signs of the times' that I'll attempt to understand by standing under the spell, the beauty, the truth, and also the burden of that selfsame Destiny which I am trying to detect under the metaphor of rhythm.[4]

Almost immediately he adds unambiguously, 'Our topic is about the very meaning of reality…'.[5]

This is not surprising. Panikkar's writings are an attempt to make sense of our pluralistic world on the background of the theanthropocosmic consciousness that is common to all cultures.[6] Concretely, Panikkar's thinking and writing have been directed towards retrieving wholeness, the interconnectedness of all Reality.[7] '… each member is an image of the Whole because the Whole is reflected in its members. Each being is unique and indispensable because the Whole is reflected in that being in order to be the whole. Reality has inter-in-dependent order. This is the sphere of *ontonomy*.'[8] The reason is, 'The interconnection of all with all is governed neither by heteronomy nor by autonomy. The relationship of all with all is not an automatic and one-to-one relationship.'[9]

Reality is cosmotheandric[10]

The cry for relevance becomes louder as the need for answers to the questions of our times becomes more acute. Everywhere we hear or read of responsible people exposing irresponsible enterprises that wreak disaster on Mother Earth and the human family, to say nothing about the instrumentalisation of the Divine for nefarious ends. Panikkar has been among the thinkers who have been reflecting on the signs of the times[11] and discerning 'what was going on in what took place'. His forthcoming monograph *Indra's Cunning* is thematically a critique of India's 'development' and its deleterious effects on 'The Wretched of India'.[12]

Regarding the trinitarian nature of reality, all reality, Panikkar employs mainly two comprehensive expressions, 'theanthropocosmic' (*theos+anthropos+cosmos*) and 'cosmotheandric' (*cosmos+theos+aner*).

They express both unity and multiplicity.[13] 'Reality' *is* and *means* a perichoretic God–World–Man–relationship.[14] The three are neither parts nor departments; Panikkar calls them dimensions.[15] God is not without World and Man; World is not without God and Man; and Man is not without God and World. The three together constitute one reality. None of them is higher or lower. Each is unique. None is independent, none can exist alone. None can be reduced to the other two. The Divine implies both the Human and the Cosmic. The Cosmic implies the Divine and the Human. The Human implies the Divine and Cosmic.[16]

In this cosmotheandric perspective there is always and already a threefold dynamic at work in every being. Each of these dimensions *is* (and not just '*means'*) a specific dynamic; all three together constitute a *perichoresis*, a *circumincessio* (a dancing together)—expressions which were coined by the early church. 'Everything is permeated by everything else in a kind of total *perichoresis*.... In all these cases, Man is 'more' than just an individual being, the Divine 'different' from a Supreme Lord and the World 'other' than raw material to be plundered for utility or profit.'[17]

Reality is rhythm, a three-fold rhythm.[18] Accordingly, spirituality would mean responding to the rhythm of Being by joining in the dance with one's whole heart and mind. However, this necessitates listening to the rhythm of Being.[19] This would be the its major spiritual exercise—*sādhana*, as it were.[20]

The expressions 'theanthropocosmic' and 'cosmotheandric' have the unique advantage of speaking of the whole of reality holistically and not separately (the Divine, the Cosmic and the Human). When our expressions are separate (as in God, World, and Man) the real danger is that in course of time our thinking assimilates them as three separate kinds of realities.[21] That seems to be the state of affairs today.

Panikkar's cosmotheandric approach helps us to revise our way of looking at reality. Ultimately, when all is said and done, reality remains a mystery. 'Mystery' means it can be experienced but cannot be expressed adequately. Mystery does not mean 'believing' blindly, but it does mean that experience is not fully under the control of reason. A good amount of our lives, it is true, is ruled by reason but not the whole of it. There is the realm of the *mythos*[22] which escapes the net of reason. It does not and cannot really come under the control of reason. *Mythos* is the background which can never be objectified but it is that area which makes possible expressions of meaning in life (*logos*). Our search for meaning can be endless but not in the sense that we can go on questioning everything and forever. We do experience situations (however rare they may be) that make sense. Such situations make sense by themselves. They cannot be questioned further. Our questioning stops there because we encounter some sort of meaning in life. In situations like these we get intimations which makes sense to us—at least for the time being.

The Three in the Trinity: *Qui incipit numerare, incipit errare*

There is, however, a problem regarding the *three* dimensions of the cosmotheandric approach. If the cosmotheandric approach remains a mystery, then what is the point in insisting on the three of the *Trinity*, the three of the cosmotheandric experience?

St Augustine's warning gives us a hint of an answer in the right direction: *Qui incipit numerare, incipit errare* (whoever starts counting, starts erring).[23] True, the number three seems to be inescapably bound to the 'three persons' in the Christian perspective, perhaps in much the same way that the number seven is bound to the rainbow in human history. Human language is unable to describe the colour-pattern of the rainbow; so it employs codes which are decoded differently from within different cultures.[24]

Besides, and more importantly, we need to remember that the three persons[25] of the Christian Trinity *per se* are not the object of our faith. They are a code pointing to the *ineffable* Mystery of the Trinity.[26] The cosmotheandric mystery remains a mystery but its function, I suggest, is that of a code.

In this context how we go about our experiences of astronomical entities is instructive. Print and electronic media constantly publish 'photos' of the farthest galaxies in space—photos mostly released by NASA which are of definite shape and size. As I understand, they are not really photos in the accepted sense, but photo-technical interpretations of electronic / radio waves or whatever. The electronic waves act like *codes* that have to be decoded and interpreted by expert astronomers for ordinary viewers.

This is nothing out of the way because we are constantly devising such codes. Do we not say that the earth is round, the moon is round, the sun is round, etc.? But in reality nothing could be further from the truth. For astronomical calculations, the real shape of the heavenly bodies is not relevant. But when, for example, astronomers retouch the pictures of the planets they always show them round or in a spiral form, etc. So the figure of a circle, spiral, etc. acts like a code. Here too, a geometrical code is employed. All this is grist to the mill of popular imagination. If the astronomers were to publish the data of the electronic / radio waves we, lay people, would not be able to make either heads or tails of it. When the astronomers pick up electronic / radio waves they interpret them for us lay people.

With this background of codes in our life, let us now return to the case of a rainbow. We count the *striking* colours and speak of the *seven* colours of the rainbow. This is what we have learnt in school. But we know that a rainbow does not consist of seven colours because one colour gradually fades and merges into the other. There are no boundaries for the colours of the rainbow. But there is a pragmatic reason for the number seven. The seven colours are 'so to speak' a way of talking of the phenomenon called 'the rainbow'. The physics of the rainbow show that we use a physical code to speak of this phenomenon. The colours that are striking are seven, so we call them the seven colours of the rainbow. But it would be incorrect if we were to take this literally. What we have devised is only 'a way of speaking' of the unspeakable.

We cannot speak of the rainbow as we experience and perceive its colour scheme. But when we make use of the code 'seven colours' we are aware that the focus of our description is not the colour scheme itself but on its function as a code pointing to a referent.

Panikkar too interprets the codes of the Christian Trinity in a language that could serve as a code for inter-cultural and inter-religious understanding. Panikkar's phrases 'pointers to the infinite' and 'decipher the code of the real' should not be glossed over.

> It all hangs together. All are pointers to the infinite. Without a tripartite anthropology, without a theory of knowledge that starts from above (the Divine) and not from below (the senses), without an adualistic vision which intuits that God and the world are not two substances, we cannot understand this *perichoresis* of Reality itself; the ultimate *pratityasamutpada* of all that exists, and in short, we cannot penetrate into the mystery of reality. However, this is not all. A more subtle anthropology, a better ontology, a more refined and comprehensive philosophy may convince us more and help us to decipher the code of the real, but the final mystery persists, the ultimate question remains unanswered and the ultimate answer keeps its secret. We cannot eliminate the Mystery. Paradoxically and significantly enough, if we could, we would eliminate ourselves. We, even in our corporeality, are parts of the Mystery.[27]

The cosmotheandric perspective is about the wholeness of reality. By 'reality', Panikkar means 'all that is'. But 'all that is' is not fully transparent, not fully intelligible to us. Panikkar says his great desire was to experience the entire reality but this reality cannot be grasped by any single organ or any one dimension.[28] Also, unless one experiences the painful tensions of reality personally, one cannot face reality fully. The experience of *advaita* witnesses a reality where differences are not absolutised and distinctions are emphasised. Ontonomy, the law that refers to the specific relationship a being has with other beings in a network of relationships, is responsible for harmony. It highlights the interrelationships that constitute their harmony. Harmony is not primarily an external order, not just limited to the level of perception. The external characteristics of harmony are symbolic of the inner characteristics. As Panikkar would have put it, harmony belongs not only to the level of the *logos* but also of the *mythos*.[29] This is true of the full reality of time called tempiternity. Time is the symbol and timelessness is the symbolised reality.[30] And the observer who discovers the symbolic nature of reality is the symboliser.[31]

Our understanding of reality—that is our own reality, the reality of the world, and not less the reality of that dimension which is unfathomable, on the one hand, and non-manipulable on the other—is the focus of Panikkar's reflections.

Today's problems have to be located here. For many of us, reality has become monodimensional. In the final chapter of his *The Rhythm of Being*, Panikkar says,

> Traditional criticism of the scientific paradigm consists in saying that it leaves no place for God, to which the scientist responds that there is no need for one. In contrast my criticism of the scientific paradigm maintains that it leaves no place for Man. The great absentee in the scientific *mythos* is Man.[32]

Panikkar's own confession regarding Man is,

> Man is not only a biped, but the meeting place of all reality, that complex being who as a mesocosm combines all that there is…. Man, the microcosm, is not a miniaturisation of the macrocosm, the bigger 'paradigm'. Man is the icon of God, the infinite Being, affirm many traditions…[33]

Reality is pluralistic[34]

With Panikkar's experience and view of reality acting as the backdrop, his understanding of pluralism becomes clear(er); this is why I shall add here a few introductory words on his complex stand on pluralism.[35] A foundational statement by Panikkar about pluralism is that it is 'a fundamental *human attitude*', not a metaphysical view of the universe,[36] pluralism is not a system. Also, 'Pluralism is not synonymous with tolerance toward a multitude of opinions.'[37] Again, reality is not totally objectifiable 'because we, the subjects, are also part of it.'[38]

The problem of pluralism is 'a philosophical question regarding reality'. 'Pluralism is precisely the recognition that there may be several centres of intelligibility....'[39] Again, 'In sum, I understand by pluralism *fundamental human attitude* which is critically aware both of the factual irreducibility (thus incompatibility) of different human systems purporting to render reality to one single centre of intelligibility, making thus unnecessary an absolute decision in favour of a particular human system with universal validity—or even one Supreme Being.'[40]

A unique aspect of Panikkar's approach to pluralism is, 'I formulate pluralism by saying that truth belongs not only to the realm of the *logos*, but that it pertains also to the order of the *mythos*.'[41] *Logos* for Panikkar is the realm of the intelligible and *mythos* is the background of the intelligible, a background which renders the *logos* meaningful. When something is understood it means something that belongs to the realm of the *logos* has been assimilated in the realm of the *mythos*. All understanding takes place in the *mythos* which is the receptacle of all that has been understood. The intelligible is intelligible only on the background of the *mythos*. *Mythos*, which cannot be objectified, is the organ of understanding. What is to be understood is the *logos*, not its *mythos* because *mythos* makes understanding possible. *Mythos* and *logos* go together. The *logos* which is the language of the *mythos* keeps on expressing its *mythos*. The *mythos* can be known only through the *logos*. Every time the *logos* is understood it enters into the magma of the *mythos* and becomes part of it. This enlarged *mythos* expresses itself afresh in a fresher understanding (*logos*). This passing over from *mythos* to *logos* to *mythos* is a never-ending process.[42]

Mythos (myth), in Panikkar's world, is not something to be exploded but something to be explored in and through its expressions (*logos*).[43] In my way of looking at things, Panikkar's specific contribution to the theme of pluralism[44] lies in the distinction he introduces between *logos* and *mythos*.[45] On the level of the *logos* there is rarely any unanimity but that is not what is to be expected. It is the *mythos* that does the uniting. The more people allow themselves to be taken up, for example, by the *mythos* of peace the more feasible will peace become. *Mythos* is the region where meaning in life originates. But people experience this in a diversity of ways. When they 'stand under' the spell of their *mythos* they are gradually taken up into a process, which Panikkar calls 'intra-religious' dialogue, that is, their self-understanding changes. So long as they stand under the *mythos* of peace, there will be attempts to mutual understanding. This is how religious, political, and social movements function.

Thus the adherents of peace, who participate in the myth of peace, understand peace differently and articulate it in divergent ways so that different aspects come to light. Similarly those who participate in the myth of pluralism, the centre of all meaning and significance regarding pluralism, will understand pluralism differently. The dynamics of a myth are such that in course of time the myth guides its participants, who come together from all possible directions imperceptibly but nonetheless increasingly to express their understanding of it as adequately as possible. Eventually they enter into the myth of pluralism more fully. Our sharing in the myth makes us part of a movement of complementing and correcting our respective stands.[46]

Here, Panikkar's view of reality as cosmotheandric can be a point of encounter. Because all reality is interconnected, he constantly takes up themes like aduality, dualism, monotheism, monism and trinity. 'Everything is interrelated, God, Being, the Trinity, Mary, and so forth. And this interrelatedness begins in our life, hence, with our attitude toward reality.'[47] Reality is such that there can be no place for 'individual', separate islands.[48]

In spite of the apparent multiplicity of things, reality is in fact adual (*advaita*) in nature. Panikkar's pluralism does not militate against this aduality. '*Advaita* is not a weakened monism or relative dualism, but an independent and third possible experience of reality.'[49] Reality is neither one nor two; it is adual. Panikkar's writings time and time again focus on this theme because it is germane to the non-duality of all reality. This problematic is common to most traditions though the attempt to tackle it intellectually is very rare. The result is that in course of time 'God', 'World,' and 'Man' tend to be separated, each having its independent 'existence'. This could change dramatically with the articulation of Panikkar's cosmotheandric intuition. It could bring everyone closer to experiencing, and speaking, of reality more holistically.[50]

The problem of the one and the many, and more specifically, the problem of monotheism and trinity, is an ever-recurring theme in all of his writings. He diagnoses our way of perceiving reality as hopelessly subjective and one-sided. We need to be guided primarily by our experience of pluralistic reality and not by our ideas of reality. This refers to the experience of all human beings, and not just a select group. *Lex entis* has priority over *lex mentis*. One comes to know this not so much by way of surveys and questionnaires but by looking at and examining the cultural heritage of diverse traditions in different parts of the world. Panikkar discovers that historically traditions,

> 'are all aware that, besides our own existence and that of our similar fellow human beings, there exists Nature or the World and an invisible and / or unknown third factor, one of whose names is the Divine. The cosmotheandric intuition is the hermeneutic of this experience expressed in some parameters that I believe could become a fairly widespread cross-cultural universal—open, of course, to diverse interpretations of the overall hermeneutic.[51]

Panikkar sees,

> … the *cosmotheandric intuition* as an adequate cross-cultural universal for the majority of cultures of our time. It is the cross-cultural interpretation of the invariant. The Christian Trinity is considered to be an 'inspired' disclosure of the triadic myths interpreted within a particular context. My conviction is that the 'radical Trinity' of the cosmotheandric intuition belongs to a mature understanding of the Christian insight and of most human traditions.[52]

These distinctions, however, have emerged towards the final stage of Panikkar's writings.[53] The first articulation of the cosmotheandric is to be found in his seminal contribution in Italian '*La visione cosmotheandrica:*

il senso religioso emergente de terzo millennio' (1976).[54] Its English translation, 'Colligite Fragmenta: For an Integration of Reality' saw the light of the day in 1977.[55]

Diatopical hermeneutics, homeomorphic equivalences, and the role of word

With the transition from theandric to cosmotheandric, many surprises began to appear on Panikkar's hermeneutic horizon. The theanthropocosmic experience of Man at the basis of all religions places them all on level ground.[56] From there they can now speak with and to one another as equals; none is higher or better or more inspired or more religious than the others. With this development, Panikkar's contributions to an holistic understanding of religion begin to appear. We find his 'diatopical hermeneutics' briefly discussed in the introduction to his *Myth, Faith and Hermeneutics* (1979), in his 'Philosophy as Life-Style', in *Philosophers on Their Own Work*,[57] and 'The Texture of a Text: In Response to Paul Ricoeur.[58]

With his pluralistic background, Panikkar is allergic to perspectives that obscure the pluralistic angle. His hermeneutics speaks first of morphological hermeneutics and diachronical hermeneutics. The former is meant 'for those who have not yet had full access to the treasure-house of meaning in a particular culture;'[59] and the latter refers to the knowledge of the context necessary in order to understand a text, because the temporal gap between the understander and that which is to be understood has obscured or even changed the meaning of the original datum.' However, both these hermeneutical approaches, important as they are, are wanting when it comes to intercultural understanding. Here in a pluralistic world *diatopical* hermeneutics answers this need.

His studies 'on the various relationships among cultures' led Panikkar to diatopical hermeneutics which 'attempts to blend fundamentally different human horizons'[60] and responds to the problem of interpreting '*topoi*' that are encountered in different cosmovisions but which apparently enjoy similar significance. Panikkar explains,

> I call it *diatopical* hermeneutics because the distance to be overcome is not merely temporal, within one broad tradition, but the gap existing between two human *topoi*, 'places' of understanding and self-understanding, between two—or more—cultures that have not developed their patterns of intelligibility or their basic assumptions out of a common historical tradition or through mutual influence.[61]

Here dialogical dialogue[62] becomes thematic as the method that diatopical hermeneutics treads.[63] 'The first step here could be a *dialogical dialogue*, which penetrates the *logos* all the way to the *mythos* and, as such, differs from a merely dialectical dialogue.'[64] Diatopical hermeneutics is realised through dialogical dialogue. It begins at the *logos*-level but does not get bogged down there. It climbs up a step higher where the revelatory potential of *logos* / Word is released at the *mythos*-level.[65] Genuine personal witness takes one beyond information, beyond *logos* / Word to transformation, the *mythos*-level. These dynamics make us aware that all real change takes place first at the *mythos*-level. Though witness expresses itself at the *logos*-level, its dynamics ineluctably derive from the *mythos*-level. Witness is active both at the *logos*- as well as at the *mythos*-level—something that is true of everything that matters in life.[66]

Homeomorphic equivalents are essential elements of diatopical hermeneutics. Though Panikkar's homeomorphic equivalents appeared in print slightly later than dialogical dialogue, they are hugely important for the dialogical enterprise to really move forward in understanding the other—person, religion, culture, and the like. The problem of interculturality is this: Every culture is a cosmovision, that is, it has its specific experience, understanding, and expression regarding 'God, World, and Man'; this is not reducible to the experience, understanding, and expression of another cosmovision. This gives rise to the question 'how can cultures communicate?' Either cultures move parallel to each other and remain (apparently) untouched (like the proverbial indian lotus in the muddy waters of ignorance and misunderstanding), or some other way has to be found for communication and mutual understanding. Panikkar speaks of homeomorphic or functional equivalents as the way to resolve the impasse. He says,

> '*Brahman*' is not a translation for 'God', since the concepts do not correspond (their attributes not being the same), and since the functions are not identical (*Brahman* not having to be creator, providence, personal, as God is). Each one of these two words express a functional equivalence within the corresponding two cosmovisions.[67]

When working out functional equivalents, belief-traditions are not being compared, as each of them is unique and incomparable. On the other hand, it is equally important to remember that no culture is an abstraction; it finds itself always and already in an interconnected world. It is this point of interconnection that functional equivalents try to identify.

Furthermore, homeomorphic equivalents are not equivalents as such. Thus when it is said that *brahman* and God are homeomorphic equivalents it is *not* stating *brahman* is God and God is *brahman*! What it is in fact stating is that *brahman* and God are homeomorphic equivalents, it is about the similarity of a certain function that is common to them.

Add to this the fact that homeomorphic equivalents refer primarily to a unique function that is operative in a cosmovision.[68] The significance that *brahman* has in the Upanishads is similar to the significance that God enjoys in the Christian tradition. In the two belief-traditions (from our human point of view) the Highest or the Ultimate Mystery has a unique significance, a unique function. This uniquely significant function is, as it were, the nodal point.

In his writings Panikkar has worked out major homeomorphic equivalents like *advaita* and Trinity,[69]...everything is in everything precisely because every being is more than an isolated entity.... The buddhist notion of *pratityasamutpada* (radical relativity) or dependent origination is a homeomorphic equivalent of the same insight.'[70] Again, 'We could perhaps adduce here the Vedic notion of *anyonyayonita* or mutual emerging from one another as an homeomorphic equivalent.'[71]

The penultimate line of Panikkar's major work *The Rhythm of Being* runs thus, 'Everything is related to everything but without monistic identity and dualistic separation.'[72] This could very well be a one line summary of his entire thought.

What dominates Panikkar's writings is the question of dualism and objectification. In this context he develops his insight into the trinitarian / adual / cosmotheandric nature of the Real, supported by his understanding of symbol, 'that which brings things together'. Connected with this is what he calls ecosophy, a life-style of listening to the wisdom of the Earth. With the expression 'cosmotheandric' we can express at one and the same time the three-fold dynamics of reality. As Panikkar puts it, 'God, Man and World are forms of three original attributes and not substances, artificially elevated as such.'[73]

In this age 'God' is unable to carry the burden imposed on 'him' by history and traditions. Panikkar, with faith as existential openness, tries to do justice to all traditions.[74] Not unconnected with this is his *sacred secularity* and his cross-cultural approach to time.[75] Here tempiternity is the intercultural corrective and complement to partial understandings of time and eternity. Panikkar's focus on the 'Trinity' leads him to the discovery that all reality is trinitarian. Deeper study and reflection could lead us to the discovery of its homeomorphic equivalents in other cultures and religions, like in *advaita* (*pratityasamutpada*), and the Shaivite *sarvam sarvatmakam*. This offers the real possibility of revising our one-sided ideas of the Divine, the World and Man, of action and contemplation,[76] of religion and politics,[77] of religion and medicine,[78] of the sacred and secular,[79] of Christian and Hindu traditions,[80] of dialectical and dialogical dialogue,[81] and of diatopical hermeneutics, and so on.

Let me posit one last word on Panikkar's understanding of word / language. It is in and through word / language that we discover reality. Language is a transparent reality. When we are in a speaking–listening situation we do not focus on language but on the referents of language. This is an insight of modern hermeneutics. But long before that the Mimamsakas of India were also aware of this and had a special expression for it—*pararthatattva*.[82] Panikkar reminds us of the importance of language. 'The word reveals reality's cosmotheandric nature.'[83] Also, 'Being speaks.' Furthermore, 'our ultimate task is not to think being, thereby hoping to arrive at the truth; instead, it is to enable being to speak by means of an active listening and obedience on our part (obedience and listening are related in English *ob-audire* and in German *Gehorsam* und *horen*). In place of the polarity between thinking and being emerges now the triadic relation of being, speaking, and thinking. We not only say what we think but also what we are. Being is not only thought of; it also speaks.'[84]

It has not been possible to refer to every one of Panikkar's insights in the present work. Even some important ones like intrareligious dialogue, the *pars pro toto* effect, the cosmotheandric Christ, spirit, *pisteuma*, interculturality, human invariant, cultural universals, technoculture, technocracy, *creatio continua, incarnatio continua,* and others, have not been mentioned.

Panikkar's relevance in a pluralistic world

Before concluding, it will be in the fitness of things to draw attention to what has been promised in the title of this paper, 'Panikkar's Relevance in a Pluralistic World'. What we have been drawing attention to is the re-vision of reality that Panikkar has undertaken.

First, reality is a mystery, that is, it cannot be adequately explained and described. Reality is not totally transparent. There is an element therein which is completely opaque where Man is concerned. Second, however we may understand reality, our approach to it has to be so holistic that nothing is left out or excluded, either programmatically and practically. Inspired by the wisdom of all religions and cultures, we have to open ourselves up to reality in the realm of all three dimensions.

Relevance is something which shows itself in the way we relate to reality. Our approach to the cosmic dimension has to avoid objectification as much as is humanly possible. It has to help us to discover the deeper dimension of reality. Our approach to the human dimension has to promote unity, not uniformity, of all human beings. The test is in the reconciliations that emerge among different groups, peoples, and nations. Finally, our approach to the divine dimension will be tested in the way our life is filled with meaning and also the lives of people around us.

Panikkar's concern has been a thorough re-vision of reality. This re-visioning has to produce a new understanding of the World, Man, and the Divine. What is being re-visioned is the way our age perceives the Cosmic, the Human, and the Divine. Briefly, the Cosmic is being relentlessly objectified, the Human is being reduced to an individual—an individual island—while the Divine, originally the source of meaning and hope, makes no sense in our times.

The Cosmos is not fully objectifiable; it is a living reality

Everywhere the world is being objectified as if inexorably. Nothing seems to escape this onslaught. Reality, under the influence of the so-called scientific mentality, is being reduced to the cosmic dimension[85] alone and words are being replaced by concepts.[86] The pragmatic and the profitable seem to constitute the major drives in Man's life. Even movements like ecology are part of the problem. The Logos in ecology witnesses to its lopsidedness. Logos is ruled by reason, which in this case is the reason for the problem.

Panikkar's answer to this is ecosophy—listening to the wisdom of the universe; reality is not a collection of objects but a living cosmos where symbols[87] are the appropriate means for holistic experience. Here concepts are out of place because they are misfits in such a discourse.[88] The cosmotheandric intuition can be the vision statement of reality where ecosophy, and not ecology, informs the pre-understanding.[89] This cosmotheandric vision is spelt out in Panikkar's ontonomy, sacred secularity, ecosophy, tempiternity, inter-independence, symbol, symbolic difference, radical relativity, technocracy, technoculture, and so on.[90]

Man is not an individual [island] but a person[91]

Human beings are being reduced to individuals, or individual islands, because they have lost their interconnectedness. As our likes and dislikes increase and multiply, *ahamkara* (false sense of identity) has arisen, grown, and begun to spread like cancer cells in our civilisations. To all this, Panikkar's 'Epilogue: Aspects of a Cosmotheandric Spirituality' is a fitting response.[92]

For Panikkar, human beings are persons, not individuals.[93] The individual is an abstraction while 'a person is a knot in a net of relationships'.[94] The net of relationships is the cosmotheandric net of the Divine, the Cosmic, and the Human. Man has to become aware of his threefold response-ability. Here the law of ontonomy rules the roost and Christophany is a trinitarian experience. Christophany is not so much a doctrine as an experience of the divine dimension of Man. From the journey from individual to person, from duality to aduality, from an island-like identity to a cosmotheandric self-understanding emerges a re-vision of reality that makes clear: appearances to the contrary, separations are illusions but distinctions are salvific. In the cosmotheandric age, this is the *mantra* that Man must cultivate.

Meaning-in-life is the core of religion, but rarely of institutionalised religions

Instead of offering religious experience which leads to meaning in life in the world, institutionalised religions have stressed culturally-conditioned doctrines and rituals which, generally speaking, do not make much sense today. That is why religion in our times tends towards private practice.

We have to experience reality as cosmotheandric. And with cosmotheandric glasses we must examine the relevance of religion in three areas: The Divine, the Human and the Cosmic. We have especially to examine whether religion helps us to retrieve the original interconnectedness of all reality *vis a vis* our *zeitgeist* that objectifies, fragments and concentrates on meaning (information) and not meaning-in-life (transformation). For a re-vision of reality, mere routine practice of religion will be of no avail. Meaning-in-life cannot be reduced to the private practice of an individual. In the cosmotheandric paradigm, neither private practice nor island-like individuals fit in. Panikkar reminds us that history is not the only measure of reality[95] and that there is such a phenomenon called trans-historical consciousness.[96]

> Nonhistorical consciousness sees life mainly in the interplay between the past and the present; the future has hardly any weight. Historical consciousness is busy discharging the past in the future; the present is just the intersection of the two. Trans-historical consciousness attempts to integrate past and future into the present; past and future are seen as mere abstractions. Not only has the two-storey building of pre-historical Man collapsed, but the one-storey building of historical Man is also a shambles. The two-storey building was the cosmological image of traditional religions: now and here are only the time and place for the struggle to attain the happiness of salvation elsewhere and after.[97]

Conclusion

Meaning arises in and from a context. Panikkar's contribution consists, first, in challenging our monochromatic understanding of reality, and second, in laying bare its trinitarian, cosmotheandric, adual structure. In this stupendous interreligious and intercultural enterprise, Panikkar has coined a good number of neologisms which like mosaic stones fill in the details of the cosmotheandric reality. However exotic they may seem to be at first glance, a discerning observation of the same reveals that each is a magnified detail of the cosmotheandric structure. Take sacred secularity[98], for example. The cosmotheandric vision is secular because it is being articulated in secular language. However, it is sacred because it shows that in today's world the secular is the homeomorphic equivalent of the sacred. The secular is not to be opposed to the sacred or the religious. As the context changes the meanings too change. Because our context has changed, Panikkar undertakes the astounding task of 'translating' traditional language / discourse / cosmovision into today's everyday language. Above all, the pluralism myth of religions and cultures is emerging. For this some commonality has to be found in order that we can speak and communicate with one another and not talk at cross-purposes. This commonality is the cosmotheandric vision—it is the intercultural and interreligious space for dialogue and encounter.

The cosmotheandric vision is not only Panikkar's flagship, it is also—and much more—a vision statement for the new millennium.

Endnotes

1. My contact with German intellectuals brought me to the realisation that not many appreciate Heidegger's efforts towards a deeper understanding of language. See Panikkar's "Philosophy as Life-Style" in his *A Dwelling Place for Wisdom* (Louisville / Kentucky: John Knox Press, 1993), 86: "My affection for the *etymos*, the origin of words, is a result of the desire to express an original human experience, though these expressions certainly seem tainted by the colors of my particular situation."

2. Panikkar, *The Vedic Experience: Mantramanjari: An Anthology of the Vedas for Modern Man and Contemporary Celebration* (London: Darton, Longmann & Todd, 1977), 347: "Now, 'becoming' can be understood in two ways: as a 'coming from be(ing)' or as a 'coming to be(ing)'." Or, 73: "That is, it [creation–sacrifice] is cosmotheandric. God, Man and the universe are correlates. God without Man is nothing, literally 'no-thing'. Man without God is exclusively a 'thing', not a person, not a really human being, while the world, the cosmos, without Man and God is 'anything', without consistency and being; it is sheer unexisting chaos." Here's another instance, Panikkar, *Myth, Faith and Hermeneutics: Cross-Cultural Studies* (New York / Ramsey / Toronto: Paulist Press, 1979), 5: "Belief articulates the myth in which we believe without 'believing' that we believe in it."

3. Scot Eastham, editor of Panikkar's English texts for many years, collaborated with him for three months in Tavertet, Catalonia preparing the manuscript of his Gifford Lectures. Unfortunately he did not edit the final version of *The Rhythm of Being: The Gifford Lectures* (Maryknoll, New York: Orbis, 2010). Eastham, one of Panikkar's first students, was a thinker and writer in his own right.

4. Panikkar, *The Rhythm of Being*, 3.

5. Panikkar, *The Rhythm of Being*, 3.

6. In his *The Rhythm of Being*, 268, Panikkar distinguishes between the two expressions "theanthropocosmic" and "cosmotheandric". See endnote 21 below.

7. Panikkar, *The Rhythm of Being*, 54: "Everything is in everything precisely because every being is more than an isolated island…. The Buddhist notion of *pratiiyasamutpada* (radical relativity or dependent origination) is a homeomorphic equivalent of the same insight."

8. Panikkar, *The Rhythm of Being*, 54.

9. Panikkar, *The Rhythm of Being,* 54. For a detailed treatment of the subject, see Panikkar, *Worship and Secular Man* (New York: Orbis; London: Darton, Longman & Todd, 1973), especially the chapter Secularisation, 28–55.

10. Panikkar's first articulation of the cosmotheandric vision, says Eastham in his introduction to *The Cosmotheandric Experience*, "began life as a twelve page piece called 'The Catholic Experience'." Later it was probably published in Italian "La visione cosmotheandrica: il senso religioso emergente de terzo millennio" in R. Corporale (ed.), *Vecchi e nuovi Dei* (Turino: Editoriale Valentino, 1976), 521–44. The English translation, "Colligite Fragmenta: For an Integration of Reality" saw the light of day in F. A. Eigo and S. E. Fittipaldi (eds): *From Alienation to At-one-ness* (Villanova, Pa. : The Villanova University Press, 1978), 19–91. The English summary appeared as "The Cosmotheandric Intuition", in *Jeevadhara,* XIV: 79, 1984, 27–35. In 1993 the full article appeared as part of the book, *The Cosmotheandric Experience: The Emerging Religious Consciousness,* Edited with an Introduction by Scot Eastham (Maryknoll: N. Y. : Orbis Books, 1993). See p. 4 fn. 9 for more details of the literary journey of the cosmotheandric experience. Interestingly the Italian version speaks of '*visione*' and '*il senso religioso emergente*', the English summary has 'intuition' and the English book has 'experience' and 'emerging religious consciousness'. *The Rhythm of Being* speaks of the divine Mystery (p. 404) and of the cosmotheandric insight (p. 404).

11. Panikkar, *The Rhythm of Being*, 3: "Speaking in the language of our times, we may say that we are at a cross-roads not only in human destiny but in the very history of reality. These are the 'signs of the times' that I'll attempt to under-stand by standing under the spell, the beauty, the truth, and also the burden of that selfsame Destiny which I am trying to detect under the metaphor of rhythm."

12. Evoking Frantz Fanon's book, *The Wretched of the Earth* translated from the French *Les Damnes de la Terre,* (1961). I have edited the original English manuscript of *Indra's Cunning*. However, it will first appear in Italian as part of Panikkar's *Opera Omnia*, Jaca Book, Milan, before the English version sees the light of day.

13. Panikkar, "The Theanthropocosmic Invariant" in *The Rhythm of Being,* 268: "The theanthropocosmic invariant belongs to human consciousness. We are all aware that, besides our own existence and that of our similar fellow human beings, there exists Nature or the World and an invisible and / or unknown third factor, one of whose names is the Divine. The cosmotheandric intuition is the hermeneutic of this experience expressed in some parameters that I believe could become a fairly widespread cross-cultural universal—open, of course, to diverse interpretations of the overall hermeneutic." On the other hand Panikkar also sees "the *cosmotheandric intuition* as an adequate cross-cultural universal for the majority of cultures of our time. It is the cross-cultural interpretation of the invariant. The Christian Trinity is considered to be an 'inspired' disclosure of the triadic myths interpreted within a particular context. My conviction is that the 'radical Trinity' of the cosmotheandric intuition belongs to a mature understanding of the Christian insight and of most human traditions." Interestingly, Panikkar hardly speaks of metaphor; most of the time he prefers to focus on myth. Perhaps because myth is a specific and important kind of metaphor and metaphor is too generic for his purpose. Be that as it may myth and metaphor are both at home in a world of symbols.

14. Panikkar, *The Rhythm of Being*, 171: "I have been saying that theisms are inadequate, that they often contradict each other, although they may also be mutually complementary if

we enlarge the horizon from which they emerge. I have also been suggesting that theisms as such do not exhaust the human ways to encounter the divine Mystery…. Yet theisms no longer seem able to satisfy the most profound urges of the contemporary sensibilities both in the civilisations that first nurtured these theisms, and in others as well…. In short, the Divine Mystery remains a mystery."

15. Panikkar, *The Rhythm of Being*, Chapter VII. The Divine Dimension, 319–367.

16, See Francis X. D'Sa, "The Significance of the Cosmotheandric Vision", in *CIRPIT REVUE, Revista Internazionale* On-Line. Centro Interculturale dedicato a Raimon Panikkar, no. 2. Marzo 2011, 27–34.

17. Panikkar, *The Rhythm of Being*, 174.

18. Hence the title of his Gifford Lectures, *The Rhythm of Being*.

19. Panikkar, *The Rhythm of Being*, 336: "The ideogram of the Japanese word for listening, *kiku*, has three graphic elements—ears, eyes, and heart. If our heart is closed, our ears are of no avail."

20. Panikkar, *The Rhythm of Being*, 347: "We listen only if we are attentive; we are attentive if we are interested; and we are interested if we are void of other conflicting interests, if our heart is pure; and our heart is pure if it has been purified by that very Silence which prompted us to listen."

21, Panikkar, *The Rhythm of Being*, 319: "I have been trying to rescue the Divine from being considered a separate entity, a supreme and absolutised Being floating somewhere above and beyond the rest of reality."

22. Panikkar, *Myth, Faith and Hermeneutics*, 4ff.

23. Panikkar, *A Dwelling Place for Wisdom* (Louisville / Kentucky: Westminster / John Knox Press, 1993), 149.

24. "The colours of a rainbow are a continuous spectrum, not a set of discrete colours", says an input in the internet. http://optics. kulgun. net/Rainbow/rainbow-faq. shtml on 19 January 2014.

25. Today, if I am not mistaken, by 'person' we mean in popular parlance, personality. There is multiple distance (not only temporal but also, and much more importantly, cultural distance) hidden in such facile translations. Karl Rahner in his article on the Trinity in *Sacramentum Mundi* advises us not to overstress the 'three persons' of the Trinity in pastoral practice because the early Church's understanding of person (and nature) was ontological which today's Christians from multiple cultural backgrounds would find difficult to understand.

26. See Francis X. D'Sa, "How Trinitarian is Panikkar's Trinity?" in *Rhythm and Vision: Conference in Memory of Raimon Panikkar*. Proceedings, George Mason University, Fairfax, U. S. A. 2011, CIRPIT REVIEW, n. 3, 2012 Supplement, 1–16.

27. *The Rhythm of Being*, 284.

28. Panikkar's "Philosophy as Life-Style" in Panikkar's *A Dwelling Place for Wisdom* (Louisville / Kentucky: John Knox Press, 1993), 90.

29. *Myth, Faith and Hermeneutics*, 4ff.

30. *Myth, Faith and Hermeneutics,* 6-8.

31. It might help to express all this in the following way: The symbol is the body, the symbolised reality is the person [and the symboliser is the discoverer of the symbolic structure of reality]. So it is good to remember that it is not just individual beings who are symbols. It is the other way round. The whole of reality is a symbol and its depth-dimension is the symbolised reality. However, we normally do not experience the symbolic structure of reality. We get so fascinated by the body that we get stuck at that level and never proceed to the discovery of the person. Thus we do not get to experience the fullness of person, time, love, beauty, selflessness, and egolessness, etc.

32. *The Rhythm of Being*, 400.

33. *The Rhythm of Being*, 400–01.

34. See Francis X. D'Sa's "Raimon Panikkar's Pluralism" in *Jeevadhara: A Theological Tribute to Raimon Panikkar* XLI: 245 (September 2011), 343–358.

35. Pluralism for Panikkar is an important theme. He has written several articles on the subject from different perspectives. It is not possible to review all of them here. It is enough to present a gist of his thinking on the subject. Especially worth mentioning is his essay "The Myth of Pluralism: The Tower of Babel" in Harry James Cargas (ed.), *Invisible Harmony: Essays on Contemplation and Responsibility* (Minneapolis: Fortress Press, 1995), 52–91. In this essay, replete with insights, two themes are worth taking notice of. One, Panikkar thematically deals with "Overcoming a threefold reductionism". This is a good background for getting into Panikkar's way of thinking. He draws attention to the threefold reductionism of our times: (i) *Reason is not the whole of Logos*, 72, (ii) *Logos is not the whole of Man*, 72, (iii) *Man is not the whole of Being*, 74. Two, his thought-provoking parable on today's world as the modern Babylon.

36. Panikkar, "A Self-Critical Dialogue" in Joseph Prabhu (ed.), *The Intercultural Challenge of Raimon Panikkar*, 250.

37. See Panikkar's "Philosophy as Life-Style", 85.

38. Panikkar, "A Self-Critical Dialogue", 250.

39. Panikkar, "A Self-Critical Dialogue", 252.

40. Panikkar, "A Self-Critical Dialogue", 254–55.

41. Panikkar, "A Self-Critical Dialogue", 249.

42. Panikkar, *Myth, Faith and Hermeneutics,* 98–100 has an interesting intercultural discussion on myth and history.

43. It might be helpful to the reader who is not familiar with Panikkar's terminology to quote the following from his *Myth, Faith and Hermeneutics,* 100–01: "To recapitulate our terminology: by *mythos*, I mean that human organ of apprehension on the same level as the *logos* and in constant relation with it. *Mythos* and *logos* are two human modes of awareness, irreducible one to the other, but equally inseparable.
"By *myth*, I understand the horizon of intelligibility, or the sense of Reality, disclosed by a certain *mythologumenon*. The *mythologumenon* is the expression, the speaking, the language.
"Finally, a myth expressed by a *mythologumenon*, i.e. by a mythic narrative, can contain different *mythemes*, which are the themes (mythic and not necessarily conceptual) the myth elucidates."

44. In his essay "The Pluralism of Truth" in *Invisible Harmony*, Panikkar expatiates on other characteristics of pluralism that witness to his deep insights on the matter. His parable on modern Babylon is a critique of what we have made out of this world and, more importantly, what and who we have become in this process.

45. Panikkar, *Myth, Faith and Hermeneutics,* 4–7.

46. Cultures do not have adequate self-critical structures. It is only in intercultural and interreligious dialogue that there is the possibility of mutual criticism, correction and enrichment.

47. Panikkar's "Philosophy as Life-Style", 106.

48. Panikkar expresses this idea differently in different places. Thus in his "Trisangam: Jordan, Tiber and Ganges" in *A Dwelling Place for Wisdom* he writes, "Reality is the 'I *am*', the 'you *are*', the 'it *is*'. Hence what exists is not the being but the 'am', 'are', 'is': the chair is; you are; I am." (154). "The phrase *tat tvam asi* would represent another possibility of expressing this insight: 'This you are' (CU VI, 8–16). The 'You' is mine, my you, and not a 'something' it is, or I assume to be. I am a 'You'. The phrase does not say 'I am *brahman*' but '[*tat*] *tvam asi*', [this] you are!'"(154).

    "Once we are well-grounded in this consciousness, we attain the communion with the self, with the entire outside world, with each other, and with the divine. After all, my identity is an 'are'; and this 'are' only exists in a 'you', pronounced by the 'I' and based on the 'it'. This truth could possibly be summed up in the unique formula *tat tvam asi*.'"(155). See Panikkar's "The Myth of Pluralism", 75: "There is a kind of *perichoresis*, a 'dwelling within one another' of these three dimensions of Reality: the Divine, the Human and the Cosmic—the *I*, the *you* and the *it*." See Panikkar's revealing statement in his "Philosophy as Life-Style", 97: "Furthermore, I have been *wrestling* with trying to formulate what I now would like to call the cosmotheandric or the theanthropocosmic intuition." [Italics mine].

49. See Panikkar, "A Self-Critical Dialogue", 274.

50. Holistic because "God [*theos*]", "World [cosmos]" and "Man [*anthropos* / *aner*]" function like a code for the whole of reality.

51. See footnote 21 above.

52. Panikkar, "The Theanthropocosmic Invariant", *The Rhythm of Being,* 269.

53. In his *Worship and Secular Man* (London: Darton, etc., Maryknoll-New York: Orbis Books, 1973) speaks repeatedly of the theandric dimension but the cosmotheandric expression is nowhere to be encountered. As early as 1968 Panikkar published "Towards an Ecumenical Theandric Spirituality", *Journal of Ecumenical Studies* (Philadelphia) V: 3, 507–34.

54. Panikkar, *Vecchi e nuovi Dei* (Turino: Editoriale Valentino, 1976), 521–44.

55. This article first appeared in F. A. Eigo (ed.), *From Alienation to At-Oneness*. Proceedings of the Theology Institute of Villanova University (Villanova, Pa. : The Villanova University Press, 1977), 19–91. Only in 1993 did it form part of the book *The Cosmotheandric Experience: Emerging Religious Consciousness* edited by Panikkar's student Scott Eastham and published by Maryknoll. N. Y. (Orbis Books). Panikkar's *The Rhythm of Being* published in 2010 is a good example of how his thought never stagnated.

56. Panikkar, "The Theanthropocosmic Invariant", *The Rhythm of Being,* 268.

57. Publishing details: *Philosophers on Their Own Work*, André Mercier and Maja Svilar (eds.), Bern, etc: Peter Lang, 1978, 193–207.

58. In *Point of Contact,* Vol. II, No. 1 (New York, 1978), 51–64.

59. Panikkar, *Myth, Faith and Hermeneutics*, 8.

60. Panikkar, "Philosophy as Life-Style", 96.

61. *Myth, Faith and Hermeneutics*, 9. Curiously, the topic of diatopical hermeneutics does not find any mention in the article dealing with his hermeneutics "The Texture of a Text: In Response to Paul Ricoeur"!

62. Panikkar, "Witness and Dialogue" in *Myth, Faith and Hermeneutics*, 232–56.

63. *Myth, Faith and Hermeneutics*, 9.

64. One would have expected Panikkar's homeomorphic equivalents too to put in an appearance at this stage. But this is not the case even when he discusses dialogical dialogue in *Myth, Faith and Hermeneutics*, 9.

65. Panikkar expresses this insight in yet another way, "Secular culture is correct in saying that being and time are 'coextensive', so that there is no being which remains untouched

by time. However, the time aspect of entire reality is only *one* aspect of the *tempiternal* nature of all things. Reality is not exhausted solely by the temporal aspect; furthermore, reality is not temporal now and eternal 'later'. Instead, reality is *tempiternal*, both temporal and eternal at once." Panikkar, "Philosophy as Life-Style", 96.

66. See Panikkar, "Witness and Dialogue" in his *Myth, Faith and Hermeneutics*, 232–56 where the thesis is "testimony is possible only in a mythic communion". Mythic communion for Panikkar stands for "participation in a common myth" (237).

67. Panikkar, "Religion, Philosophy and Culture" in *Polylog: Forum for Intercultural Philosophy* 1 (2000), http://them. polylog. org/1/fpr-en. htm, 21–22.

68. Another less frightening and more reader-friendly name is 'functional equivalents'.

69. See Panikkar's "A Self-Critical Dialogue", 273: "I am not identifying in an unqualified way Father, Non-being, Baselessness (and Abyss), sunyata, *wu-wei* and similar notions. Nor is God a cultural universal. None of these notions is the 'same'. They are *homeomorphic equivalents*.... We have also stated that *advaita* and Trinity are homeomorphic equivalents for the ultimate structure of reality."

70. Panikkar, *The Rhythm of Being*, 54.

71. Panikkar, *The Rhythm of Being,* 53.

72. Panikkar, *The Rhythm of Being*, 404.

73. Panikkar, "Philosophy as Life-Style", 97. Panikkar has revised his original formulation as stated in "Philosophy as Life-Style" in André Mercier and Maja Svilar (eds), Bern, etc: Peter Lang (1978), 206.

74. The seven-page folder giving the gist of each of the Gifford lectures says in the Introduction: "They [the lectures] give vent to the suspicion that most of the traditional ideas about 'God' are inadequate for carrying the burden imposed upon the word by our present day consciousness. This fact may reflect a corresponding event in Being itself."

75. See Francis X. D'Sa, "Sacred Secularity: Raimon Panikkar in a Pluralistic World" in Johnson J. Puthenpurackal (ed.), *Raimon Panikkar: Being Beyond Borders.* A Commemorative Volume (Bangalore: Asian Trading Corporation / Eluru: Association of Christian Philosophers of India. ACPI Special Series, 2012), 545–64.

76. Panikkar, "Action and Contemplation as categories of Religious Understanding" in Y. Ibish and I. Marculescu (eds.), *Contemplation and Action in World Religions*. A Rothko Chapel Book (Seattle and London: University of Washington Press, 1978), 85–104.

77. Panikkar, "Non-Dualistic Relation between Religion and Politics" in *Religion and Society*. Bangalore, XXV, 3, 53–63.

78. Panikkar, "Medicine and Religion" in *InterCulture*, XXVII. No. 4 (Fall 1994), 1–39.

79. Panikkar, *Worship and Secular Man*, 28–55.

80. Panikkar, "Das Verhaltnis Christentum-Hinduismus" in *Gott, Mensch und Welt: Die Drei-Einheit der Wirklichkeit* hrsg. von Roland R. Ropers (Petersberg: Verlag Via Nova, 1999), 19–28.

81. Panikkar, "The Dialogical Dialogue" in F. Wahling (ed.), *The World's Religious Traditions: Current Perspectives in Religious Studies*. Essays in Honour of Wilfred Cantwell Smith (Edinburgh: T. T. Clark, 1984), 201–21.

82. Francis X. D'Sa, "Sabdapramanyam" in Sabara and Kumarila, *Towards a Study of the Mimamsa Experience of Language*. De Nobili Research Library Vol. VII (Vienna: University of Vienna, 1980), 165: "It is one of the interesting phenomena of the Mimamsa that some of its more important categories like sabdah, akṛtih, *yagaḥ*, etc. have this characteristic—*pararthatva*, that is, 'for the sake of the other', their purpose is to serve another aim."

83. Panikkar, "Philosophy as Life-Style", 98.

84. Panikkar, "Philosophy as Life-Style", 98.

85. Panikkar, *Cultural Disarmament: The Way to Peace* (Louisville (KY): Westminster John Knox Press, 1995), Obstacles to Peace, 85 expresses in nine pithy but nonetheless profound Sutras what I am referring to.

86. Panikkar, "Words and Terms" in M. M. Olivetti (ed.), *Esistenza, Mito, Ermeneutica*. Scritti per Enrico Castelli. Archivio di Filosofia Padova (CEDAM, 1980) II, 117–33.

87. See Panikkar, *Myth, Faith and Hermeneutics* for a brief but relevant understanding of the wholeness of reality through symbol. 6f.

88. See Panikkar's "Anima Mundi / Vita Hominis / Spiritus Dei" in *The Cosmotheandric Experience*, 137: "The modern Western world has undertaken a thoroughgoing deanthropomorphisation of the meaning of the word *God*. It has also tried to denontologise God. In the same process, Man has equally devitalised the Earth. The Earth has been left for dead by the same token that Heaven has been deserted. Modern Man seems to have forgotten what the Vedas, the Bible and the Chinese Classics affirm: that Heaven and Earth have the same destiny. With Heaven fading away, the Earth becomes no longer a living Being, but simply matter and energy; and the forces of nature are no longer living spirits and qualities, but merely 'attributes' of nature."

89. Panikkar, "Okosophie, oder: Der kosmotheandrische Umgang mit der Natur" in H. Kessler, Okologisches Weltethos im Dialog der Kulturen und Religionen (Darmstadt: Wissenschaftliche Buchgesellschaft, 1996), 58–66.

90. Elsewhere I have spoken of the sacramentality of the Cosmic, the sacra-mentality of the Human and the Sacrum of the Divine in *Sacramentum Mundi: Preface to a Cross-Cultural Re-Vision of Sacraments* in Francis X. D'Sa, Isaac Padinjarekuttu, and Jacob

Parappally (eds), *The World as Sacrament: Interdisciplinary Bridge-Building of the Sacred and the Secular.* Essays in Honour of Josef Neuner on the Occasion of his 90th Birthday (Pune: Jnana-Deepa Vidyapeeth, 1998), 239–93.

91. See Francis X. D'Sa's, "On Becoming a Person: Panikkar's Trinitarian Approach" in Johnson J. Puthenpurackal, *Raimon Panikkar: Being Beyond Borders*. A Commemorative Volume (Bangalore: Asian Trading Corporation / Eluru: Association of Christian Philosophers of India. ACPI Special Series, 2012), 591-605.

92. Panikkar, *The Cosmotheandric Experience*, 135–152.

93. Panikkar, "The Law of Karma and the Historical Dimension of Man" in *Myth, Faith and Hermeneutics*, 376–79.

94. See Panikkar, "A Self-Critical Dialogue", 264.

95. Panikkar, *Christophany: The Fullness of Man* (Maryknoll / NewYork: Orbis Books, 2004), 162: "Christophany does not contest the historicity of Jesus. It merely affirms that history is not the only dimension of the real and that Christ's reality is thus not exhausted with Jesus's historicity." More exhaustively in "Is History the Measure of Man? Three Kairological Moments of Human Consciousness" in Panikkar, *A Dwelling Place for Wisdom*, 134–44.

96. Panikkar, *The Cosmotheandric Experience*, 122–33.

97. Panikkar, *The Cosmotheandric Experience*, 124.

98. See Francis X. D'Sa, "Sacred Secularity: Raimon Panikkar in a Pluralistic World" in Johnson J. Puthenpurackal (ed.), *Raimon Panikkar: Being Beyond Borders*. A Commemorative Volume (Bangalore: Asian Trading Corporation / Eluru: Association of Christian Philosophers of India. ACPI Special Series, 2012), 545–64.

The Encounter of Religions in a Globalised World: Provocations from Panikkar

Joseph Prabhu

Among those who have made the transition [to the future] some become mediators of the future for others who can make passage…. I suggest that Raimundo Panikkar is such a spiritual mutant, one in whom the global mutation has already occurred and in whom the new forms of consciousness have been concretised…they are cross-cultural, for in them the great cultural traditions—formally distinct through their diverse historical origin and development—now converge, making these mutants heirs, for the first time in history, to the spiritual heritage of humankind. As such they become multi-dimensional, for they combine the polarities of the East and the West, outer and inner consciousness, science and mysticism, mythic and rational thinking, pragmatic involvement in the world and spiritual detachment.

Ewert Cousins[1]

One of the consequences of contemporary globalisation has been the encounter of religions and religious personalities. While it is true that in pluralistic countries like India and the United States, religions have for long been in contact with one another, this contact intensifies under the compression of time and space that is a structural feature of globalisation. This meeting of religions has had decidedly mixed results. On the one hand, there has been genuine dialogue and the transformation that goes along with such dialogue; but on the other hand, the encounter has also produced much antagonism and, often, violence. In circumstances such as these, it is instructive to revisit the thought of Raimon Panikkar, one of the pioneers in the twentieth century of inter- and intra-faith dialogue. Panikkar's rich reflection on dialogue was, however, part of a comprehensive world-view which both framed and reflected it. It is important to emphasise this because his contribution is often, especially in parts of the West, restricted to his practice of dialogue. As a corrective to this reductive view, it is salient to point out that his practice of dialogue was itself part of an overarching philosophy of dialogue, and the latter in turn can be seen as an offshoot of his pluralistic world-view.

I shall accordingly divide this paper into two sections—the first will deal with his metaphysical world-view and the second with the different dimensions of his philosophy of dialogue including one very important aspect of the theory and practice of dialogue, namely his philosophy of peace and the alternative it provides to some contemporary forms of politics.

Panikkar's cosmotheandrism

What for long has driven and unified Panikkar's thinking has been his cosmotheandric vision of reality, what he calls the 'trinity' of cosmic matter, human consciousness, and divine freedom in co-constitutive relationality. These three basic and irreducible dimensions of reality interpenetrate each other and exist only in relation to one another. 'There is a kind of *perichoresis*, "dwelling within one another", of these three dimensions of Reality—the Divine, the Human, and the Cosmic.'[2]

And then again, 'There is no matter without spirit and no spirit without matter, no World without Man, no God without the universe, etc. God, Man, and World are three artificially substantivised forms of the three primordial adjectives which describe Reality.'[3]

Panikkar's use of the theological term *perichoresis* taken from the discussions about the Trinity by the Greek Fathers and paralleling in a loose manner the three moments of the eternal dance of Siva Nataraja—creation, preservation, and destruction—is deliberate and is designed to articulate its 'trinitarian' structure.

The main thesis that Panikkar wants to proffer is the triadic structure of Reality comprising the Divine, the Human, and the Cosmic in thoroughgoing relationality. By saying, 'God, Man, and World are three artificially substantivised forms of the adjectives which describe Reality' Panikkar is pointing to his own version of the Buddhist *pratityasamutpada*, the espousal of what he calls 'radical relativity'. There are no such things or beings as God or Man or World considered as completely independent entities. Not only are they dependent on each other, but this dependence is not just external, but rather internal, i.e., constitutive of their being. Panikkar coins the term 'interindependence' to express this relationship.

As to the appropriateness of taking a Christian theological symbol to describe what is essentially a philosophical and poetic vision, Panikkar makes at least three responses.

First, the symbol of the Trinity is not a Christian monopoly, but in fact is common in many other traditions.

Second, the relationships and movements within the Trinity provide a precise and vivid model for the dynamism of the different dimensions of Reality that Panikkar wants to articulate. Rowan Williams, the current Archbishop of Canterbury and a significant theologian in his own right, has captured this dynamism well in a perceptive essay on Panikkar entitled, 'Trinity and Pluralism', in which he writes,

> For Panikkar, the Trinitarian structure is that of a source, inexhaustibly generative and *always* generative, from which arises form and determination, 'being' in the sense of what can be concretely perceived and engaged with; that form itself is never exhausted, never limited by this or that specific realisation, but is constantly being realised in the flux of active life that equally springs out from the source of all. Between form, 'logos', and life, 'spirit', there is an unceasing

> interaction. The Source of all does not and cannot exhaust itself simply in producing shape and structure; it also produces that which dissolves and re-forms all structures in endless and undetermined movement, in such a way that form itself is not absolutised but always turned back toward the primal reality of the source.[4]

Third, even for Christians, Panikkar feels that the doctrine of the Trinity should not be treated, as it often is, as a recondite teaching about the inner life of God cut off from the rest of life and experience. Rather, it is so potent and rich a symbol that it invites further deepening and development, preferably by intercultural and interreligious communication. Panikkar is by no means alone in wanting to articulate the logic of the Trinity philosophically, and with reference to the whole of reality. Hegel, likewise, saw the Christian Trinity as the *Grundstruktur* for his entire dialectic and conceived of his philosophy as a translation of the doctrinal core of Christianity.[5] Of course, Panikkar's is a quite different philosophical style than Hegel's, but the aim in both cases is the same—to 'expand' and articulate Christian doctrine as a model of Reality. In offering the Christian symbol of the Trinity as a resource for interpreting reality, and in showing its homeomorphic equivalence to the Hindu notion of *advaita*, Panikkar is engaging in an exercise of comparative theology where symbols of particular traditions are shared with the idea of testing their applicability and fruitfulness to contexts beyond their original ones. This is a process that Panikkar describes as 'mutual fecundation'.

This ontological pluralism matches a corresponding epistemological pluralism where Panikkar attempts to fuse three different modes of thought, sensibility, and consciousness which he calls *mythos, logos,* and *pneuma*. The mutual relation between these three notions can be succinctly expressed—*mythos* is the unthought, *logos* is that which is thought, while *pneuma* is the unthinkable. *Mythos* is the unthought because it is the background, the source, and origin of what is thought, and, therefore, cannot be made the object of thought. *Logos* covers the whole range of thought from sensibility at the 'lower' end of the cognitive spectrum to speculative ideas at the 'higher' end, what the tradition of German idealism designates as *Verstand* and *Vernunft*, and what the medieval Latin tradition calls *ratio* and *intellectus*. *Pneuma* is the ever-new, the unpredictable, the wind that blows where it will. As Panikkar expresses it, 'the unthinkable does not exist in itself as a fixed dimension. At any given moment it is the provisional, the historical that accomplishes itself in the future, in hope.... Receiving the *pneuma* is permanent passage, a *pascha*, a pilgrimage. The procession from *mythos* through *logos* to *pneuma* is endless. Precisely the pneumatic dimensions guarantees the constant openness into which we may take a step forward.'[6]

Panikkar's *advaita* in a sense is a *via media* between the rationalistic, dialectic of a Spinoza or a Hegel tending toward monism and the non-rational *advaita* of a Sankara or a Ramanuja. Like the former, Panikkar regards the world as fully real and reason as an essential instrument in our engagement with it. Unlike them, however, for Panikkar it is only an aspect, crucial and essential as it is, of a wider dance or procession of consciousness that also incorporates the mythic and the pneumatic. Like the latter, he wants to overcome the dualism of knower and known without, on the one hand, postulating the 'self-thinking Thought' (*noesis noseseos*) of Hegel, who follows Aristotle here, or, on the other hand, wanting to transcend reason completely. Furthermore, unlike Sankara, Panikkar does not see the world as mere appearance.

There is thus at both ontological and epistemological levels a relational energy at the heart of Panikkar's *Weltanschauung*, an energy that he refers to by various symbolic notions—'*advaita*', '*pratityasamutpada*', 'trinity', '*perichoresis*', 'dance', and finally the 'rhythm of being', the title of his last book, and unfinished symphony, all of which are homeomorphic equivalents. The Trinity is the ontological foundation of Panikkar's multifaceted doctrine of pluralism, which is quite a different notion from what is usually understood by that term. In the debates between exclusivists, inclusivists, and pluralists, 'pluralism' has come to mean the liberal idea of many equally valid paths to salvation or the view that the various religions constitute phenomenal manifestations of one transcendent *noumenon*, a *Ding-an-sich*. Panikkar's view is almost the opposite. He does not think that one can trump religious pluralism by metaphysical universalism because there is as much diversity in metaphysics and in conceptions of the Ultimate as there is in religion. Furthermore, the Mystery by definition cannot be objectified or made into some neutral transcendent essence of which the different faiths are manifestations. Panikkar adopts a radically apophatic attitude towards the Mystery. He is deeply sympathetic to the '*neti, neti*' (not this, not this) of the Brhadaranyaka Upanishad, the mystical doctrine of the indescribability of the Absolute. In the same vein, he is sympathetic to the Buddhist idea of *sunyata*, the radical 'emptiness' of Reality. This emptiness is compatible with, and can contain a relational core, because it is to be interpreted in dynamic rather than static terms.

If the liberal view of religious pluralism can be expressed cryptically as 'many paths to one and the same mountain', as in the influential view of John Hick,[7] Panikkar's might be described as many paths up different mountains, paths which thus remain incommensurable with one another. Pluralism for Panikkar is the negotiation in respect and love with such incommensurability.

Panikkar's philosophy of dialogue

The relational energy at the heart of Panikkar's ontology is given expression in his theory and practice of dialogue for which he is best known, at least in large parts of the West. Dialogue can be seen as a personalising of this relational energy. At its deepest level, it can be regarded as a mutual recognition of the cosmotheandric Mystery expressing itself in oneself and the other. But given the inter-relatedness and co-relationality of all being, the other should not be seen as an alien other (an *alius),* and even less as an 'it' (an *aliud*). The other is properly speaking another self, or in Paul Ricoeur's felicitous phrase, 'oneself as another', and conversely the other as oneself. The idea that the 'I' would not, strictly speaking, even *be* without the other, that the other is my own self externalised, and that both selves are expressions of the Mystery—it is this idea that provides the ontological ground for Panikkar's philosophy of inter-personal dialogue.

Of course, Panikkar is quite aware that much of what is called dialogue operates at a purely cognitive level where the focus of the dialogue is doctrine or ideas. This is what sets up the important distinction between dialectical and dialogical dialogues. Dialectical dialogues take place at the level of doctrines and ideas. When conducted at the interpersonal level, they tend to treat members of other religions either as objects of cognitive inquiry, or as subjects that are to be objectively examined and discussed. Needless-to-say, such dialogues have their legitimate place at the institutional or organisational level. Thus, when the Catholic church changes its official position of 'no salvation outside the Church' (*extra cathedra nulla salus*), or when Hindu society decides to make *sati* (or the self-immolation of widows) illegal, we can speak of these changes coming about as a result of dialectical dialogues.

By contrast, dialogical dialogues involve the whole person and not just his or her cognitive dimension. They treat others not primarily as purveyors of objective thoughts or ideas, but as other selves (an *alter*), who are independent sources of self-understanding and of a world-view not reducible to one's own. As Panikkar says,

> The dialogical dialogue is not concerned so much about opinions as about the different viewpoints from which the respective opinions are arrived at. Now, to deal with a perspective means to deal with very fundamental springs in the knowing subject. A new epistemology is required here. Just as any knowledge of an object requires a certain con-naturality and identification with the object to be known, any knowledge of the subject necessitates also a similar identification. This is what has led me to formulate the principle of 'Understanding as Convincement'. We cannot understand a person's ultimate convictions unless we somehow share them.[8]

This thesis of 'understanding as convincement' needs to be carefully understood because it is often misinterpreted. Panikkar is saying that one has to enter into the very *mythos*, the fundamental well-springs of the thought and sensibility of one's dialogue partner and in the process to touch on one's own *mythos* without being fully aware of its shaping power. To understand is in a sense to 'stand under' the thinking and feeling of the other, not as an alien other (an *alius*) as is very often the case, for example, in psychoanalysis, where the methodological move of distanciation operates in the interests of so-called 'objectivity', and still less as an 'it' (an *aliud*), as in the objectifying stance of much social science. When Panikkar talks of 'standing under', the new epistemology he refers to in the quotation above points to a loving knowledge, an attempt to participate sympathetically, but also critically in the other's myth or horizon of intelligibility,

> The dialogical dialogue challenges us on a much deeper level than the dialectical one. With the dialectical dialogue we are unable to explore realms of human experience, spheres of reality, or aspects of being that belong to the first and second persons, that is, to the '*am*' and '*art*' aspects of reality. In other words, with the dialectical dialogue, we can only reach the '*it is*' aspect of the real and cannot be in full communication with other subjects and their most intimate convictions. With the dialectical dialogue, we may discuss religious doctrines once we have clarified the context, but we need the dialogical dialogue to discuss beliefs as those conscious attitudes we have in face of the ultimate issues of our existence and life.

In the dialogical dialogue, I trust the other not out of an ethical principle (because it is good) or an epistemological one (because I recognise that it is intelligent to do so), but because I have discovered (experienced) the *'thou'* as the counterpart of the I, as belonging *to* the I (and not as not-I). I trust the partner's understanding and self-understanding because I do not start out by putting my ego as the foundation of everything. It is not that I do not examine my partner's credentials (he could be wicked or a fool), not that I fall into irrationalism (or any type of sentimentalism), giving up my stance, but that I find in his actual presence something irreducible to my ego and yet not belonging to a non-ego. I discover the 'thou' as part of a Self that is as much mine as his, or to be more precise, that is as little my property as his. [9]

This seeking of our common divinity, the *atman*, in one another in and through dialogical dialogue and making it a methodological requirement is the challenging new element that Panikkar adds to the general discussion on dialogue. It requires us to transcend and go beyond our egos to a genuine communion with the other seen as a Thou to one's I. At the same time, it is important to see this requirement both as hermeneutical and existential, both as a requirement of sympathetic understanding and of respect for the other as a source of independent thinking and feeling, not reducible to one's own. It is also salient to stress that this sympathetic understanding by no means implies either an uncritical acceptance of the other's views or a surrender of one's own.

It should also be clear that dialogical dialogue, as Panikkar understands it, has two vectors—the deep and searching conversation with the other seen as an *alter*, but equally a dialogue with oneself where the views of the other challenge one's own. Both elements are intertwined. The dialogue with the other is also the occasion for a profound dialogue with oneself opening the way to a possible transformation. Otherwise expressed, the inter-religious dialogue implies an intra-religious dialogue and vice versa.

Both dialogues, dialectical and dialogical, presuppose a dialogical attitude, a disposition to be in relationship with the other. Dialogue may be regarded as expressing Panikkar's pluralism in its operational aspect. Pluralism is not just diversity but the engagement with differences and otherness, differences which may sometimes be incommensurable. Needless to say, such stark and incommensurable differences may well lead to conflict, and, in fact, there are some like Samuel Huntington, for example, who see conflict as inevitable. Panikkar, of course, recognises the risk of conflict but embraces the dialogical attitude with the goal of avoiding conflict and attempting to reach deeper understanding for the sake of both social harmony and personal growth.

It is worth spelling out the presuppositions and implications of such a dialogical attitude, because it is at variance with a more common attitude that sees difference and otherness as intrinsically conflictual. By contrast, the dialogical stance is one that seeks mutual understanding and respect, even when, and especially when, there are sharp differences between two or more positions. As a way of highlighting the contrast between these two sharply differing stances, I shall designate them the dialogical model vs the 'clash' model, named after perhaps the most well-known proponent of such a position, the late Samuel Huntington.

First, a dialogical attitude expresses a broadmindedness and an appreciation of the complexity of truth, as expressed, for example, in the Jain notion of *anekantavada*, the many-sidedness of truth. It follows that dialogue between these different sides enriches and enlarges one's perspective. By contrast, the clash model tends to see matters of truth in univocal and ideological terms and frequently criticises the dialogue model for being indeterminate and relativistic.

Second, given the recognition of the many-sidedness of truth, the dialogue model implics both openness and tolerance. This does not at all entail indeterminacy or relativism. Panikkar used to employ the image of people looking out at a mountain from respective windows or viewpoints. It is quite possible, especially if one is unaware of other windows in the vicinity, to absolutise the view from one's own window, until others point out their different views of the mountain garnered from their own windows. One may, of course, try to experience these different views for oneself, but even without doing so one may no longer absolutise one's own view once one is made aware of other viewpoints. One may still want to argue for the relative superiority of one's own view, depending on what particular features of the mountain one considers crucial. The clash model, however, tends to think that there is only one valid view, or at most a very limited number, and is quite convinced of the absolute superiority of one's own viewpoint.

Finally, the clash model tends to see cultures as largely monolithic, homogeneous, and oppositional to one another, whereas the dialogue model sees cultures by and large as heterogeneous and interactive. Samuel Huntington, in his *The Clash of Civilizations* presents Islam as a largely homogeneous civilisation, ignoring the fact that the 1. 6 billion Muslims who comprise the present Muslim world population span many different cultures, Indonesian, Indian, Pakistani, Central Asian, and Arab, to name just a few. Given that internal diversity, it is highly problematic in analytical terms to talk of a homogeneous 'Islamic civilisation'. Together with this attitude towards culture, the picture of politics in the clash model is invariably oppositional and ideological—'the West vs the rest', or 'Us' vs 'Them'. Needless to say, the dialogical model sees cultures and political systems as being diverse rather than oppositional, and it is precisely this diversity that makes dialogue both possible and necessary.

Given both the conflicts that exist in the world and the arms arsenals that nations and terrorist groups possess, it is quite obvious that we live in dangerous times. Whether it is religion, political ideology, race, ethnicity, or economic inequalities, or a combination of these factors that contributes to the discord, it is clear that viable ideas of dialogue leading to understanding and peace are badly needed in our war-torn world. Peace is not just a wish or an ideal, but a state of affairs that has to be actively worked for. The path to a true and lasting peace requires more than just dialogue. It requires at a more fundamental level a dialogical attitude, a disposition of heart, mind, and will which aims at, and works for, the overcoming of absolutism, greed, selfishness, and egoism. Panikkar's notions of pluralism and dialogue, which I have tried to explicate and comment on in this essay, have much to contribute to the building of both inner and outer peace.

Endnotes

1. Cousins, Ewert, *Christ of the 21st Century.* Rockport MA: Element, 1992, pp 73-73
2. Panikkar, Raimon, "The Myth of Pluralism: The Tower of Babel—A Meditation on Non-Violence," *Cross Currents*, 29, no. 2 (1979): pp 214-216.

3. Panikkar,"Philosophy as Life-style," in *A Dwelling Place for Wisdom, op. cit.*, p. 97.

4. Williams, Rowan, "Trinity and Pluralism," in *Christian Uniqueness Reconsidered: The Myth of a Pluralistic Theology of Religions*, ed. Gavin D'Costa. Maryknoll, NY: Orbis Books, 1990, p. 3

5. Splett, Jorg, *Die Trinitaetslehre GWF Hegels*. Freiburg: Herder Verlag, 1965.

6. Panikkar, *Myth, Faith, and Hermeneutics*. New York: Paulist Press, 1979, p 347.

7. Hick, John, *An Interpretation of Religion*. New Haven: Yale University Press, 1989.

8. Panikkar, R. *The Intra-Religious Dialogue*. New York: Paulist Press, 1999, p. 34.

9. *Ibid*, p. 38.

Understanding Panikkar and Making Him Understood: A Threefold Hermeneutic Structure—*Graphe, Bios, Autos*

Maciej Bielawski

We are only beginning to realise the extent and the depth of Raimon Panikkar's work and vision. Personally, I am convinced that his work is a particular—possibly even unique—testimonial of the timeless human spirit, and a special tribute for our epoch.

In the evening of his life, Panikkar said that his writings were not 'simply speculative but rather autobiographical' and it strikes me that his writings (*grafe*), his life (*bios*) and the mystery of his person (*autos*) are inter-in-dependent. If we want to understand his writings we have to know his life. One way to understand the deeper dimension of his life is to read it through his writings. And yet both Panikkar's writings and his life are rooted in the mystery of his person (*autos*), which is found in something deeper and bigger than the events of his life and pages of his writings. Yet none of these three elements can exist without the other two and none of them can be exalted above or separated from the two others, because the three of them are one, united or, as he would like to say, inter-in-dependent, and they have to be taken into consideration together.

Grafe

This is the most material, most concrete, and the very first dimension through which people today shall be able to find access to Panikkar's vision.

Panikkar was many faceted. Even if he used to say that he had given the best of himself in liturgies, conferences, and relations with others, it is certain that he was also a writer. And today his vision is found primarily in his texts. In order to understand him it is necessary to pay attention to these, their formal aspect.

Panikkar wrote in at least seven languages (Latin, Spanish, Catalonian, German, English, French, and Italian) and his work remains multi-linguistic. Even if today we are gradually unfurling his 'Opera Omnia' as a single-language work (starting with an 'Italian matrix' subsequently translated into Catalonian, Spanish, French, English or German), Panikkar's thought is multi-linguistic, too. Panikkar was a pluralistic man even from the linguistic point of view.

Panikkar expressed himself primarily in the Anglo-Saxon and Romanic branches of Western European languages. Even though he knew basic Sanskrit and Hindi, his famous neologisms are all rooted in Greek or Latin (such as 'cosmotheandrism', 'tempiternitas', 'christophany', and the like). Although it is relatively easy to translate him into one of these Western European languages, one finds different obstacles when we try to introduce him into more distant languages, such as Slavic, Hindi, Chinese, or Swahili. Panikkar used to say, 'Not everything can be said in English'. It could be added, 'Not all Panikkar is translatable', which, of course, emphasises the whole question of understanding him and making him understood. In other words, can Panikkar's universal vision be made worldwide? And if so, how?

Panikkar wrote for more than 70 years, and, for a certain level of understanding, a chronological approach to his works cannot be avoided. It is not an easy task, yet it is an indispensable one. There is a certain evolution in Panikkar's works, and though he tends towards a harmony, one finds some contradictions in his writing. Of course, we can only speak to a certain extent about the 'first', the 'second', and maybe even the 'third' Panikkar. For example, the first Panikkar is clearly theocentric and the second one is cosmotheandric, or rather, pluri-centric. The first is clearly Christ-centric, the second Chistophanic. The first Panikkar speaks about the object of faith; for the second one, faith has no object. The first one is radical, the second revolutionary, the third tends toward a harmonious synthesis of the first and the second ones. It is fascinating to see how and why he changed, and to reflect on what it means.

The whole question is not purely academic or theoretical, because, following the evolution of Panikkar himself, whoever trails his development can participate in it and experience it. For example, following the steps of Panikkar from a Christocentric vision into a Christophanic one, one can make a qualitative leap, a real spiritual experience, which can involve an interior transformation.

Along the way of understanding the writings of Panikkar, different interpretations will appear. The question is, does Panikkar, being pluralistic by definition, allow different interpretations? Are we going to have a variety of different Panikkars after Panikkar? Yes, and yet, they are one.

In my opinion, the most urgent thing to do today is to collect Panikkar's entire patrimony and make it accessible to people without any exclusivity or censorship. To have everything collected and available is not enough, yet it is the condition *sine qua non* to understand Panikkar.

Bios

The work of Panikkar is like a great sea, and his life like a mountain, rising above the water and reflected in it. Navigating on the lake in different directions we can see the mountain from different perspectives and contemplate different aspects of the personality of Panikkar, yet if we want to see the whole lake we must climb the mountain. In other words, we have to understand his life if we want to see his whole work in a proper perspective. Panikkar's work and life belong to each other. Any honest study of his writing sooner or later must include his biography.

Yet climbing this mountain is not an easy task, because the rock from a distance looks nice yet as we come closer it seems difficult to climb, sometimes unpleasant and even disagreeable. Looking closer at Panikkar's life we see that he made errors, created conflicts, hurt persons, and felt ashamed. There were bright and dark spots within him, and in his life, as in all human beings. It would be wrong to judge him and his work only from the perspective of these errors, yet it is useless and dishonest to try to hide them. Panikkar was great not because he was innocent, but because he was sometimes wrong. We can see his greatness and better appreciate his search for freedom when we contemplate also his limitations, that is, his humanity.

There are numerous explanations for Panikkar's reluctance for any biography about him to be written. His life was so rich and original that he himself probably had difficulties understanding it or talking about it. He knew that the richness and complexity of life could not be reduced to a biographical narration. He had a certain mystical tendency according to which a wise man, a mystic, should not be known, should not have a biography, should be hidden and should have only a message. He was quite resistant to any kind of psychology, which, from one point of view, is somewhat correct and yet on the other hand can hide some psychological problems of his personality. Panikkar was quite aware that during his life he made mistakes and it was not easy for him to reconcile these facts with the image of a wise philosopher.

Similarly, there are several reasons for the inevitability of a biographical approach to Panikkar. First of all, Panikkar did not only have only a spiritual experience but also a full life; a very rich, interesting and, in a certain way, a beautiful life which should be known. Second, behind his quite speculative, metaphysical, and mystic writings, an understanding of the concreteness of his life is needed in order to appreciate his message. In other words, a reader somehow needs to know the answer to the question which had been put by his friend Abhishiktananda, who, after he had read his *The Unknown Christ of Hinduism*, wrote in his diary, 'Did he (Panikkar) accomplish all of that in his life?' The question cannot be avoided and the answer to that question has to pass through the knowledge of Panikkar's life. Whoever reads him, eventually asks, 'How did he live it? How did he accomplish all of that in his life? Is that real or are those only words?' Biography is not the only answer but without this no other answer can be given. In other words, the life of Panikkar can demonstrate the validity of his teaching and so it has to be known. We need to create a dialogue with the thoughts of Panikkar, we need to 'speak with' his life, and we need to juxtapose his life and his work.

The elderly Panikkar said, 'As soon as I had a hunch I started writing a new book or at least an article in order to check, clarify, deepen, and finally formulate my experience—although dressed in philosophical language that I believe is necessary.' This means that all his theories are rooted in his personal experience, and in order to understand them well, it is useful, if not necessary, to know the circumstances and the events that generated his reflections and in order to accomplish it the knowledge of his life is inevitable.

I think that Panikkar is going to keep many researchers busy for a long time yet, and from time to time we are going to be presented with a new discovery of letters, notes, or confessions which will call us to review what we know about his life and how we understand his vision. Also in the case of his life we are going to have different biographies of this man and different interpretations of the events, which are going to influence the comprehension of his ideas.

Right now, a widespread effort should be made to collect any kind of testimony about his life. This must be done quickly because time is passing and many witnesses are leaving us. It is obvious to me that Panikkar's personal archive should be accessible for this biographical research.

Autos

One of the verses from the *Veda* Panikkar loved the most was, 'What thing I am I do not know, I wander secluded, burdened by my mind" (RV I, 164, 37). This indicates the unknown, hidden or *apophatic* dimension of his existence as well as of his writings. This dimension is present everywhere in his life and work. It is present, yet it can be neither eliminated nor explained. Panikkar was in touch with this inexplicable and silent dimension, with his '*autos*', which, in keeping with the tradition, could be called *atman* (which is also Brahman), void or *sunyata* (which also indicates plenitude), and which has to remain in silence and in darkness. Using another image, we could say that his work is a circle, his life is its radius and yet the wheel moves because of the void at the pivot in the centre.

In the existence of Panikkar there is something which cannot be understood. Yet this 'something' is communicated to us by his life as we know it. Also, his writings cannot be reduced either to quotes, pages, or exegetical studies, yet in poring through his letters, words, sounds, and meanings we have access to their deepest dimension. In passing through the visibility of biography we reach the invisibility of life. We reach the silence of the word of Panikkar through the words and sounds of his teaching.

All three dimensions (*graphe, bios,* and *autos)* are inter-in-dependent. To the corresponding images of the lake (his writings, *graphe*) and the mountain (his life, *bios*), one more element should be added—the cloud that covers the top of the mountain and by reflecting on the surface of the water is mixed with the depths of the sea. One can neither pierce the cloud atop the mountain nor fathom the depths of the sea. They both symbolise the mystical character of Panikkar's writing and the enigma of his personality.

And so I see the challenge of understanding Panikkar and making him known as a practice of the threefold structure of *graphe-bios-autos*. These three words are symbols in a needful and dynamic interrelationship. In my opinion, it is only by facing each of the three dimensions of this structure and putting them together that the misunderstanding of Panikkar's work can be avoided and his thought can be fruitfully received in order to influence the life of other people.

The Relevance of Panikkar's Understanding of Symbol for Interreligious Education

Clemens Mendonca

Why do we need interreligious education?

We live in a multicultural and multireligious milieu and are experiencing a necessary interaction of our cultures, religions, and spiritualities. The major concern of all religious and secular traditions should have been to prepare the people to face life realistically. For this purpose religions need to learn from one another the way to reconciliation and peace. This entails coming together on the part of our traditions, encountering one another in dialogue and working in collaboration for the wellbeing of all. But we are far from this ideal. Formation of youth and children should have been the first priority of all traditions. Youth and children are the hope-bearers of the future. In order to do this, religious traditions need to broaden their understanding of reality. They need to understand one another, their cultures, and traditions. Understanding is a process. In this process, critique and creativity have to go hand in hand. Creativity has to do with being open, open to receiving. But in receiving we can go astray; here is where critique has to come in. Cultures and religions are not self-corrective; they need each other to do this. Without mutual critique there is no mutual enrichment. This is the principle and foundation of interreligious and intercultural formation.

Furthermore, interreligious education is essential because all traditions are aware today how our society functions at large. We note two dominant features in the functioning of our society—the *symbolic* (*syn-ballein*—to put things together, that which brings us together, that which unites) and the *diabolic* (*dia-ballein*—that which fragments, that which puts asunder, that which divides). On the one hand we are confronted by unimaginable diabolic forces that are bent on destroying our world and the humans. The ancient oppressive structures like the caste system, dictatorship, the exploitation of indigenous people and internal strife often control our lives. There is widespread corruption at various levels of government and private enterprises. We are also painfully aware of the rise of communalism, religious fundamentalism, and terrorism which continue to bring division and devastation to many people. In brief, we live in a culture of violence and death. This culture of violence is prevalent not only among humans, but has affected our ecosystem, the way we go about with the planet and its resources. It also affects our religious ideology, i.e. the way we understand God and deal with religious matters.

On the other hand we experience something like 'world consciousness'[1] for peace and harmony, for justice and equality. There is a common quest that unites all people of goodwill today—the quest for a healthy world—a healthy environment; the quest for unity in the human family beyond race, colour, caste, religion, gender, politics, nations, and continents; and the quest for meaning in life. These are the common concerns that affect people of all traditions, secular, and religious. Consequently, we find movements towards integration and peace. People all over the world are gradually becoming aware of their responsibility towards their fellow human beings especially in times of grave human and environmental disasters. Dialogue is becoming a catchword in all sectors, secular and religious. Yet we have not moved forward to deal with these common concerns in a deeper and methodical way barring a few NGOs and some committed individuals who work for these common concerns. In brief, the symbolic dimension in our life in this world has either already disappeared or is fast disappearing. Hence it needs to be retrieved through relevant religious education.

What all this highlights is the need for developing sensitivity to the world of symbols and its expressions (symbol-language) through deepening of awareness. Religions belong to the world of symbols and are expressed in symbolic language. Interreligious education will have to focus on how to discover the world of symbols, and deepen familiarity with the symbolic expressions of religious experience. It will also have to develop formative approaches through which this symbolic dimension can become part and parcel of human consciousness. This is the path all traditions will have to tread if they wish to heal humans and their world. Indeed, retrieval of the symbolic dimension is the essence of religious education today.

Panikkar's understanding of symbol and symbolic language

According to Raimon Panikkar, human beings are endowed with awareness and at the same time pervaded by an element of mystery, an element of the unknown. They are aware that this 'Mystery embraces something we call World, something we call Man,[2] and something that many cultures call the Divine. The awareness of this triad belongs to our very nature, though the names and conceptions of the three differ widely. There is some sort of connection between the three. We are together with other Men, on a common Earth, under the same sky, and enveloped by the Unknown. There is interconnectedness among the three. The triad is a Trinity. I call this Trinity, the theanthropocosmic invariant. Man as Man is conscious of this Trinity.'[3]

The theanthropocosmic experience is holistic and natural to Man, whatever be Man's cosmovision, culture or religion. It is a fundamental experience. But the expression of this fundamental experience differs from culture to culture, from cosmovision to cosmovision, from religion to religion. As we said earlier the worlds of religions and cultures are worlds of symbols and metaphors (symbolic language). So the basic theanthropocosmic experience can only be expressed through symbols and symbolic language of respective cultures. Experience belongs to the realm of symbol, and expression to the level of symbol-language, namely, metaphor. This is the hallmark of all religious experience. Consequently we have to examine how best we can go about with symbols and symbolic language in a multireligious and multicultural world.

The history of religions is full of conflict and misunderstanding. The effort of understanding other cultures and religions in the past was peripheral and self-centred. Till recently we were used to a monocultural mentality (Western culture) and our attitudes and dealings with other cultures and religions were rather strange and negative. An extremely important implication of the plurality of cultures often overlooked is that we have in fact different approaches to reality, truth, and history. Besides, there is a world of difference between 'knowing' and 'knowing about'. Hence it is not enough to know about a neighbour's culture and religion. To understand a religion it is imperative that we have to know its culture in the first place because culture and religion, though not synonymous, are a closely-knit unity. According to Panikkar, culture gives religion its language and religion gives culture its vision or content.[4] The awareness of cultural and religious diversity challenges us to move towards a new way of thinking and a new way of dealing with this problem. Awareness and acknowledgement of the fact that others have their own understanding and criteria of truth and right just as I have mine, will open us up towards a more holistic understanding of religions and cultures. It is here that the major problem of dialogue and interreligious awareness/education has to be located.

Panikkar's approach to reality is phenomenological. Reality, according to him, is all that there is, and 'all that there is' is interconnected and interrelated. 'By reality, we understand all that is, or is thinkable, all that can enter our consciousness, the representation (whether realistic or idealistic), the *idam* of the Upanishads…We exclude neither Being nor Nothingness, nor do we limit ourselves to what can be expressed by the verb to be.'[5]

Panikkar points out that the theanthropocosmic experience is a conscious experience but thematisation of this experience belongs to another realm of consciousness—self-consciousness. We do not find adequate words to describe an experience. That is to say expression, however communicative it may be, is not the experience, although they are intimately connected with each other. Panikkar thematises this theanthropocosmic experience and calls it unitary experience of reality, or the cosmotheandric experience.[6] He speaks of reality as the integration of three dimensions—cosmic, human, and divine. These three dimensions form a single community because they interpenetrate one another. Each dimension is unique and irreducible to the others. 'God, World, and Man', as he rightly puts it, are not and cannot be three separate entities but are three common invariants that form one fundamental unity in radical relativity.[7]

Symbol belongs to the material or cosmic dimension of reality. We encounter reality through its body, the material element, the cosmic dimension. Symbol makes present that which it symbolises, that is, symbolised reality. Symbolised reality is the 'depth' dimension of reality. The depth dimension makes us enter into a world of the meaningfulness of symbols. A symbol also needs a symboliser, a human person to symbolise (the 'human' dimension). The symboliser is the one who discovers symbols. Humans are the discoverers of symbols in their encounter with reality. A symbol is the meeting point of three worlds—the cosmic, the human, and the divine. It is a bridge-builder, because a symbol symbolises the symbolised reality.

A real symbol does not need any interpretation because it is self-expressive. For example, if we destroy a symbol we destroy that which it symbolises, the symbolised reality, along with it. 'If you kill the one, the symbol, you also kill the other, the symbolised thing. Symbols can die in the consciousness of the people.'[8] Panikkar remarks, 'The symbol is always immediate, non-mediated. The symbol is symbol precisely because it does not require mediation. There is no possible hermeneutics of a symbol. The symbol is symbol because it symbolises—not because it 'hermeneuticises' (i.e., because it gives an interpretation of itself).'[9]

Symbol is transparent because it contains the reality in itself. It carries within itself the reality it symbolises. Symbol and the symbolised reality are distinct but inseparable. One does not exist without the other but one is not the other. For example, the human body is the symbol of the person. We cannot separate the body from the person and the person can only be expressed through the symbol body.

Symbol belongs to the realm of both the ontological and the mythical. Panikkar says a symbol is an 'ontomythical reality'.[10] A symbol is not a product of *logos*; it is also not subject to analysis and verification. It is on the level of experience and of mythos, but to speak about it we need the help of *logos*.

Symbolic experiences are expressed in metaphors or symbolic language. We constantly make use of symbolic or metaphoric language in our day-to-day life without even being aware that we do not mean it literally. When we say 'my heart is burning' or 'my soul is thirsting', we normally do understand this language very well. These are symbolic phrases; they are not literal. There is no physical or literal burning or thirsting of the soul, yet we know these realities are very real and deep. Similarly, religious language is symbolic because the worlds of religions and cultures are worlds of symbols. Symbolic language operates at the level of understanding. In order to understand, we need openness. Informative language, though needed for practical purposes, does not do justice to religious beliefs. Informative language is literal and descriptive with univocal meaning. Symbolic language is transformative. Here we enter into a world of personal relationships.[11] A symbolic experience does not derive from reasoning, but through an awareness that is inherent in and immediate to our very (ontological) being. It is this symbolic awareness that we need to capture through interreligious education.

The relevance of 'symbol' for interreligious education

Symbol is the way to wholeness and has intercultural relevance. Consequently a cross-cultural approach is basic in any interreligious venture. When we enter into the world of 'the Other' (other traditions), their cosmovisions, we become familiar with their mythos, their forms of worship, the stories, symbols, and rituals they use in their worship of God, the feasts they celebrate and the significance of those feasts, etc. We are a step closer to understanding the other traditions. So far religious traditions have lived in isolation like strangers and quite often even as enemies forgetting that diverse religious traditions are meant to reveal the different perspectives of the Ultimate Mystery. Once we are familiar with other traditions, we have a space where we can correct, criticise, learn, and discover the wealth of each other's tradition. Awareness of the Other (culture, religion, etc.) leads to a genuine dialogue. Dialogue has to open us up to a process of deepening awareness, to see things as they really are, to see the world, the humans, and the divine as an interrelated organic unity in diversity. This is a new perspective, not a literal seeing and understanding but a seeing and understanding on the ontological level, that is, on the level of being-and-understanding. In this respect Panikkar's understanding of symbol is relevant to interreligious education.

Panikkar speaks of education as truly religious education because it touches the very core of the religious dimension of human person. He describes the religious dimension of secular education as 'the human face implicit in any human venture'. For example, mathematics, physics, chemistry, politics, and music are human activities that touch the human spirit (though they come under secular learning) and, insofar as they touch the human face, they also touch the religious dimension of the humans. [12]

Accordingly, for Panikkar education is the art and science of converting the polarising tensions into polarities. Tensions are dialectical and polarities are dialogical. Polarity implies awareness of complementarity, wherein 'without the position of the other, my position disappears'. Our positions should not, and cannot, be absolutised. Education should deal with symbols and not concepts alone, but today's education gives more importance to concepts. Symbolic awareness is a *via media* between the solipsism (that is, belief in 'self' as the only reality—the belief that the only thing somebody can be sure of is that he or she exists, and that true knowledge of anything else is impossible) of the thing and the abstraction of the concept. Symbol overcomes any solipsism and monism by involving us in the symbolising process.

Panikkar points out to a paradigm shift from concepts to symbols in religious and interreligious education. This does not mean that we should totally get rid of concepts in the educational field; we need them, but we cannot remain content only with them. They are supported by reason which is very important. However, we have to cross over to the next important step of 'awareness' that brings about a change in life. Symbol plays an important role in creating this awareness.

Interreligious education cannot be restricted to concepts alone simply because religion belongs to the realm of being. Concepts are abstractions and not things, not symbols. A concept is univocal and is valid and meaningful only where it is conceived. Symbols, on the other hand, unfold the real. They are 'polysemic' and 'polyvalent'.[13] A symbol is not interchangeable. It is holistic because it includes all the dimensions of reality. It is not static, but dynamic. Thus, for example, a song that is not sung is not a song.[14] It is not merely sound, but is rather something deeper that the music reveals. A symbol includes the symboliser, the subject. At the same time it reveals the symbolised. Such awareness is symbolic that genuine religious education should promote and deepen.

Symbolic awareness, says Panikkar, is an art or *techne*. There is a basic distinction between technique and *techne*. *Techne*, he points out, is an art, a craft, a human invariant, and is concerned with inherent beauty, its value in itself. It has to do with the intrinsic relationship between the human person and the thing made. Here no total objectification is possible. The approach of *techne* is holistic—that is, the relationship between the doer, the doing, and the done is a whole. Every culture has *techne*; every culture has its own ways and means to transform things for the benefit of the humans and the welfare of the society.[15]

In the light of awareness, one sees things differently because it is a stage beyond reasoning and reflection, beyond the push and pull of likes and dislikes, beyond the stage of grasping to the stage of being grasped by the Mystery. Awareness happens best in an atmosphere of freedom and truth and of letting go. It is not a magical formula attained as and when one likes. It is a gradual process, a process of awareness which opens our being and leads us to an experience of integration.

The challenge facing interreligious education is to enter into the arena of the real world, into today's concrete life situations that threaten our integrity and dialogue with the most pressing issues of our time. How do we transform these inhuman and unjust structures and systems that are threatening our world without collaboration? Religions have a responsibility of criticising, opposing and taking their clear stand against these systems and of inspiring the people to reach their human/communitarian destiny. In this sense, every genuine religious tradition has a mission to fulfil in today's world. This mission is to be reconcilers and bridge-builders between cultures and between religions. Propagating a doctrine of hatred and cultural superiority only worsens the global situation.

Interreligious education has to take upon itself this responsibility of making the people aware of the dangers of these systems. This entails a dual task—reflection and analysis of the situation in which we find ourselves, and a deepening awareness of what such a situation does to us in the depth of our being. The former functions at the level of the *logos* and the latter at the level of the *mythos*. There are two types of dynamics involved here—reasoning and analysing at the *logos* level and becoming aware at the *mythos* level. This is how we can develop sensitivity to the symbolic dimension of the world.

Finally, developing sensitivity to the symbolic dimension of the world—sensitivity in the symboliser (the humans), sensitivity to the symbol (the world of symbols), and sensitivity for the symbolised reality (the Mystery). Awareness of the symbolic dimension of the world is an experience of wholeness. But a holistic experience is not a product of mere reasoning, although reasoning through reflection deepens up our convictions. An experience of the working of these convictions belongs to the realm of the *mythos*.

Once religious traditions learn to be open to one another in dialogue, then taking joint responsibility for common concerns of our society will follow spontaneously. This is a praxis-oriented test for all religious traditions. The question is not as to which religious tradition I belong to, but what inspiration my tradition can give to shoulder my responsibility to bring about justice, peace, and healing to a broken world.[16]

The praxis of interreligious education

Finally, we come to the question of 'how'. How do we come to this symbolic experience? Panikkar often used to say that there is no 'how'. It happens just as love happens. One cannot produce or create love; so too, we cannot produce or manipulate symbolic awareness. But still, we can facilitate its happening. Every symbol is cosmotheandric because a symbol (in its 'cosmic' dimension) is a bridge-builder between the divine and the human. Every symbol has three main functions to fulfil (a) to work for the wholeness of creation (its cosmic commitment), (b) to work for the wholeness of humanity (its human welfare), and (c) to discover spirituality for our times ('cosmotheandric spirituality'). These three functions are oriented towards a triple openness, i.e. openness to the cosmos, to other humans, and to the divine. The function of interreligious education here is to sensitise the people to this triple openness.

There are some universal symbols that can be meaningful for all traditions secular and religious; for example, breath, bread, and religion (*dharma*). These symbols could be used in the interreligious community through a process of reasoning and awareness. Reasoning helps us to build up convictions and awareness opens us to the depth dimension of reality. These twin exercises of reasoning and awareness can guide us to the roots of our problems and open us to a new awareness.

True awareness is dynamic. It opens not only one's heart but also one's entire being to go out in service, in commitment to the wellbeing of all. The process of awareness and discovery naturally leads to collaboration in genuine action. It is an action that is selfless because it does not seek the fruits of its labour. Such action has two characteristics—an internal freedom and an external commitment to the welfare of all. Let us examine a few examples.

Breath, the symbol of the life of the world (ecological issues)

Breath has a vital significance in almost every religious tradition. It is the symbol of life—our earthly life would be impossible without the life-giving element of air, breath, and wind. Life from the beginning to the end is related to breath. It is this all-penetrating breath that opens one up to the infinite, without which one would not exist on earth.

In the Vedas 'breath' is the primordial symbol of life. The hymn to the breath of life (*prana*) in the Atharva Veda[17] speaks of its creative power which brings forth life on earth. According to Panikkar, wind, breath, and life, though not identical, belong together and form an interrelated and integrated unity on earth. Though named differently, they are experienced holistically. For example, if the wind disappears breath would be impossible. Wind, breath, and life have also a common feature, that of physical movement. Panikkar further points out that movement is the life-principle or the soul of every phenomenon in the wind, breath, and life. Wind is not just air but air in movement; breath is the same movement of the air within living beings. Finally life is intrinsically a movement for it moves without being moved.[18] Indeed, life is the 'interiorisation and ontologisation' of the breath, remarks Panikkar.[19]

In the Christian tradition, breath is the symbol of the Spirit of God and the Spirit of God is the Life-giving and Creative Spirit. The Spirit of God fills the universe. Psalm 104 speaks of the Spirit as being sent forth from God who renews the face of the earth. The Spirit blows where it wills. In the second chapter of the Acts of the Apostles, at the feast of the Pentecost, the Spirit of God is likened to the strong Wind. We see here a connection between the breath, wind, earth, and life, the source of which is the Spirit of God. They are interrelated realities, all pointing towards life. They signify wholeness and sacredness.[20]

Reality is structured in such a way that it revolves around all-pervasive life. Panikkar notes that the wind manifests the life of the earth, breath reveals to us the intimate connection between life and non-life (matter). Life is an abstraction if there is no living being. Further, wind, breath and life are not only interrelated, but there is an existential cooperation between these three in order to preserve life. For example, the wind gives life to the plants and comforts animals. The plants in their turn breathe in and out and complete the 'ecologically essential purifying function' and humans live because of this process.[21] In other words, the breath of life is the 'symbol of life itself, that is, life as it manifests itself in living beings'.[22] The breath of life is the gift that the earth gives to all those who are born in her.

The breath animates our entire being, i.e. our whole being is alive with breath. All living beings breathe the same breath provided by the same cosmos. Here there is no hierarchy, no discrimination. Breath is a sacred gift. It is life, mystery, communion, and interconnection. Breath is communion among the cosmos, the human, and the divine.

All the three dimensions of reality are visible here—the cosmic, because it is the earth that provides us with this atmosphere, the breath of life; the human, because humans exist because they breathe the breath of life; the divine, because ultimately breath *is* Mystery. We cannot produce breath. We cannot comprehend its depths and heights. We do not know where it comes from and where it goes. Breath connects us to both the Ultimate Mystery and the cosmos. The exercise of 'Breath' could be used to create awareness on ecological issues.

Bread, the symbol of communion (humanitarian issues)

Like breath, bread too is a very rich symbol of life and life is wholeness and communion. Communion is not possible without collaboration and mutual interdependence. For example, bread does not exist by itself. One single grain of wheat does not make bread. Bread is bread only in communion, in togetherness.

Bread is the symbol of a cosmic process. It expresses the symbolised reality of self-giving. Bread is a community, a communion, a presence of the divine working in the world and in the humans. Here is the cosmotheandric mystery at work. It is a mysterious work of collaboration between the cosmic, the human, and the divine.

Further, bread is a continuous process of life and death; at each stage there is a self-giving, a death, so that the other might come to life. The cosmic elements like sun, water, earth, minerals all have to 'die' to give life to the grain. The seed dies and gives life to the plant, the plant dies in the sense it gives itself up so that many other plants are born, again the plants 'die' in that they have to be ground in the mill to become flour, the flour has to be kneaded and formed into dough, and the dough has to be baked in the fire in order to become bread. The bread 'dies' in order to be transformed into life-blood in the humans. The process goes on and on. One who eats this bread has to become bread for others, if the process is to go on. All this reveals a deeper truth—self-emptying process, a life and death experience. This is so because reality itself is kenotic. Self-giving is the navel of Reality.[23]

The Hindu understanding of *yajna* is also very relevant here. According to this understanding, the world is understood by the metaphor of *yajna* or sacrifice. Again, it represents the kenotic activity of the cosmos. According to this world-view, everything in this cosmos lives for others, sacrifices itself for the sake of others. Everything dies in order that others might live. One lives because of the other and for the other. In other words, *yajna* symbolises that everything is food (bread) for everything. For example the sun shines not for itself but to give warmth and light for others, the water is there not for itself but for others, the rain, the trees, and the whole creation exists not for itself but for others. The process of self-giving is the life of the world according to this tradition. The *yajna* symbol reveals this ontological interrelationship.[24]

Kenosis (self-emptying) is the central mystery of Christianity. Where there is self-giving there is life; that is why Jesus is the 'Bread of Life'. The life of Jesus is a life of kenosis; he came to serve and not to be served. Hence, 'bread' is not only the symbol of a cosmic process, it signifies to us Christians the Life, Death, and Resurrection of Jesus. The Eucharist is the symbol of Life and Communion.

Bread is the symbol of communion. Communion is possible only in a world of self-giving and collaboration. The process of self-emptying is a continuous process. We all eat the same bread that has undergone this kenotic process. But unlike the bread, humans can turn out to be selfish. Thus, this cosmic process of self-giving stops only with the blindness and selfishness of human beings. It is because of this selfishness that today our bread contains blood and exploitation. It is profit-oriented bread which causes division, destruction, and death. Symbolically expressed, humans, though they exist because of the kenotic process of the cosmos, refuse to continue this process. Hence, instead of communion, what we have been mostly experiencing today is fragmentation.

Bread, a natural symbol of self-giving and communion, has in our present context become a symbol of dehumanisation, division, sectarianism, discrimination, and marginalisation on the basis of class (the rich and the poor), caste (the problem of untouchability in India), gender (the patriarchal system that denies humanity to females), creed (interreligious conflicts), and the like.

Religion (dharma), the symbol of integration (religious issues)

Whereas breath and bread are intercultural and interreligious meeting points, *dharma* goes one step beyond. It is a special meeting point because *dharma* has to do specifically with the divine, the ultimate goal of every human search. But it is also a specific historical search since each religion has a specific foundational experience. Here again, reasoning and awareness have their place. The first brings out the specific character of *dharma,* and the second its specific experience.

Dharma is a comprehensive word which derives from the root *dhr*—to uphold, to support, to nourish,[25] and hence has something to do with holding, holding together, sustaining, maintaining, and supporting. *Dharma* connotes the 'source' of this holding together, hence the implication of a 'being held-together in being'. It comprehends wholeness, interrelation, interconnection, interactivity and the final destiny (and thus the fulfilment) of both humans and the cosmos.[26] As such, *dharma* is the symbol of integration and leads to harmony, peace, and meaningfulness in life.

Every religious tradition ultimately tries to offer to its followers meaningfulness in life. But it is expressed differently according to the diversity of cultures and traditions as peace, justice, liberation, salvation, and so on. According to Panikkar, 'religion is the way to peace' and is equivalent to the interpretations of salvation. Further, says Panikkar, peace is the blend of harmony, freedom, and justice, and is often clothed with a particular cultural garb. Some cultures call it freedom—often spoken of as individual freedom for they are sensitive to those elements that hamper human fulfilment; some cultures stress the aspect of justice—collective justice while these are sensitive to the structural obstacles that hamper just social order; some other cultures stress harmony—an interconnection with nature as they are sensitive to those elements that promote both human and cosmic harmony because for them life is of highest value.[27] By whatever name it might be called, *dharma* is a symbol of peace and wholeness. But here comes an important point we often tend to forget—peace cannot be partial. It is holistic and integral because it has that triple characteristic—ecological (cosmic wellbeing), human (human welfare) and divine (meaningfulness of life).

Conclusion

Interreligious education enables all religious traditions to listen to the Spirit to discover in which direction the Spirit is leading us. Listening to the Spirit means the openness of being and readiness to move in that direction which brings wholeness, healing, justice and peace to all. It is becoming aware of unity in diversity. It is above all going beyond all relativism and syncretism, sectarianism and absolutism. It is opening oneself to the happenings of today's world, among today's humans wherever/whoever they may be. It is listening to the story of the earth and taking up joint responsibility to bring about this wholeness.

Second, Interreligious education is a sure means to take other traditions seriously. The responsibility of philosophers, theologians, animators, and directors is to perceive the 'signs of the times', or the common concerns. Having perceived these signs, they have to work towards holistic movements, be they political, social, economic, cultural, religious, or gender-based.

Third, it involves people of good will of different religious traditions, networking and working together. Various movements, such as ecological, justice, and peace movements, would be powerhouses if backed by such networking. The motivating force for this networking should be service to the earth, welfare of humans, and openness to the Mystery. The insight of Nicholas D. Kristof could give us an impetus towards this move. 'Religious people and secular people alike do fantastic work on humanitarian issues—but they often don't work *together* because of mutual suspicions. If we could bridge this 'God gulf', we would make far more progress on the world's ills."[28]

Our task is threefold—to keep alive the quest for a healthy world, to deepen our belongingness to the one common human family, and to open ourselves to the ever-elusive meaning in life. Only then can our shared dream of 'a New Earth' become a tangible reality. If our religious traditions could take the lead in this undertaking then our world would be a much happier place to live in! Instead of comparing and competing with one another, they could begin to discover the significance they have for their respective traditions and share this richness with one another.

Endnotes

1. C. Murray Rogers, "A New Millennium – Nearly!" in *Hindu-Christian Studies,* 8 (1995), 36–37.

2. Panikkar employs the word Man with a capital letter for 'human being'. In this usage, 'Man' refers to the human being in its totality. Such an expression is in no way a language of sexism and thus should not be taken as antifeminist. Panikkar himself says the following, 'Two reasons compel me to write Man with a capital letter – (a) to indicate that it means the human being in its totality and thus includes the male and the female; – (b) to imply that Man is an irreducible reality standing side by side, with all the necessary ontological distinctions, with God and the world.' *Raimundo Panikkar*: *The Unknown Christ of Hinduism,* Asian Trading Corporation, Bangalore, 1982, footnote 1, ix.

3. Raimon Panikkar, *The Rhythm of Being*, The Gifford Lectures, Orbis Books, Maryknoll, New York, 2010, 268.

4. Raimon Panikkar, "Religious Identity and Pluralism" in *A Dome of Many Colours, Studies in Religious Pluralism, Identity and Unity* by Arvind Sharma and Kathleen M. Dugan (eds.), Trinity Press International, Pennsylvania, 1999, 27.

5. Raimon Panikkar, "Religion, Philosophy and Culture" in Polylog, Forum for Intercultural Philosophy, 1 (2000), 43, http://them. polylog. org/1/fpr-en. htm

6. See Raimon Panikkar, "The Cosmotheandric Intuition" in *Jeevadhara,* XIV, 79 (1984), 27–35.

7. ibid, 27–28.

8. ibid, 21.

9. Raimon Panikkar, "A Self-Critical Dialogue" in Joseph Prabhu (ed.), *The Intercultural Challenge of Raimon Panikkar,* 1996, 227–91, 235.

10. R. Panikkar, *Myth, Faith and Hermeneutics,* Asian Trading Corporation, Bangalore, 1983, 6.

11. Francis X. D'Sa, "The Language of God and the God of Language" in Robert P. Scharlemann and Gilbert E. M. Ogutu (eds), *God in Language*, Paragon House Publishers, New York, 1987, 35–59.

12. R. Panikkar, "The Challenge of Religious Studies to the Issues of Our Times" in *Nucleus: Reconnecting Science and Religion in the Nuclear Age*, by Scott Thomas Eastham, Foreword by Raimundo Panikkar, 1987, xiii–xxxviii, xv.

13. Raimond Panikkar, "The Power of Words" in *The Dharma of Jesus,* Interdisciplinary Essays in Memory of George M. Soares-Prabhu, S. J, Francis X. D'Sa S. J. (ed.), Institute for the Study of Religion, Pune and Gujarat Sahitya Prakash, 1997, 408–17, 413.

14. Colloquium with Raimond Panikkar, Sadhana Institute, 1999.

15. Raimond Panikkar, "Present Day University Education and World Cultures" in *Asian Cultural Studies: Religious Consciousness and Modern World,* M. Uozumi and M. Kasai, Mitaka (eds), Special Issue, 4, 187–98, 194–95.

16. Cf. Clemens Mendonca, *Dynamics of Symbol and Dialogue: Interreligious Education in India,* The Relevance of Raimon Panikkar's Intercultural Challenge, LIT Verlag, Münster, 2002, 231–32.

17. Cf., R. Panikkar, *The Vedic Experience: An Anthology of the Vedas for Modern Man and Contemporary Celebration,* All India Books, Pondicherry, 1989, AV XI, 4, 206.

18. Ibid. 204–05.

19. Ibid. 208.

20. In Hebrew the word '*ruach*' means air, breath, wind, all signs of life. Ruach Elohim hovers over the waters – Gen 1, 2; Cf. . also, Gen 1: 7, 7: 22, 8: 1, 15: 10, Joel 3: 1–4, Is 11: 1–16, EZ 37: 1–14, 1Sam 10: 9–12, Ps 104: 24–30, Lk 1: 15b, 1: 35, 4: 16–21, 11: 20, 23: 46, Mk 1: 10, Mt 28: 1, Jn 20: 22, Acts 2, II Cor 3: 17, Rom 8: 15, etc.

21. R. Panikkar, *The Vedic Experience*, 204–05. According to the Vedas the mystery of personal consciousness is identified with the person with this same Breath of Life (*prana*). 205; See also the hymn Prana, AV XI, 4, 206–08.

22. Ibid. 205.

23. The *Eucharist* in Christianity and the *Yajna* (cosmic sacrifice) of Hinduism use the symbols of Bread and Food respectively as central to their faith experience.

24. Cf., R. Panikkar, *The Vedic Experience*, 347–56.

25. P. V. Kane, *History of Dharmasasthra,* Revised and Enlarged Edition, Vol. 1 Part 1, Bhandarkar Oriental Institute, Pune, 1966, 1.

26. Francis X. D'Sa, "Dharma as Delight in Cosmic Welfare: A Study of Dharma in the Gita" in *Biblebhashyam* VI (1980), 335–57, 336–41.

27. R. Panikkar, "The Challenge of Religious Studies to the Issues of Our Times" in *Nucleus: Reconnecting Science and Religion in the Nuclear Age*, by Scott Thomas Eastham, Foreword by Raimundo Panikkar, 1987, xiii–xxxviii, xxv, 'Freedom points to truth. Justice points to goodness. Harmony points to beauty. A genuine peace would be to blend these three values, visions, experiences, both in a time-less/time-full (tempiternal) way and in a personal/cosmic manner. The traditional word for this blend is Love.'

28. Nicholas D. Kristof, "Evangelicals without Blowhards" in *Sunday Review, New York Times*, July 30, 2011, http://www. nytimes. com/2011/07/31/opinion/sunday/kristof-evangelicals-without-blowhards. html

Raimon Panikkar's Quest for Rhythm of Being (*Rtatattva*)

The challenge of being true to one's faith tradition while admitting the truth-claims of other religions

Anand Amaladass

Preliminary Remarks

In this paper an attempt is made to look for a vision of Panikkar, if possible, a common thread that runs through his thought, thus uniting all his writings. To remain with Panikkar's choice of formulation of his own mission in life, one can trace back to one of Panikkar's earlier essays "Towards a Hindu–Christian Theology: Rtatattva" (*Jeevadhara*, 1979). Significantly enough, his last book carries the title *Rhythm of Being* (2010).

Obviously, *rtatattva* is a metaphor, one which sums up Panikkar's understanding of his life's mission. The metaphor stems from the worldview of the *Rig Veda*, wherein *rta* is the cosmic order which keeps the universe dancing[1] in rhythm, governing the whole universe and holding it together. The last hymn of the *Rig Veda* sums up what is meant by this rhythm as follows,

> Gather together, converse together!
> Your minds be of one accord,
> Just as in harmony the Gods of old
> Took their ritual shared of oblation!
> United be your counsel, united your assembly,
> United your spirit and thoughts!
> A single plan do I lay before you;

A single oblation do I offer!
United your resolve, united your hearts,
May your spirits be at one,
That you may long together dwell
In unity and concord. (*Rig Veda*, X, 191, 2–4)[2]

Rhythm, harmony, concord, are the key words in Panikkar's vocabulary, for he would like to highlight the interconnectedness of everything in the universe. He repeats this idea in different forms and finds parallel formulations in different traditions like the Greek *perichoresis*, the Buddhist notion of dependent origination (*pratitya samutpada*), the basic philosophy of the Mallavadins, later adopted by Abhinavagupta, 'everything is interconnected' (*sarvam sarvatmakam*) and the underlying principle of the cosmic solidarity in the *karma* theory.

Panikkar accepts that all religions are ways towards freedom and happiness. He does not claim to speak for any particular religion, not for Christianity, not for Hinduism. He seems to distance himself from an exclusive loyalty to any religious tradition. He has taken the Buddhist symbol of *pratitya samutpada* as his motive, for, as he himself says, a radical relativity of all that exists can only maintain a harmony without abuse of power. The reason is 'no single religion, not even all traditional religions taken together, has a monopoly on religion'. But he participates in all the worldviews that exist, otherwise he cannot claim to understand really any religion or tradition which he talks about, whose texts and myths he translates and interprets. That is why he could say that he discovered in India that he was a Hindu and returned to Europe as a Buddhist without ceasing to be a Christian.

Panikkar's Pilgrimage to Gangotri

Now, how does Panikkar go about his mission of finding this harmony or rhythm by his writings? Panikkar formulates this quest as a thesis thus: On the one hand, if Hinduism goes on in the traditional way without Christian input, it would run out of inspiration and become irrelevant. On the other hand, if Christianity also goes on in its traditional way without Hindu input, it would also become counter-productive and even dangerous. Thus he means to say that both need to interact with one another in order to get enriched and find fulfillment. This process he calls cross-fertilisation or mutual fecundation. He refers to St. Paul's theology as an example of cross-fertilisation of Hebrew and Greek thoughts. So too, as Panikkar puts it, the Vedic world is another example of the cross-fertilisation of the Arian and Dravidian—the *materia* is Dravidian, autochthonous, but the *forma* is Aryan and the language is Sanskrit.

So he pleads for a Hindu–Christian theology valid for both. All his later works seem to go in the direction of realising this dream come true. What did that mean for Panikkar and what does it mean for us today?

He was communicating to a wider world, in that he was mediating between the East and the West, between Christian and Hindu worlds, as he was placed in a historical situation which was not his choice, inheriting the two world-views of his Hindu father and of his Catholic mother. He was trying to be true to both these two traditions he inherited. Obviously he was sharing the views of others as a precondition for understating the other. Hindu and Christian worlds were not foreign to him. He was not an outsider to any of these traditions, as he says.

His first major publication was to discover the *Unknown Christ*, unknown to both Hindus and Christians, by writing a commentary on the second *Brahmasutra* in 1965. He develops this insight of discovering the Christic principle hidden in everything over the course of time, and comes out with a fully developed thesis in his book *Fullness of Man: A Christophany* (in Italian, 1999). Even on his final journey in life he wanted this double loyalty to be symbolised by half of his ashes being immersed in the Ganges and the other half buried in his family grave in Tavertet (Barcelona), and a Catholic Mass celebrated in the Basilica in Montserrat.

Through the historical predicament Panikkar had many natural advantages from being exposed to two worlds, with their differing forms of faith and ways of thinking, and from his exposure to different nationalities and training—but not without corresponding ambiguities and the consequent tensions to live up to what he said and did. He was also trying to integrate or find ways of accounting for his belongingness to different worlds of faith. Brought up as a Christian and deciding to be a Catholic priest meant a lot to him, but did not want to alienate his Indian family connection through his Hindu father. Obviously he could not make a choice between his father and mother. As a result perhaps he found a way to explain at what level he remains part of these two traditions.

Panikkar's Philosophical Quest

Panikkar himself sums up his philosophical quest under three headings (i) *the existential venture,* (ii) *the intellectual burden, and (iii) spiritual freedom.* [3]

The Existential Venture

The existential venture is the venture of a life at home in more than one culture and religion. In this process he says that Indic teachings concerning one's personal *karma* (*svadharma)* became a new, vivid symbol for him. He does not consider himself deliberately both Indian and European, both Hindu and Christian. He says,

> Instead, my birth, my education, my initiatives and my practical life have made me the person I am, nurtured by the basic experiences of both the Western and the Indic traditions. Thus, I am participating, on the one hand, in both the Christian and the secular realms and, on the other, in both the Hindu and the Buddhist. It took three-fourths of my life to be able to express this view with confidence. (p. 131)

His interest in mythos taught him two things, one, to accept the *dharma* of his concrete existence, and two, to dedicate himself to living a new kind of spirituality. 'Only *pratitya samutpada,* the radical relativity of all that exists can maintain a harmony without abuse of power.' (p. 131)

The Intellectual Burden

Then Panikkar tries to express these existential experiences in an intelligible way. A few pointers could be mentioned here. There arises a polarity which is able to endure tension and that is the ultimate characteristic of what is real.

The concept of *ontonomy* highlights mutual relation, a radical relativity which shows us that reality is ultimately a non-dualistic polarity and, therefore, it is best for every living being to seek a harmonious integration in the whole.

The *symbolic difference*. A symbol is simply an epiphany of what appears in the symbol itself. Viewing existence as a symbol opens, in his opinion, a new chapter in the encounter of cultures and worldviews.

We need *pisteuma* in order to understand the ultimate phenomena of religious beliefs. Two assumptions are made here—first, faith is a fundamental, basic phenomenon of the human being; and second, the human self-understanding is a fundamental element of Man's essence.

The notion of *diatopical hermeneutics*. This starts out with the awareness of the *topoi* (the *loci* of the various worldviews), which normally could not be understood within the categories of only one culture or tradition. It is an attempt to blend fundamentally different human horizons.

Then comes the *tempiternal* nature of reality. Reality is at once both temporal and eternal.

Cosmotheandric or the *theanthropocosmic* intuition. Reality is non-dual and all existence has three constituting dimensions—the cosmic, the human, and the divine; the material (space-time), the intellectual (conscious) and the mystical (eternal). There is no matter without spirit and no spirit without matter, no world without God and no God without the universe and so forth. The threefold-world view (*triloka*) is found in all traditions.

Spiritual Freedom

All that has been said results from a personal adventure, from an experience that is neither individualistic nor sociological which takes place in any small mirror that reflects all of reality and thus comprises the whole, in the intimate microcosm of the person, in the depth of the contemplative love.

Concrete Way of Living His Mission

Panikkar was not an armchair philosopher fabricating a theory for world peace and harmony. He plunged into action, into the world of Hindu tradition and translated and interpreted its texts. Panikkar's usual explanation of 'understanding the other' means to stand under the spell of the other. In that sense Panikkar was also convinced that one cannot understand a text without participating in it. We can cite several such sayings of Panikkar. But Panikkar was not merely making theological statements to justify his position, like some other experts who stand at the platform and discuss for hours without ever getting into the train, with their counter-argument that they want to make sure where the train will take them.

Panikkar sees the urgency of the need to take his spiritual calling earnestly, standing before a burning house, a metaphor from the Buddhist parable of the *Lotus Sutra*, to rescue a manuscript containing the message of salvation for mankind. There is an act of faith in the inevitability of the choice by allowing circumstances to guide his intellect, his spirit and indeed his whole life, as he says.

We shall concretely take one work of his and see whether one can derive some conclusions out of that, namely his translation of Vedic hymns called *The Vedic Experience* (1977), for he himself did not say much about his personal life. He wanted no biography to be written about him. He wanted his readers to know him through what he has left behind. His publications speak for him.[4]

What does that mean? What does it involve? The task is not just finding equivalent symbols in another language or dressing his thoughts in another set of linguistic codes. Panikkar started translating Indian texts like the Vedas and the Myths to the modern man, as he says, mediating Indian culture to the European world. In that process he created his own vocabulary, his own world of thinking which is not easy to be understood. First of all, let us see what he says about his own task of translation and the hermeneutic principles involved in his process of communicating Indian thought to the modern man, as he calls.

Panikkar as Translator and the Challenge of Intercultural Communication

One well-known work of Panikkar is *The Vedic Experience: Mantramanjari—An Anthology of the Vedas for Modern Man and Contemporary Celebrations*.[5] This is not the first time the Vedas were translated into English. He mentions a few prior works, and admits that he makes use of them at times. Then what is unique about his translation? What is different in his translation compared to those of others?

He admits that the 'Vedic epiphany belongs to the heritage of mankind'. He seems to be aware of his identity as a Christian when he says that 'we do not want to hurt the feelings or invade the rights of the different religions of the world grouped under Hinduism' (p. 4). 'We do not intend to loosen the roots from their historical identity, but we believe that this rootedness does not preclude further growth' (p. 5).

Panikkar writes a long introduction to his translation of the Vedas explaining the difficulties involved in such a venture. First he considers the introductions themselves as integral parts of the translation, and second, the criterion of selection of the hymns is another constituent element of the translation. That is why he suggests 'that the introductions be studied twice, before the texts as prologues and after the texts as epilogues' (p. 26).

He spells out some principles which are involved in his enterprise of translation. He says that 'the aim of any translation is not to be mere transposition of signs', but to make the text intelligible to the reader. He also admits that 'any translation is provisional in the sense that it is only for the time being, until the moment when illumination comes by itself, the translation is forgotten and the reader is converted that is convinced'(p. 20). Even then 'a certain technique, a particular methodology, and a whole cluster of disciplines are needed'. There are as many forms of interdisciplinary help as possible but they remain discretely in the background. Its function is to promote the understanding of the underlying intuitions.

Another principle implied in his translation is that the translator shares the world-view of what is interpreted. 'If we try to report other people's beliefs without in some way sharing in them, we prevent ourselves from expressing what we think is the correct interpretation.' In other words, 'the belief of the believer belongs to the phenomenon itself. Our own interpretation has to face the challenge of meeting both our own convictions and those of the representatives of the document we interpret' (p. 22).

There are no fixed and immutable translations; words are much more alive than we tend to think, and all of them have a personal 'face'. The ambivalence of words and concepts constitutes proof that we are dealing with subjects that are still alive (p. 22). This should 'add to our sense of responsibility to find on each occasion the right words, the proper atmosphere'.

Another problem related to translation is that nearly all Western languages have been moulded by the Jewish–Hellenic–Christian tradition against a Gothic, Celtic, or other indigenous background.

> Transcultural translations disturb or even destroy the otherwise neatly defined difference between proper and common names. Substantives like 'grace', 'revelation', 'democracy', and even 'lord' and 'god' are undoubtedly common names within a certain cultural area. Yet to speak of Vedic Revelation, the God of Hinduism, the Grace of Vishnu, the Lord Buddha and the like would make at least some people uneasy. The same can be said the other way around. Are the words *agni, karman, dharma, mantra, brahman, advaita*, and the like the exclusive property of the Indian religions? In other words, 'words are more than mere labels and thus we cannot deny the fact that words have their proper orthodoxies'. We cannot accept as a criterion of translation the existence of a 'thing in itself' apprehended differently by two interpretations of the same word (pp. 23–24).
>
> For a long time it was forbidden to translate the Vedas or to teach them to the non-initiated. Nowadays, there is a universal trend, which abhors artificial esotericisms and sectarian separations.... So long as the symbolism of the Vedas was alive, so long as it needed no

> trans-mythologisation in order to be understood and lived, translation amounted to a betrayal; but when Vedic symbolism is no longer alive, survival may well demand emigration, that is, translation (p. 24).

The process of translation is not just transcultural. It begins within a particular culture. The work of the great *bhashyakaras* or commentators consists precisely of such translations, including the translation of the proper names of the tradition itself. When those names cease to stand for a living symbol within a 'lived' myth, they are 'trans-lated', that is 'shifted', so as to designate henceforward the same 'reality' but beyond its proper or native horizon (p. 25).

In fact Panikkar tries to play the role of the *bhashyakara* by translating the mind and perspective of the Indian sages into the modern culture. Consciously or unconsciously Panikkar carries over this Indian cultural trait of *sutra-bhashya* mode to another culture, another language-milieu. He is fond of formulating nine sutras on any theme and then writing *bhashya* or commentary on these sutras. His nine sutras on 'Peace and Interculturality' is one such example. Thus Panikkar trans-lated, or 'shifted', not only the intuition of the Indian *rishis*, but also the special *sutra-bhashya* style of writing into the cultural milieu of the West.[6]

The World of Translators and the Challenges Confronting Them

Translators are intercultural communicators and they are global players. Panikkar says in his introduction to his Vedic experience, 'The intention of this *mantramanjari* is not translation, but representation; that is, its goal is an existential reenactment.' He elaborates it further, 'The aim of this anthology is to make available to modern Man the riches of the elders and thus to globalise human experience" (p. 27).

This process of translation has been a challenge between India and the Western world; this has changed the world of cultures and brought about a revolution in human understanding. Al Biruni, for example, translated two Greek texts on mathematics (by Euclid and Ptolemy) into Sanskrit and brought Patanjali's *Yoga Sutras* into Arabic and attempted to synchronise it with the Qur'an. Likewise, Dara Shukoh translated some 50 Upanishads into Persian to show that they are commentaries on the Qur'an. This was then translated into Latin by Anquettil Duperron, which found its way to the European world. The Christian missionaries translated the Bible into Indian languages. Thus they introduced the exegetical method of translation to India. There was also an indirect 'missionary' attempt to capture the mind of the audience by translations. However, Panikkar's approach was different—there was no missionary overtone in Panikkar's endeavour.

Panikkar's Theological Position Amidst the Multiple Identity Debate

How do we place his theological position relating to the plurality of religions? It is ambiguous to call it simply a 'trans-religious theology', for what transcends the religious realm cannot be called theology. Panikkar is against any absolutising tendency, though 'relativising one's position' might sound too negative and so not acceptable. In 1965 Panikkar wrote that Christians have no monopoly of goodness, no monopoly of truth, and no monopoly of salvation.[7] What are the implications of his theological position in a pluralistic world of religions? Monotheism is said to be the presupposition for dictatorship or violence. How does Panikkar's vision sustain the world of religions, which have the inbuilt violence potential?

Panikkar makes a distinction between Religion and religions in his earlier work (1965). He identifies nine dimensions which constitute Religion and they are mentioned here briefly.

1. The ontic–mystic dimension: It is comprised of the inner ontic side and the outer mystic side; in other words, the objective and subjective aspects of this first dimension.
2. The dogmatic–doctrinaire dimension: On the one hand, dogmas are the underlying intellectual interpretation of the religion and on the other hand, there is an understandable and accessible system, a darsana, a world-view.

3. The ethical–practical dimension: The means of reaching the goal—cult, laws, sacraments, rites on the one hand as well as a way to show people how this stage could be reached.
4. The emotional dimension: There is a difference between the inner aspect of Man as an emotional being and an external response to the religion, which covers the entire world of feelings of Man.
5. The ecclesial–sociological dimension: The organic body, the inner structure of the community on the one hand, wherein prayer, suffering for the sake of others, preaching, serving, and love of neighbour and the like are part of this aspect and this requires on the other hand a certain sum of traditions and prescriptions through the bunch of history, geography, and race.
6. The material–cosmological dimension: A human being is not only soul and spirit, but also body and its material structure on the one hand and is also part of the universe. The fate of the human and of the cosmos are connected with one another.
7. The angelic–demonic dimension: On the one hand, the human being is immersed in the world of spirits; the angelic relation of the spirit which is personal, free and invisible, which helps and inspires to reach man's goal, and on the other, there are also spirits which tempt and mislead, known as demons—the religious spirit involves a struggle between good and evil.
8. The immanent–transcendent dimension: Religion is not only a response to the deeper human longing but also to a transcendent call to complete and fulfil our human nature.
9. The temporal–eternal dimension: Religion strives to lead the temporal humans to the timeless state; that is why religion claims to be as temporal as are the humans, yet also eternal like God.[8]

He goes on to highlight three levels—the mystic, the intellectual, and one of cults and norms of behaviour.

In his own words, 'Religion is a theandric reality, which can only be understood if we consider human beings not as isolated self-sufficient beings, but as mysterious, wonderful, place of encounter, in which God and the evil, spirit and matter, individual and society, person and universe, struggle with each other and come together. Human being is no microcosm, but a megacosmos.'[9]

On the other hand, 'religions show an inner constitutive development towards the only religion and all contribute to the enrichment of the true catholic religion, whose only leading power is God, who calls from above all people of good will by truth, goodness, and beauty and draws to Himself. There may be in the world of religion lights of many colours, but all proceed from a pure white ray.' That would mean, 'Till not all colours meet together again in a new white ray, they are ray particles, though one may be more intensive than the other. According to Christian understanding the Church is the inverted prism, which restores the fullness of the human nature. The claim to be a catholic religion proceeds on the assumption that this religion has no special colour, but the white light.'[10]

Panikkar also points out that the plurality of religions can only have a provisional meaning. Either this plurality exists for the time being, for a particular period of time, or there is this plurality at all only because the religions have not yet reached their maturity and perfection. Panikkar's study was only to show that there is a historical dialectical development which leads all religions together and creates space for a single true religion. This development is still in the process. Panikkar also explains why he was using Christian terminology and Christian foundation to explain this process. He says that it is the only way to provide fuller expression to one's own thought in order to express the dynamic development and integrating dialectics without any hidden agenda of Christian apologetics. If the followers of other religions see theirs as the true catholic religion to explain the formal structure of these reflections, as he has done, they would have served Panikkar's purpose. For, this genuine effort awakens the required spiritual 'competitive fervor', which is needed in us, to not fall asleep on the way or to be pharisaically satisfied with our own thoughts which stagnate within our own group.[11]

Some others would like to emphasise the difference and not to rush to the conclusion that both the Hindu and Christian traditions mutually enrich each other. For instance, in another context, Albert Cuttat is emphatic, 'In the world of the spirit it is the clear differentiation which really unites without mixing up, while a uniform type of blurring the borders only separates in reality, because genuine values could never be exchangeable, never actually be equivalent.'[12]

But what Panikkar is trying to show is the interconnectedness, in keeping with his vision of the rhythm of being. His concept of homeomorphic equivalent is an example in this regard. They are not identifying the concepts of different traditions, but showing the functional similarity between them while acknowledging difference. This is one way of showing how mutual fecundation or cross-fertilisation of Hindu–Christian world takes place.

Being faithful to his vocation of creating a Hindu–Christian theology, Panikkar attempts to bring in specific doctrines of both the traditions together. For instance, the Trinity is a core doctrine of the Christian tradition and *advaita* is basic to the Hindu tradition. Panikkar calls them homeomorphic equivalents. He is not speaking on behalf of Christian tradition nor for Hindu tradition. Moreover he considers that the Trinity is not exclusively Christian and *advaita* is not exclusively Hindu. In the Christian tradition God is understood to be 'Trinitarian', but Panikkar says that not only God is Trinitarian, but that the whole of reality is Trinitarian. He admits that it is through Christian theology he came closer to the notion of Trinity and his exposure to Hindu concept of *sat-cit-ananda* has strengthened his understanding of Trinity. This sort of mutual input has enriched his philosophico-theological vision of cosmotheandric intuition.[13]

Foundation of Hermeneutical Pluralism

In one of his essays on the hermeneutics of pluralism, Panikkar summarises what we could learn from Hinduism. First, there is possibility of a pluralism which does not imply that one need fall into an agnostic relativism.

Second, this pluralism which underlies true tolerance finds its justification in the difference between orthodoxy and orthopraxis. If I identify Christianity with orthodoxy, the other who does not think like me is in error and must be contested. But if Christianity is identified with orthopraxis, then there lacks neither in me nor in the other, who has a different kind of thinking and understanding of the teaching, the honesty, brotherhood, and compassion granting that he is in good faith and participates with me in the same mystery. Here is the place of true tolerance, since one recognises a communion which stands above the teaching position.

Third, pluralism of teaching necessarily arises from the transcendence of the truth-reality on the one hand and the imperfection of our knowledge on the other.

Fourth, the logical possibility and natural probability of a hermeneutic does not justify its existential truth. Here it needs another kind of authority, of another criterion—like that of the Church (scripture and tradition), which stand above the hermeneutics.

Fifth, the fact of hermeneutics itself obliges us to cross over this, since it is not the final and ultimate way of truth and salvation. In other words, the hermeneutics can be multiple, because it is not the last authority, because one must always go beyond, transcend—in life, in being, in faith, and in mystery.[14]

How Do We Formulate Panikkar's Position? As a Religio Triplex?

The renowned Egyptologist Jan Assmann in his book *Religio duplex*[15] writes

> Everyone should practice his/her particular religion *as if* it is the true religion, in full recognition of the possibility that the truth resides in another or much more: that the truth is hidden and all religions strive towards it in their own way. Since there is now and there will be religion only in the plural, this form of *both-and*, both true to one's own and at the same time respect for the other, is a reasonable solution.

Assmann suggests that the *religio duplex*, that is, the contrast between a universal religion of reason and a positive religion, is a normative perspective for a proper self-understanding of religion in the global modernity.

> In this form this model fits in, in which the cultures and thus the religions of this earth are brought together in a way, which does not allow any one of them to understand itself in possession of the absolute and universal truths as 'alone making holy'. Only as *religio duplex*, that is, a religion at two levels, which has learnt to see itself as one among many and with the eyes of the other and however does not lose sight of the hidden God or the hidden truth as converging point of all religions, that religion has a place in our globalised world.[16]

The enlightenment-based reformulation of the original meaning of the *religio duplex*, namely, the opposition between public and private religion (according to Jan Assmann) is clearly articulated by Moses Mendelsohn.[17] 'Out of the "folk religion" arose the concrete world religions like Christianity, Judaism, and Islam, from the 'mysteries' came naturally the foundations of a universal theology, which is common to all men, the world-citizens. 'The *religio duplex* aims at a complementarity between a philosophically fixed religion of humanity, that is, of reason, and of the plurality of particular religions, which should not be eliminated, but preserved in an attitude of 'as if''.[18]

Panikkar's position could be expressed in terms of *religio triplex*.[19] First, regarding the experience of the Absolute Nothing (mystical), Panikkar talks of the 'primacy of the mystic and inexpressible nucleus of Christianity—the cosmic Christ in the strict Pauline sense'[20]—which must be established if Christianity has a chance to survive; second, interpretations of the Absolute Nothing, whether it is in atheistic form or religious form, out of which particular moral-political perspectives arise; third, rites and symbols, which are connected via their content with the second level.

This distinction would correspond to some extent to Panikkar's formulation of religion at three levels. Panikkar says that in every religion there are three dimensions—sociological, sacramental, and transcendental.[21]

1. A *sociological dimension*, where there is a fixed code of behaviour, doctrines, and belief system (e. g. Christendom, i.e., the socio-historical

crystallisation of Christian principles) and in this sense one cannot be a Hindu, a Christian, and a Jew at the same time.

2. A *sacramental dimension* (e. g. Church structure, which is not totally dependent on the sociological and cultural fluctuations), where there is a change taking place at the human level which cuts deeper into the human nature, we may, for instance, share the sacramental religiousness of the other without belonging to it.
3. A *transcendental dimension* (e. g. Christ), includes the above two while transcending both and cannot be manipulated. The question remains, at what level does one relate himself/herself to other religions?

Panikkar points out that this threefold division is valid in any religion. A Christian would call the three levels Christendom, Church, and Christ; a Buddhist may call them *sangha, dharma, nirvana*; a Hindu, *sampradaya, karma,* and *brahman*, and a Muslim, *umma, Qur'an,* and *Allah*.

Monotheism under Suspicion of Violence

The relevance of this consideration by Panikkar becomes clear when one looks at the history of religions. In spite of all achievements by Judaism and Christianity, a new source of violence broke out, namely, violence in the name of 'true' religion, which targeted not only against the outsiders (pagans and non-believers), but also against the insiders (heretics and schismatics).

The potential sources of violence in the monotheistic religions are many such as the concept of revelation, which is a model of authority. The traditional claims of revelation are a foreign body, which makes undue demand on the individual for a *sacrificium intellectus*, that is, *quia absurdum.* In the history of positive religions consequently it comes to philosophical self-exclusion of the concept of revelation, as for instance in the Mutazilite movement in the Medieval Islam (which in Islam led to the marginalisation of philosophy), or in Nicholas of Cusa (which led to reformation and counter-reformation). The violent excesses of re-dogmatisation of Christian religion and the wars between confessions have led finally in Europe to the radical atheism which tried, like the early Sophists, to suggest religions on the whole as human inventions.

It is not out of place to bring in Gandhi in this context as he expressed his voice against the dogmatic concept of revelation in the name of reason,

> I pronounce my judgment on every scripture including the Gita. No historical text can enter in the place of my reason. Even when I accept the most significant books as revelations, still I know that they suffer under the process of double distillation. First of all, they are communicated by a human prophet and then commented upon by the exegetes. Nothing comes direct from God.[22]

Are the Modes of the 'Sacred Nucleus' 'relativisable'?

In order to strike a balance between the absolute claim on the one hand and its interpretation on the other, one can suggest the concept of the 'sacred nucleus' ('sacred core)[23] of the forms of life. In the 'sacred nucleus' the unconditional claim of the Absolute Nothing is present; the 'sacred' thus marks a border for discursive fusion. However, the 'sacred nucleus' of a form of life, according to the niveau of critical self-reflection, is surrounded by interpretations, in which even the respective meaning of the 'sacred' itself is explained together. The 'sacred nucleus' together with the revolving process of interpretations builds a middle path between the inexpressible mystery of the Absolute Nothing and the rites and symbols of the 'positive' religions. That is why a model of *religio triplex* of Panikkar which opens the possibility of perspectives for a normative differentiation of religious and even secular worlds.

First of all, the 'sacred nuclei' are not historically stable, but 'shift' in multiple ways. The Exodus-narrative in the Bible is a proto-typical example for shifting of a sacred nucleus. The old theology of Israel partially de-sacralises the institution of the divine monarchy of the Pharaohs of Egypt, and at the same time takes up the moral content of the Ma'at concept (the Egyptian goddess of justice), especially in support of the poor, widows, and orphans, which was made sacred (sacralised) by the prophets. In the shifting process of 'sacred nucleus' the religion of peace could also come to a dangerous re-sacralising, as in the case of the protest of the Maccabees in the Bible.[24] Even in the Buddhist critique of the belief of the Creator God and the caste system many forms of ridicule and abuse are to be found. In other words, the cultural development of mankind is determined by the shifting of sacred nucleus, in which the de-sacralising and re-sacralising enter into one another.

Second, the differentiation between the religion of reason and revelation is not that clearly demarcated, since even in cosmotheism there is an element of reason at work. The experience of the world-alienation is not connected to an irrational claim of the revelation, but a possible and in principle legitimate self-interpretation of the *conditio humana.* The idea of creation, that is, freedom of the Absolute, thus emerges again and again in European philosophy (not merely in theology); a prominent example would be the late Schelling.[25]

Third, if cosmotheism and radical transcendence are to be taken earnestly as two different yet (in principle) possible interpretations of the claim of the Absolute Nothing, the relativistic variant of a religious pluralism will forbid itself from doing that which *religio duplex* tends towards. Not all positive religions are indifferent to call the Divine merely by various names. Much more, they show (on the horizons of meaning and of the moral–political) options between the religions—both on the level of content and in relation to the niveau of self-enlightenment—clear differences which are not eliminated, but should be carried over as far as possible by dialogical exchanges.

This could be exemplified by referring to Gandhi. Gandhi understands the concept of religion in a double way—religion in the sense of concrete faith communities, for example, the various religions, and religion which transcends all concrete religions and which coincides with the truth. Religion in the second sense permanently relativises as well as purifies the concrete religions in the plural. By identification of religion with truth, Gandhi removes not only the walls between religions, but also between religion and secular world. Even the secular world is rooted in religion in the sense of

Gandhi. Consequently according to Gandhi it has no meaning to change from one religion to another, to convert. The decisive task consists much more in the *relativising of one's own religion in the light of the comprehensive truth.*

When one, however, looks at the self-understanding of Gandhi away from the religious and political interactions in the Indian decolonisation process, especially at the conflict with Ambedkar, it becomes clear that the religious worlds are not so simple in the scheme of *religio duplex*. For as a Dalit leader, Ambedkar aggressively confronts the 'sacred nucleus' of the Indian caste system which is supported on the authority of 'holy scriptures'. To maintain the caste system in the sense of 'as if' and at the same time to relativise in the name of comprehensive truth was thus not an acceptable option. On the contrary, Ambedkar supports in all openness fully desacralising the entire 'religious' legitimation of the caste system.[26] Since such a radical reform of Hinduism met with insurmountable obstacles, Ambedkar recommends to the Dalits the conversion to Buddhism, in which the caste system was already desacralised.

On the other hand, even Gandhi does not limit himself to an 'as if' model of relativising Hinduism, but in fact in a creative way he advocates a comprehensive revision of Hinduism. So he defends, for example, the principle of non-violence in the *Bhagavadgita* against other types of interpretations, takes up the elements of Christianity and criticises the Brahminical system.[27]

Conclusions

Panikkar works at different levels in understanding the phenomenon of religion. One can identify at least three levels in his writings, (a) removing misunderstanding in the East–West encounter, (b) redefining certain concepts with an exclusive understanding, and (c) identifying homeomorphic equivalents in different traditions. At the initial stage Panikkar tries to 'free' from many a misunderstanding in the Hindu–Christian encounter and 'de-sacralises' or 'relativises' certain attitudes ('sacred nucleus') in the Christian consciousness like idolatry and revelation.

a. Removing misunderstanding in intercultural communication

In his earlier essays Panikkar talks about the misunderstanding involved in the East–West communication and as a result Christianity and Hinduism did not meet at the intellectual/spiritual level. They spoke on parallel tracks.

> One does not speak the same language and if one believes to have understood the other, at the end one discovers that the vocabulary does not have the same meaning. The major concepts, the underlying attitudes, the silent presuppositions, the 'original' moods are not the same. Even at the intellectual level this misunderstanding continues.[28]

Then Panikkar gives some examples such as 'pantheism' being applied to Indian philosophy. 'The entire Hellenistic state of affairs of a *materia prima (protohyle),* out of which a demiurge shaped the world (against which the Christian response was the *creatio ex nihilo*) is foreign to India.'[29] This does not mean that there are no pantheists in India, as there are also in the West, but pantheism is not the basic Indian spirit. Today this basic idea is expressed by the word pan-en-theism.

Advaita is not monism, which does not express what is meant by *advaita. Advaita* highlights the basic attitude that the God and the world are not two, nor are they one, but non-dual (the whole of Thomistic problematic of *relatio rationis*, of creation by God, should not be very different from the Indian teaching of *advaita*).[30]

Maya is not illusion or unreality of the world. *Maya* is 'a technical term in order to describe the uniqueness of that non-divine form of reality, which is neither being nor non-being and as such cannot be grasped *in toto, in statu quietis, in esse completo*, but only *in fieri, in statu viatoris, in esse imperfecto,* is something which cannot be placed along with Brahman on the same level as the Absolute, because it has no reality of its own.'[31]

Another example is that of the concept of *karma.* 'The modern West is so proud of its discovery of the historical dimension of man that it has become almost blind to the recognition of an ontological and human historicity in the Indian *karma*. The past carries forward by the law of *karma* in to the present and the human solidarity finds an ontological and historical bond.'[32]

Many more examples of misunderstanding could be cited here like idolatry, the concept of *avatara*, and others. Idolatry, for example, presents a normal dimension of the religious life of the human being, if it is not a consequence of the epiphany of God. Now is it really idolatry that the prophets attack or is it not much more the false idolatry, that of the rival of Yahweh? The God of Israel is a jealous God. The Christian West, the heritage of Jewish prophets, has always found a kind of instinctive aversion against idolatry, which had the consequent tragic misunderstandings, as Christianity in the modern time came in contact with the religions of Africa and Asia, says Panikkar.[33]

b. Re-defining exclusive understanding of some concepts

Panikkar brings in concepts like sacred secularity, secularisation and tolerance to 'relativise' the sources of potential violence—dwelling on the fleeting nature of the '"sacred nucleus'. Secularisation, for instance, is seen as athe healthy metabolic process by which a certain society gets rid of obsolete cultic forms in order to acquire new ones.'[34] He even offers a not-so-exclusive interpretation of the 'infallibility' claim of some religious traditions, as a 'concern for the entire cosmos, humankind in particular, and a vision that sees the act of Christ in a universal perspective'. Infallibility may thus be seen as grand awareness that Man now has the burden of this dignity… We are all thrown together in this adventure that propels us closer and closer to the perfect Man…. to the free reception of the Spirit: to be a Man, a fallible being who must believe himself infallible in order to survive. The experience of the *We* amounts to the realisation to the *atman* (*brahman*).'[35]

Another concept Panikkar presses into service to achieve harmony is accepting a mystical tolerance (besides the political, philosophical, and theological tolerance). 'Mystical tolerance represents a non-objectifiable vision of the world and implies the conviction that every human act has a value that is not purely objective. This notion of tolerance implies that all reality is redeemable because it is never immutable. It also supposes the existential character of truth and the radical relativity of personal being. Tolerance is then the way one being exists in another and expresses the radical interdependence of all that exists.'[36]

c. Identifying homeomorphic equivalents in different traditions

At the final stage of his writings Panikkar brings in his concept of homeomorphic equivalents to build bridge between different religious traditions.[37] His goal is to see the harmony in living together. Granting the religious core in all religious interpretations, without absolutising any of them, Panikkar seeks to perceive the underlying unity. He thus highlights the harmony that prevails and that alone matters in the end for salvation.

Endnotes

1. The Dance of Shiva is later developed as Saiva theology in the *Tirumantiram* by Tirumular (around the 7th century AD), included in the 10th Book of Saiva Canon, divided into nine books (*tantras*); the ninth book treats the dance of Shiva in detail.
2. Raimon Panikkar, *The Vedic Experience*, Motilal Banarasidass, Delhi, (1977), 1994, 854.
3. Cf. Panikkar, *Life and Word* (*vita e parola. La mia Opera*), Jaca Book, 2010, 130–134. The English version is not yet published and so the reference is to the Italian version.
4. There are several scholars on Panikkar's thought and they are contributing to Panikkar's heritage by research on his works, editing and translating them into different languages. Dr Milena Carrara Pavan, for example, has succeeded in translating all his works into Italian and started a series of publications in Milan by Jaca Books. This is a great initiative and she deserves our appreciation and thanks for the yeoman service rendered to the humanity as a whole. The need is also felt to make him known to the Indian readers in Indian languages. For my part, I have tried with the help of another Tamil scholar to make Panikkar accessible to Tamil-speaking readers through translation. So far, four volumes have appeared (a) *Introducing Panikkar* with select articles; (b) *Peace and Interculturality*; (c) *The Fullness of Man – a Christophany;* and (d) *Sunahsepa: A Myth of the Human Condition.* In addition to these, his *Life and Word* is now in the process of publication.

5. This work has gone into several editions. The references to this work are from the 1994 edition, published by Motilal Banarasidass, Delhi.

6. The Shrivaishnavas of South India employed this model of writing commentary as they wrote in Tamil. Pillai Lokacarya, the founder of the Tenkalai or Southern branch, wrote his *curnai* (not *sutras*) and Manavalamamuni (Varavaramuni) wrote *vyakhyana* commentary on these *curnais*. They created a further subculture in the process, as 6000-, 9000-, and 12000-syllable-works and their commentaries are known by this name.

7. Raimon Panikkar, "The Relation of Christians to their Non-Christian Surroundings?" in *Christian Revelation and World Religions*, Edited by Joseph Neuner, *Indian Ecclesiastical Studies* IV, 3–4, 1965. Reprinted by Burns and Oates, London, 1967, 143–184.

8. Raimon Panikkar, *Religionen und die Religion*, Max Hueber Verlag, München, 1965, 42–112.

9. Raimon Panikkar, *Religionen und die Religion*, 1965, 113.

10. Raimon Panikkar, *Religionen und die Religion*, 1965, 151.

11. Raimon Panikkar, *Religionen und die Religion*, 1965, 169–170.

12. Jacques Albert Cuttat, *Asiatische Gottheit: Christliche Gott*. Spiritualitat der beiden Hemispharen. Johannes Verlag, Einsiedeln, 1965, 22.

13. Panikkar takes up the basic elements of Indian philosophy and builds his own vision of cosmotheandric vision. For instance, Ramanuja's understanding of the organic whole (with his body–soul metaphor) with *cit-acit-isvara* components has to be kept in mind as the background.

14. R. Panikkar, *Die vielen Götter und der eine Herr*, 1963, 112–14.

15. Jan Assmann, *Religio Duplex: Egyptische Mysterien und europaische Aufklarung*, Berlin, 2010, 221. Some object to this position: How can a believer proceed like this: that God came out of the hiddenness and revealed himself once and for all; both to remain true to one's conviction and at the same time to recognise that the truth is possibly still hidden? Is it not a concept of divided truth?

16. *Religio duplex*, 2010, 23.

17. Moses Mendelsohn, "Jerusalem oder Uber die religiose Macht im Judentum" (1783). Assmann, *Religio duplex*, 173.

18. Assmann, 210.

19. This phrase is borrowed from Johann Schelkshorn's response to Jan Assmann. Cf. Hans Schelkshorn, "Religio triplex – Uber den 'Ort' der Religion in der globalen Moderne. Eine Auseinandersetzung mit Jan Assmann.' Text yet to be published.

20. Raimon Panikkar, *Die vielen Gotter und der eine Herr*, Otto Wilhelm Barth Verlag, 1963, 128.

21. This idea of Panikkar is expressed in different places. For Example, Cf. "Response to Harold Coward" in *Cross Currents*, Vol. XXIX, No. 2. 1979, 190–91.

22. Mahatma Gandhi, *What is Hinduism?* Frankfurt/M. 2006, 46.

23. Cf. Paul Ricoeur refers to the 'creative nucleus of great civilisations and great cultures, that nucleus on the basis of which we interpret life – the ethical and mythical nucleus of mankind', which constitute the cultural resources of a nation, in which the moral depth-views are articulated in narrative form. Cf. "Universal Civilization and National Cultures", in: *History and Truth,* Northwestern University Press, Evanston, 1965, 276; also cf. Habermas' concept of an 'opaque nucleus' of religious and aesthetic experiences. Jurgen Habermas, *Between Naturalism and Religion*, Polity Press, Malden, USA, 2008.

24. Jan Assmann brings in the example of Antiochus IV, whose step becomes violent, not something through forced Hellenising culturally and religiously, but 'by the heroic protest', which the Jewish leader Yehuda Maccabee offered resisting these efforts. This protest is the first religiously motivated war in the world history. He introduces the new religion in their political consequences before our eyes. The people fight for the Law, for God. In this connection for the first time there is the talk of martyrdom, who would prefer to suffer horrible death rather than to bow themselves before the images of the idols or eat the meat offered to the image of the idol.' (Jan Assmann, "Ist der neue Mensch ein Eiferer? Uber den Preis des Monotheismus" in NZZ 30, 10, 2004, Nr. 254, 67, quoted by Schelkshorn.) From the Maccabees proceeds the line up to the Taliban, according to Assmann.

25. Schelkshorn refers to this trend in the Western philosophy in his paper.

26. Cf. B. R. Ambedkar, "Annihilation of Caste" in Valerian Rodriques (ed.), *Ambedkar. Essential Writings*, Oxford University Press, 2002, c. xv–xviii.

27. This illustration comes from Schelkshorn in his paper referred to above.

28. Raimundo Panikkar, *Die vielen Gotter und der eine Herr*, Otto Wilhelm Barth-Verlag, Oberbeyern, 1963, 57. In this book Panikkar avoids any sort of syncretistic or exclusive or apologetic attitude.

29. *Ibid.* 58.

30. *Ibid.* 58.

31. R. Panikkar, *Die vielen Gotter und der eine Herr*, 1963, 59.

32. *Ibid.* 60.

33. Raimon Panikkar, *Kerygma und Indien*, Herbert Reich, Hamburg, 1967, 104.

34. Panikkar, *Worship and Secularization,* Paul Brand, Bussum, Holland, 1970, 36–37.

35. Panikkar, *Myth Faith and Hermeneutics*, Cross-Cultural Studies, Paulist Press, 1979, 413–14.

36. *Ibid.* 23.

37. There are several functional similarities suggested by Panikkar, eg. *advaita* and the trinity, the *sanatana dharma* and the *ecclesia ab Abel*; between the idea of the incarnation and the concept of *istadevata,* etc. Cf. Anand Amaladass, "Raimon Panikkar, the Bridge-Builder among Religions and Cultures" in *Jeevadhara*, 2011, 386–400.

The Hermit above a Sea of Music: A Poet's View of Raimundo Panikkar[1]

Grevel Lindop

Friendships, for I regarded Raimundo Panikkar as a friend, do not depend primarily upon time. We can meet people regularly over many years without becoming friends. This is sad but true. Equally, we may meet certain people for a few hours, or for a few minutes, and take away the impression that something deep inside us has changed; that the encounter has altered us, that something within us has opened up which was closed, or at least unrecognised, before. That person will never be forgotten, and they have contributed something of value which will remain with us perhaps for ever.

Something like this was my experience of Raimundo Panikkar. I met him only quite briefly, I think, on just three occasions, during 2000–2001. We met twice in Tavertet, at the Vivarium and also in his house; and once in Switzerland, where we spent several days together at an international conference. I am not a scholar of religions, though I suppose as an Englishman who, if pressed, describes himself as Buddhist, I necessarily have an interest in interreligious dialogues, or perhaps embody something of it in myself in an unspoken way. My contact with Panikkar was altogether non-academic and informal. But in a way that is difficult to define. It left something permanent with me, something which has been present frequently not so much in my thoughts as in my feelings ever since.

Panikkar has remained with me not primarily by the things he said, though several of his sayings have reverberated in my mind ever since; and not by anything in particular that he did, though his way of doing things was indeed distinctive. Yet both of these contributed to the impression, as did his visual appearance—his distinctive clothing, his facial expression, and his way of speaking. Much, I think, was communicated by his surroundings—by his house and its setting, into which he seemed to fit so perfectly. Perhaps it was his smile which above all endeared him to me. It was a smile boyish, slightly mischievous, full of fun and enthusiasm, and seeming entirely spontaneous.

Owing to the nature of the circumstances, I never heard him deliver an academic paper or lecture, and I never heard him give spiritual advice. I felt no inclination to regard him as an infallible guru. He was simply a companion—a fellow-worker in a project which, as it turned out, did not last very long; and a friend with whom, one day, Dr Kapila Vatsyayan and I enjoyed a few hours exploring some Swiss mountains, the three of us feeling very much, I believe, like children who for a few hours had been let out of school, and could run wild without the stern supervision of parents or teachers. And yet from this minimal contact, and after a decade during which I remember little about the many other people I encountered around the same time and in the course of the same project, it is Raimundo Panikkar who stands out, and whom I see in my mind's eye as vividly as ever, not with nostalgia, and not merely with friendship, but with love.

Panikkar was connected, through his friendships with both Dr Kapila Vatsyayan and the poet and scholar Kathleen Raine, with the Temenos Academy in London. Temenos had begun simply as a journal of arts, ideas, and traditional spiritual wisdom; but it had grown into almost a miniature university, holding lectures, seminars, and reading groups on philosophy and the arts in the light of the sacred traditions of East and West. Panikkar had lectured at the Temenos Academy in London, and thereby made an important contribution. It was partly through this connection with Temenos, I believe, that both Panikkar and I came to be invited to work on an international project.

It was a project which aimed at those ever-elusive objects, nuclear disarmament and world peace. Its basic idea was at once so ingenious and so simple that it had immediate appeal. Everyone, from heads of state to the waiter in the restaurant where we held some of our meetings, was eager to sign up. I believe that, left in its original simple form, it might actually have worked. But, unfortunately, it did not. Like so many human endeavours, it lost impetus, became mired in disagreement, and gradually fell away. Now, like a thousand other well-intentioned schemes, it has vanished as if it had never been, and probably no trace of it now remains.

And yet that is not quite true, for without it I would not have met Raimundo Panikkar. For it came about one day in the year 2000 that I and my two or three companions found ourselves in the remote village of Tavertet, in the rocky and precipitous limestone hills outside Barcelona, late in the autumn. We had been given permission to stay at the Vivarium, a little way above the village, for a few days whilst we worked on a draft of our manifesto, which, we believed, would change the world forever. During the days, we worked in the seminar room; we went down into the village twice a day to have our meals in the village *cantina;* no simple business, since none of us spoke a word of Spanish. And at night we slept in makeshift beds, I think, on mattresses or perhaps with sleeping-bags, on the floors of small side-rooms in the Vivarium. Sleeping was not altogether easy; not only because of the hardness of the floor, as I remember it, but because outside the window a bird persistently and beautifully sang with the most piercing sweetness. Perhaps it was a nightingale. I like to think so, though I never found out.

On the day after our arrival we were invited to go and meet Raimundo Panikkar himself. We walked across the meadow behind the Vivarium, up the slopes and terraces of the white rock to his house, his hermitage. The hermitage was, as I remember it, a single-storey building of white stone, perched at the highest point of the slope, so that it overlooked the vast sweep of the valley which spread out below the limestone cliffs. (I know now that it had two storeys; but in memory I see it as a low building, with only one.)

And there was a bell, a Tibetan bell. Did we ring it to gain entrance? I can't remember. I can see the bell quite clearly, its greyish metal sides decorated with Tibetan characters and other figures, and it has something red at the top. A tassel, a ribbon? Perhaps it hung from a red cord at the door. I don't know. But the bell itself seemed to have something important to say. I knew that we were here to visit a Christian Catholic priest; but it was the voice of a Tibetan Buddhist bell that would summon him.

A secretary or assistant opened the door and welcomed us in. We were taken to meet Panikkar. I was at once struck by two things. One was the warmth of his welcome, which was not effusive but gentle and quiet, yet given with a smile which seemed to treat each person there as an intimate friend who could be entirely trusted. His politeness was not a thing of etiquette or good manners, it was an outflow of complete kindness. He seemed to be welcoming us, not so much into his house, as into his heart. I was tongue-tied, but I felt that had I been alone with this man, he was someone to whom I could have opened my heart without hesitation or holding back.

The other thing which struck me was Panikkar's clothing. Rather than any form of priestly garb—the black suit and the white 'dog-collar' of the off-duty English priest, or the cassock of the Catholic priest—Panikkar wore a shawl or robe of what I can only describe as a greyish-gold colour, which seemed to be made of very fine wool. I was used to the company of Buddhist monks, and his garb seemed closer to their traditional yellow robes than to any ecclesiastical dress I had ever encountered. Instead of making him impressive or intimidating, in some curious way his robe seemed almost to make him appear vulnerable. Rather than being an armour that set him apart from use, this soft radiant robe invited one to touch and stroke it. Subliminally, one could not help catching a hint of the small child in its blanket. Together with Panikkar's delightfully spontaneous smile, it rendered him an utterly unthreatening presence.

He took us into his study, where there was a long wall completely covered with books—a whole large library which I could not help regarding with both awe and, I confess it, envy. And then, as one turned away, still astonished, from the riches of his books, one was stunned for a moment by a still greater richness in the form of the view from the window, which looked out over the slopes that ran down to the edge of the limestone escarpment and over the cliffs to a vast valley of fields and forests, edged by precipitous white outcrops of rock, with a river and a dam just visible in the far distance and the deep blue of the sky, just darkening towards twilight, arching over the whole.

Given the keynote struck by that Tibetan bell at the entrance to the house, one found oneself half-consciously visualising the whole scene as a Tibetan *thangka*: Panikkar's house perched on the summit of a mountain, perhaps as the abode of a minor deity of an incarnate master such as Milarepa, with the world of *samsara* unfolding below on its various levels—humans and animals, titans, ghosts, and unfortunate beings arrayed on the stone shelves of the land amongst the trees and streams down to the valley floor. It seemed a place from which the world could be serenely surveyed. Yet not with indifference or unfeeling detachment, for we were there with our plans and our ideas. Panikkar listened patiently and sympathetically as we sat round his table and explained our project. He offered us drinks—I do not think I am fantasising when I say that he gave us wine, though I am not certain—and he agreed to give us his active help.

For our first visit, that was all. We left, I think, the following day, having secured his promise of co-operation and drawn up preliminary plans for some kind of manifesto or statement. We returned a few weeks later for a longer stay. This time Panikkar worked with us at times to help us draft our document. He also dined with us. Knowing that he had been a friend of Martin Heidegger, I took the opportunity to ask him what he thought about Heidegger's relationship with the Nazi party—something which was being much discussed in Britain at the time. Panikkar answered readily, telling me that he had in fact discussed the same matter with Heidegger himself. Panikkar told me that in his opinion it had been a matter of sheer human egoism. Heidegger had admitted to him that he had been tempted with the Rectorship of Freiburg University, the University's highest office, and that out of pure vanity he had been unable to resist. Heidegger had joined the Nazi party as a mere matter of form because it was required in order for him to hold the post. He had had no interest in Nazism or in politics.

While we were at Tavertet on this second occasion, I gained some other impressions of Panikkar. One was that he was not altogether happy in his role as a public guru. He was willing to do what he could, when people demanded of him that he give talks and make pronouncements on all kinds of matters, but he did it out of duty rather than inclination. He felt that there was something subtly false about the persona he had been forced to develop in response to his local disciples, where he was required to offer public advice and opinions to large audiences almost on a weekly basis. His natural simplicity and humanity were ill at ease in such circumstances. He preferred, I think, to speak to just one or two people. Here he need have no public persona.

I have since wondered whether some small tinge of such feelings also formed an ingredient in Panikkar's ingenious coinage of so many novel technical terms such as cosmotheandric, or, contrariwise, theanthropocosmic; ecosophy; tempiternity; katachronism; sophodisy; and others. Academic scholars are well known for their love of technical terminology, which the unsympathetic term 'jargon'. Most often, such terminology has the aim of narrowing meanings, of making finer and more exact distinctions between things. On the contrary, most of Panikkar's terms seem to function quite differently. They tend to bring things together, to merge opposites, or to embody a critique of artificial separations. They are, if you like, synthetic rather than analytical. But I believe that Panikkar rarely did anything from just one motive. A complex man who looked at things from many sides, he took, I think, a certain delight in playing with language in this way. I suspect that for him, coining neologisms was amongst other things a game. He simply enjoyed it, rather as Lewis Carroll did, seeing it as a kind of solemn linguistic joking. I also suspect that he enjoyed playing more conventional scholars at their own game. 'They like technical terms?' I imagine him saying, 'Then let them have technical terms, more than they bargain for.' To confront sober scholars, accustomed to putting everything into sealed compartments, with terminology that spliced their concepts together or dissolved their boundaries, was perhaps a source of quiet amusement to him.

But to return to the year 2000. On our last day at Tavertet, after Panikkar had again been down to the Vivarium to help us with our work, I walked back with him in the later afternoon up to his hermitage. As we climbed the hill, I was struck by the sounds around us. The long grass of the hillside was alive with a many-toned chorus of insects—buzzing, humming, droning, chirping on different notes; over this, from the trees at the edges of the fields, were the songs of the birds, fluting, calling, echoing. I stopped, and Panikkar stopped also. His face lit up with a beatific smile. For a long time we stood and listened. We were surrounded by, immersed in, music. The whole hillside was an ocean of unceasing natural music. At last I said to Panikkar, simply, 'Music!' Panikkar turned to me with absolute delight on his face. 'Yes!' he whispered with a kind of delighted intensity. He seemed to rejoice, as if at last someone had solved a puzzle when he had almost given up hope of their ever seeing the point. We stood there together a little longer, surrounded by the sea of music, above which the hermitage seemed to float, weightless, and above time.

It was nearly a year later that I met Panikkar once again. This time it was in Switzerland, at a grand hotel near Interlaken where the organisers of our project had arranged an international conference of politicians, philosophers, religious figures and philanthropists. We were a motley crew, but perhaps for that reason no less fitted for our task. I was delighted to find some friends among the crowd, among them the Poet-Laureate of Taiwan, and Dr Kapila Vatsyayan. And there was Raimundo Panikkar. The conference made its difficult way over several days, with drafts of documents written, amended, rejected, written again. How little I now remember of all that!

What remains clear in my mind is the day when, during a break in the conference, Dr Vatsyayan, Panikkar and I thankfully escaped from the velvet prison of the hotel, with its enormous meals that nonetheless seemed to contain so little real nourishment. We took a taxi into the nearby mountains, and there we found a chairlift, which silently and magically floated us one by one—Dr Vatsyayan in her elegant sari, Panikkar in his golden robe of wool, and me in my English coat and trousers, like three unexpected minor spirits or *gandhabbas*—up through the air, over the vast and silent spaces of the forest, and at last to a landing-place among the snow-covered peaks, where we could contemplate a small lake of the most radiant turquoise. We strolled along by this lake, we talked and laughed, and we felt, as I have already said, like a group of children released for a few hours from school. We discussed many things, and Panikkar had an original and striking view on each. I remember him saying that the Chinese desire to control Tibet stemmed from an understanding that the Tibetan snows were the source of Asia's rivers; water would become the world's most precious commodity, and who controlled Tibet would one day control the water. He speculated upon the plight of the so-called 'developed' world at the future time when the supply of oil would be exhausted, as one day it must. It was clear that his perspective on the world was not that of the moment, but of broad stretches of time. He thought in centuries or millennia; our own situation was always related to vast reaches of time, or the whole human situation on earth.

And he had aphorisms. He said things which stayed in my memory and which even now I find myself quoting almost every day. 'There is no such thing as a chemically pure religion,' he would say when people argued about orthodoxy or correctness. And 'It is not possible for everyone in the world to have a job; but it is possible for everyone in the world to have work,'—a thought which he attributed to his friend Ivan Illich. His utterances were pieces of very simple wisdom, but extremely profound.

At the end of our conference, when we had failed to solve the world's problems and were dispersing, from the Swiss town of Zug, a taxi came for Panikkar. We embraced, and I tried to tell him how much his friendship had meant to me. The intensity of the moment has made me forget what either of us said, but he had already given me one of the last copies of his great masterwork, *The Vedic Experience,* a book which my friend and mentor, the poet Kathleen Raine, in her last years used to read every night before sleeping. Panikkar has inscribed it to me as 'These songs which reverberate in us as remembrance of a meeting of hearts and minds'. As I embraced Panikkar there in Switzerland, I was certain that we would never meet again.

And indeed we did not. I tried to arrange for him to visit and speak to the Temenos Academy in London, and it seemed that it might happen. But in reality he was not strong enough and the visit was cancelled. However, there was one further practical result of our meeting. One morning in Switzerland, Panikkar had announced at breakfast that he had been unable to sleep the previous night, and had found himself writing a story. The story, entitled 'The Tragedy of the Grand Inquisitor', was a continuation of the narrative of the Grand Inquisitor from Dostoevsky's novel *The Brothers Karamazov*. At the time I was editing a journal, *Temenos Academy Review*, which had been founded by Kathleen Raine; and so, by letter and email, I succeeded with some difficulty in persuading Panikkar to send a copy of his story for publication. It appeared in the journal in an English translation in 2008.[2] I have been unable to find any mention of this story elsewhere. Nor have I been able to locate the original Spanish text; it survives only in English translation. So it may be that it is otherwise unknown. That would be a pity, because I believe it to be important.

Panikkar's story is extremely cryptic. After summarising Dostoevski's parable, it follows the Inquisitor himself, who after the departure of Him who is Christ, collapses into his chair in a state of shock. The Inquisitor admits to himself that, despite the cunning arguments he has just used, he has not brought people happiness by depriving them of their freedom. He is due to sign the order for another execution but cannot bring himself to do it. Instead he shuts himself into his room and broods. In a dream he foresees a time when the Church 'no longer sent people to the stake but continued to condemn them in other ways.' In vision, he sees himself in the future, as a Pope who longs to ask forgiveness for the past but is so enmeshed in bureaucracy that he can do nothing to alter the present. Around this Pope are crowds who are not pilgrims but 'tourists and curious passers-by'. 'His churches were empty of true believers; those who surrounded him in the administration [...] were motivated by ambition alone and by a faith which lacked both hope and love.'

Panikkar's story is puzzling and ambiguous. Not being an expert either on theology or on Panikkar's ideas, I cannot tell how to interpret it. But it seems to me that the story contains some of his last reflections, from many different sides, on the church, on Christ, and on history. I believe it deserves to be better known and to be interpreted by those more knowledgeable than I.

Having mentioned Panikkar as the nocturnal creator of fiction, I will digress here to mention a point that has puzzled me greatly. Indeed, if I were asked to point to the passage in Panikkar's writings that has perplexed me the most, I should have to choose one sentence from his essay 'Philosophy as Life Style' in his book *A Dwelling-Place for Wisdom*. The sentence is this: 'Throughout my life I have hardly dreamed; that is, I can hardly remember any dream.'[3] I find this profoundly strange.

Most of us can recall childhood nightmares. Many of us can recall from adulthood what Emily Bronte, in *Wuthering Heights*, called 'dreams that have stayed with me ever after, and changed my ideas—they have gone through and through me, like wine through water, and altered the colour of my mind.'[4] Dreaming, if only occasionally, is the state in which every one of us can still experience the world of the shaman—to fly, to speak with the dead, to visit other worlds, or to encounter animals who bring messages. If Panikkar's statement is true, what can it mean that he seems largely to have lacked this experience? And if his statement is *not* true, why did he want us to think it was the case?

In conclusion, Raimundo Panikkar remains for me a warm and loving presence, an example to aspire to, of someone who followed the true spiritual path to which historical institutions can only point. Radiating love, a delight in existence and a sense of comedy, looking at the problems of his time from a standpoint of many centuries and perhaps of eternity, he seemed a man who had chosen to live within forms and yet attained a freedom which transcended them. Like all such people he was unique, and his living presence was different from anything that can be found in his writings. It is right and natural that a scholarly edifice should be erected around his work that translations and commentaries should appear. But for me Panikkar will always, most profoundly, be the softly-robed figure floating silent and weightless on his chair lift up the mountain, and smiling with a radiant childlike delight as the ineffable beauty of the world opened up before him. This is the vision which I would wish to share.

Endnotes

1. I must express my gratitude to the India International Centre, the Kapur Surya Foundation and the Instituto Cervantes, Nueva Delhi for their generous invitation to participate in the seminar on 'The Work and Legacy of Raimundo Panikkar', 30 November–1 December 2013, for which this paper was written.

2. Raimundo Panikkar, 'The Tragedy of the Grand Inquisitor', trans. Austen Ivereigh, *Temenos Academy Review*, 5, Autumn 2002, 138–46.

3. Raimundo Panikkar, *A Dwelling-Place for Wisdom*, Lousiville, Kentucky: Westminster/ John Knox Press, 1993, 82.

4. Emily Bronte, *Wuthering Heights*, Chapter IX.

Raimon Panikkar: Prophet of Samanvaya

George Gispert-Sauch, S.J.

It is always difficult to speak about Raimon Panikkar. Those who know him only through his writings are often lost in the whirlpool of paradoxes, neologism, philosophical insight, and references to almost every culture of history that seem to rush pell-mell into the printed pages of his books and articles, and to leave one quite perplexed. Those who knew him personally perceived intuitively that there was a profound unity in his complex personality, a unity which gelled, I think, during a lifelong journey from the culture of his native country through the cultures of antiquity, the modern West, the Asian continent and post-modernity. Through this long pilgrimage he preserved, as he always acknowledged, the roots of his original education and surely also of his biological DNA. How often did we hear him to correct people and affirm that he was one hundred per cent Indian and one hundred per cent Spanish, and prove so with reference to the laws of genetics!

Panikkar, however, was not a modern polymath, a sort of twentieth century Leonardo da Vinci born in Spain - nor, if one prefers, a really 'new' Abhinavagupta of the twentieth century who through a kind of universal culture can point to a bridge between East and West. He was more than that. He was a forerunner, a leader of the cultural transformation the world is called to undergo and to perform during our millennium, a transition *from* a culture that still suffers from the remnants of ethnic rivalries and racial wars that have filled the pages of history for a few millennia, *to* a world that accepts plurality and the equal dignity of individuals and cultures in solidarity. Dr Anand Amaladass develops the theme of *rtatva* or the Rhythm of Being, the title of what may have been his last publication in book form, though the ideas were developed quite earlier. There is also the theme of polyphonic music which expresses unity in plurality through the aesthetic experience. Politically, solidarity is acquiring prominence in the world of ethics for a peaceful future. Perhaps it could be better expressed by its Indian version that would be *samanvaya*, at least in its etymological significance implying togetherness and mutual inner inherence (*sam-anu-aya*) that goes beyond co-existence. Panikkar might have called it a 'homeomorphic equivalent'. In such a vision of religion based on *sruti*, the 'hearing' or 'listened to' transcendence may paradoxically lead to a 'trans-religious theology' if the expression makes any sense, as was proposed in the Concept Paper by Professor Carpentier de Gourdon.

Samanvaya is neither the mere tolerance of differences nor a mere celebration of plurality for its own sake. Panikkar was too much the philosopher and mystic to be satisfied with mere pluralism. Like Plotinus, he was in search of the One that binds the many together. Also he did not reach out for the One at the cost of plurality. The man who had obtained a German doctorate in chemistry 55 years ago could not forget the world of *the many* that constituted his early love. Both had to be integrated in a *samanvaya*. In such plurality there is an immanence of each in the heart of the other without destroying it. Towards the end of his life, Panikkar published *The Cosmotheandric Experience*. It developed the insight that had inspired most of his intellectual journey. He may have been influenced by the Gospel of St John, wherein Jesus speaks of being with the Father and the Father in him, the 'Father' standing, of course, for the Divine Principle. But he also drew much from philosophies and theologies both of the East (including the Indic and the Chinese traditions) and the West (whether Platonic or Aristotelian, via Aquinas).

Relation

Well-known in Western philosophy is the long history of reflection on what 'relation' is. Aristotle placed it as one of the ten categories of reality. It is not, he said 'being' (*ti*), it is rather 'towards being' (*pros ti*), on the border, something about to give birth to being or reality. This is perhaps something like the Indian *maya*. Panikkar realised that both his faith and his theology made him want to rescue 'relation' and put it at the top of the pyramid of the categories of being, even above Substance, their Queen, and above accident, quantity, quality, and action. 'Relation' is in truth *the Real*, for the universe is constituted by a web of relations not only at the human level where our very names bear our relation to our ancestors, but also at both extremes of the scale of being. His faith told him that the Divine Real was a web of what Aquinas called Subsistent Relations. Physics too told him that the relation of mass and energy is constitutive of what we call the *jada* world. Pierre Teilhard de Chardin had similar insights about the 'heart of matter'. It is not unlikely that Panikkar was influenced in this area by the Buddhist tradition of *pratityasamutpada*, the rise of the world of plurality by 'interrelated production'. One of Panikkar's last books presents his vision of 'the cosmotheandric principle', which is the *samanvaya* or mutual immanence of material reality, the mental world and the Divine Principle. For him, 'relation' leads to dialogue and in dialogue we come to glimpse the new vision for our future.

Truth

Even before he reflected on the issue of 'relation', Panikkar had developed deep insights on the question of Truth, the Truth of God, the Truth of logic, the Truth of metaphysics, and, in the Christian context, the Truth identified with Jesus Christ or the Logos (the word) of God. One should read the dense final chapter of a book published in Spanish as early as 1969. Significantly, he signed the book on the 2nd of October of that year, when the world was celebrating the centenary of the birth of Mahatma Gandhi. The book, titled *Misterio y revelación: Hinduismo y Cristianismo: Encuentro de dos culturas*, is a collection of essays. It offers an organised whole under three sections, (i) *Mystery*, on Hindu spirituality and philosophy, (ii) *Revelation*, on the articulations of the Mystery in India, and (iii) *Hinduism and Christianity*, on a dialogue of the two traditions, ending in profound insights on Truth and Reality. Permit me to translate a few sentences as closely to the original as possible, and omitting the footnotes.

> *Truth is the manifestation of Being. We could specify this by saying that Truth is the self-manifestation of Being not as an object and not to anybody. Truth is a revelation of Being, not a discovery of being from outside, so to say. There is no onlooker, there is nothing outside Being (*out of which, for which, *and* to *which* it *Being could be revealed or unveiled).*
>
> *In spite of this, Truth is an un-veiling* [allusion, I think, to the etymology of *a-letheia*, the Greek work for Truth] *of what was 'hidden'. Truth is that reflection of the 'Simply One', or the 'image'* (eikon) ['icon'] *of what is 'un-image-in-able'. Truth is the 'plenitude' of what is Absolute (Latin solutus, freed). We call it the 'Logos' of 'Silence', of the 'thatness' of what is 'Not That'; this just stresses the inadequacy of words and the particular specific meaning of these and of many similar conceptions that are applied to the Absolute.*
>
> *Being is truth because Being is not empty; it is full, full of life, of truth, of love. Truth is the manifestation of epiphany of Being as Being. This is why Truth is the way that leads to Being. Being manifests itself as Truth.*

Panikkar: The Missionary for the Future?

Panikkar did not speak much about any 'mission', though in the mass of material he left us it will always be possible to find implicit or explicit references to a 'mission'. He knew that in the popular mind and the media the word has a negative connotation. The 'mission' is simply identified with the sad story of aggressive colonialism—cultural and economic. Moreover, etymologically the 'mission' is based on the dualism of the sender and sent, with an inevitable element of cultural superiority, open or hidden. On both accounts the mystic in Raimon would have been allergic to the popular meaning of the 'mission'. Even if we discount as accidental the physical or economic violence associated with it, the 'mission' implies organised action for concrete results, not necessarily evil; and in the popular mind these are just 'conversions', whether forced or free.

I hope nobody will be offended or misunderstand if I suggest that Raimon Panikkar represented a model of the missions for the future, whether political, economic, cultural, or religious. Mission cannot be crypto-colonialist by manipulating the other to accept my personal view. Yet one who has a vision for a future new world wants first of all to make that vision a reality within oneself, and then to share that vision with the rest of humanity so as to work together for a better world by discovering 'what is questionable and what is genuine in oneself and in others, and allowing others to remain *other*', in his own words.

Panikkar was surely not a post-modernist who paternally allows everybody to be different and gives up the search for the One underlying all plurality and making it meaningful. It is this search for unity at the heart of plurality that made Panikkar put relation at the top of philosophy and theology. Relation is needed not only to understand reality but also for authentic living; in other words, for the welfare of the universe. 'Conversion' for him can only come from inside, as the word itself and sound theology teach. For the effort to 'convert' others boomerangs on the would-be converter, and makes him change.

Peter and Cornelius

There is an amusing story in early Christian sources that seems to be a critique of the practices of proselytism common to the Jews settled outside Palestine, and also of a section of the first disciples of Jesus. We are told in the Acts of the Apostles that when Paul had converted as a result of a mysterious personal experience and joined the company of the disciples of Jesus in Israel, there was a time of peace for the community of the followers of Jesus during which the church grew in Judea, Galilee, and Samaria. Peter, the acknowledged leader of the disciples of Jesus went around strengthening the communities in the towns of those regions.

Once when in the coastal town of Joppa, at around noon he climbed onto the terrace of the house to pray. He was hungry, and while the meal was being prepared below, he fell into a trance in which he saw a large sheet coming down from heaven held by the four corners and containing all sorts of living animals, four-footed, reptiles, and birds. He heard a voice commanding him, 'Get up, Peter, kill and eat'. Peter was neither a Gandhian nor a vegetarian. But he was a devout Jew, though a disciple of Jesus, and knew the distinction between pure and impure animals as classified in his ancient scriptures. Horrified at the order received he replied, 'No way, Lord. I have never eaten impure animals!' But the voice insisted, 'What God has made clean you must not call profane!' Three times the vision happened and then disappeared.

As he was reflecting on what the vision or the dream could mean, two men knocked at the door of the house sent by an official of the Roman colonial army with the request of the official to come and visit him at the headquarters a few miles north. Peter had never been to a pagan's house; neither his patriotism nor his religion permitted it. But the arrival of men at that moment made him understand the meaning of the vision. He must not be afraid to extend his hand of friendship and his help to a foreigner, even if he belonged to an enemy power. Nothing that God has created is impure, and God has created all in Heaven and on earth! By then Peter may have already known from the diaspora that the new apostle Paul was bringing 'pagans' into the pure-blooded community of Jews who had given allegiance to the prophet of Galilee. They hoped he would finally establish the order of the world according to the Jewish expectations and interpretation of the promises in their Bible.

But the command in the vision led to another direction. He had to be converted before he could convert others. Conversion had boomeranged on him. He had to change even his own basic identity as a Jewish disciple of Jesus and break out of the protective walls of his own community's understanding of the faith. His 'Jewishness' had to take a back seat. It was no longer very important. Peter, therefore, went somewhat reluctantly to the house of Cornelius and listened to what he wanted to say. Only after that he could share with him and his family his own experience of the crucified prophet who, incredibly, was still alive. It would take years for Peter to assimilate this lesson; not long after these events, when visiting Damascus he was still reluctant to mix with Christians of pagan origin. Paul challenged him openly.

The 'Mission' of Raimon Panikkar

Panikkar must have understood the meaning of this story, and he put it into practice in his own life. He explained often how he travelled from his maternal Christian faith to an oriental understanding, to Hinduism, Buddhism, and secularism, and yet realised that he had never left his original home. He lived the conversion implied in the comment of Badrinath Chaturvedi a few years later. Commenting on the well-known saying of Karl Marx, 'The philosophers have only interpreted the world, in many ways; the point, however, is to change it' (in his *Thesis on Feuerbach*), Badrinath tartly said, 'Missionaries tried to change India. What matters is to understand it.' How can you change what you do not understand? Panikkar's primary concern was not to bring about change at once. He wanted to understand the other, and he wanted all committed people to make an effort to first understand the others' points of view, economic, social, cultural, or religious, and finding within oneself a place for the other without destroying them, without distorting their own self-explanations or subordinating them to one's convictions. In other words, by practising *samanvaya*.

I think that with these principles Panikkar outlined the meaning of 'mission' for the new millennium, whether the mission of the UNO or of political leaders and national diplomats, or of the churches of any religion, or of anyone concerned with the welfare of the planet. He wanted first to ensure that human freedom is fully respected and protected, for true change can only emerge out of the depths of freedom. Second, he wanted to spread the awareness of the other, particularly of the East in the West and of the West in the East, and also of North and South, and across ages and cultures, past and present, in order to programme our future; for the world is entrusted to the hands of humanity. Third, he wanted to work for equal rights and equal responsibilities for all cultures and peoples. Fourth, he was tolerant of the tension within us between patience with the slow pace of nature that take ages to mature, and the impatience of the human spirit that wants change and happiness *now*. Both have to be accommodated.

This is now our task, enlightened as we are by the insights of the master to continue the mission that he had.

Opera Omnia: The Philosophical and Spiritual Pilgrimage of Raimon Panikkar In Dialogue with Other Cultures and Religions

Milena Carrara Pavan

I feel greatly honoured and grateful being invited to participate in this seminar organised by the India International Centre, the Instituto Cervantes, Kapur Surya Foundation, and the Embassy of Spain in honour of Raimon Panikkar. As co-ordinator and curator of Panikkar's *Opera Omnia*, I suppose I am expected to speak about its development and diffusion in the world.

The decision to publish the collection of his writings was not easy for Panikkar. More than once, he had to overcome the 'temptation' to abandon the attempt, the reason being that, though he fully subscribed to the Latin saying '*scripta manent*', he also firmly believed that what actually matters in the final analysis is to live out Life.... 'The great masters, Pythagoras, Socrates, Buddha, Jesus, did not actually write a single word, other than in the hearts of their disciples', he used to say.

It took years of working alongside the author to collect and systematically organise his writings, which include not only all his books but also the most important articles that help to give the most complete picture of his thinking. This work involved selecting and classifying these into different subjects, and at times also editing and updating them, as he frequently felt the desire to change or add something. The work led us to draft the general outline of the *Opera*, which consisted of some twenty books, each one with an introduction by the author himself. He managed to see only three of these in print. He left me the task of continuing and completing the work, along with instructions on how to proceed.

I have been supported in this arduous task by the Vivarium Raimon Panikkar Foundation, continuing the work of the Centre for Intercultural Studies, whose founder and driving force was Panikkar. In compliance with his wishes, the Vivarium inherited his intellectual work, with the specific task of publishing and spreading his thinking in the world.

I must emphasise that without the initiative of Sante Bagnoli, the president of the Italian publishing house Jaca Book, which had already published some of Panikkar's important works, the Opera Omnia would not have come to light in Italian, and certainly not in other languages. Sante Bagnoli, whose relationship with Panikkar was one of reciprocal respect and friendship, wisely suggested to him while he was still fully active that he should organise the entire *Opera Omnia* so that it could be published. And it is thanks to the renowned reliability of Jaca Book that other foreign publishing houses have then had the courage to embark on such a challenging enterprise.

To date, eight books have been published in Italian by Jaca Book. The ninth is in the process of publication; so in five years we are already halfway down the road. Seven have been published in Catalan by Fragmenta publishing house, and three in French by Editions du Cerf. Herder of Barcelona will begin to publish books in Spanish at the rate of two volumes per year, starting 2014. Last but not the least, the English version will be published by Orbis Books of New York. The announcement was made recently in Baltimore at the prestigious American Academy of Religions, where I had the honour to present it.

We can say, therefore, that the project of spreading Panikkar's philosophy throughout the world is well underway. The Vivarium Raimon Panikkar Foundation and I myself, both as President of the Foundation and close assistant of Panikkar in this great work, as well as Jaca Book, which is also the international agent, are extremely satisfied with what has so far been accomplished and planned for the future.

*

Allow me some words on the content of the *Opera Omnia* and on how it is structured.

Each volume is enriched with an introduction by the author. I am very glad to have managed to convince the author to write all these introductions, of which some are new drafts and some are edited writings adapted to introduce the topic of a volume. Jaca Book then collected and published them in a single book, *Life and Word*, which in a certain way represents the *summa* of Panikkar's thought. I remember how, after gathering the material into the various volumes with their related introductions, Panikkar himself realised—almost with surprise—that this was a good representation of the phases of his life's journey, both philosophical and spiritual, and he said with a smile, 'I have been asked several times for a text which could be entitled *My Work* and I always refused to write it, and here we have the synthesis of my life and my thought.'

It is fascinating to see how in each volume, apparently on the most varied topics, there always appears reflected the life of its author, in his mystical vision of reality. I will, therefore, report the itinerary of his journey as he himself described in general terms in *Life and Word*, a true overview of the life and thought of Panikkar, adding in *sutra* style, typical of Panikkar, a phrase which grasps the essence of the meaning.

I was attracted by spirituality since my youth
(Vol. I, *Mysticism and Spirituality*)
This was the most important theme of the author's life, which subtly inspired all his writing, so that it became an indispensable hermeneutical key to all his intellectual intuitions. Mysticism is the integral and joyous experience of life, which we feel beating in us and which manifests itself increasingly in Panikkar as *sat* (Being), *cit* (Consciousness) and *ananda* (Bliss), equivalent for him to the Christic experience to which we are all called and which is not exclusive to a select few.

I approached the study of religions

(Vol. II, *Religion and Religions*)

Herein, 'religion' (singular) is understood to be the constitutive opening of man to the mystery of life and the journey towards fulfilment or salvation, while in the plural it indicates the diverse religious traditions.

...firstly examining the religion I was born into and brought up in depth, Christianity

(Vol. III, *Christianity*)

This shows the threefold embrace of Christendom (a civilisation), Christianity (a religion) and 'Christianness' (a personal religiosity which belongs to the mystical sphere, to the field of experience); the three moments are mutually correlated and cannot be completely separated, even though they must be distinguished. We can say that the experience of Christian maturity is threefold—it is the meeting with Christ in the centre of one's self, in the centre of the human community, and in the centre of reality. Christophany is the manifestation of Christ, icon of all reality—every being is a Christophany, but needs to become aware of it.

I then discovered my father's religion, Hinduism

(Vol. IV, *Hinduism*)

The richness and profundity of Hinduism was discovered by Panikkar as an adult during his long stay in India, through the fundamental texts of Vedic revelation, which would lead him to draft his anthology *The Veda, Mantramanjari*. It will be said of Panikkar that only a *rishi* (seer) could perform the arduous task of rendering accessible to people of today the wisdom attained by man in the past when he lived in awareness of Reality.

...and later became fascinated by Buddhism, while nevertheless remaining faithful to my Christian origins

(Vol. V, *Buddhism*)

Panikkar could not help but be fascinated by the subtle analysis of the mind and the consequent Buddhist spiritual search, which takes the form of a way of liberation through the integral experience of reality in every aspect of life, yet remaining aware of its ineffability in that the human mind is constrained to think of the Absolute as Being or non-Being, thus using related hermeneutic categories.

With this store of experience and knowledge I spontaneously opened myself to dialogue with the different cultures and religions, having already experienced this opening internally. The fact is that one cannot discover the truth of another religion if one has not 'lived' it profoundly from within.
(Vol. VI, *Cultures and Religions at Dialogue*)
The profound encounter with other cultures and religions, unfettered by prefabricated patterns, will lead Panikkar to his vision of the 'pluralism' and 'relativity' which abolishes any type of absolutist claim and has its foundations in the diversity and radical variety of reality itself. All of Raimon Panikkar's life was 'dialogue'. Indeed, he says,

> Dialogue is not simple discussion. It comes from a source deeper and more internal to the stimulation we receive from others. If dialogue wants to be something more than the simple manipulation of ideas, it must emerge from the deepest recesses of our being. This means that intra-religious dialogue is the necessary foundation of inter-religious dialogue.

Dialogue begins in the vacuum of the heart, where neither space nor time separate. The time of the vacuum of the heart is the Present, 'the point at which all times are present'.

This religious dialogue has mainly been carried out between the two religions of which I am made up—Christianity and Hinduism
(Vol. VII, *Christianity and Hinduism*)
Like brothers who meet again after a long separation and try to share their experiences, Hindus and Christians see the end of life in the terms of the

complete and fulfilled human person. Panikkar hopes that their meeting may create a cross-fertilisation which leads the Christian to recognise levels of perception and degrees of cognition which exceed the general cognition of the rational mind, and that living life means finding joy in discovering reality and achieving harmony with it, rather than trying to control and conquer it. Hinduism, in turn, can learn from Christianity to consider the structures of the world more seriously—that human social order must be governed also on the basis of an immanent and direct justice; and, finally, that historicity is itself also an element in the human striving for salvation.

I reached the formulation of my vision of Reality, which I have named cosmotheandric, through a reworking of the Trinity which I consider to lie at the heart of Christianity

(Vol. VIII, *Trinitarian and Cosmotheandric Vision: God–Man–Kosmos*)

Panikkar overcomes both monotheistic and dualist vision and opens up to the a-dualist or *advaita* one, which pure intellect cannot grasp without the participation of love. Reality is constituted of three dimensions in constant inter-in-dependent relation among themselves—God–Man–Cosmos which, taken separately, are simple abstractions of our mind.

To communicate to others what cannot be described directly I have made use of myth, symbol and cult, which are at the foundation of every faith, by developing their hermeneutics.

(Vol. IX, *Myth, Symbol and Ritual*)

It is through these three forms that man opens to the mystery of reality, a triple veil which does not impede the vision of reality but rather, only upon recognising it as such can we see.

I have always been attracted to philosophy as the love of truth and of Mystery

(Vol. X, *Philosophy and Theology*)

The separation of philosophy from theology is, according to Panikkar, fatal for both. Panikkar's mother defined him a 'passionate philosopher' and in fact his passion for philosophy not only as 'love of wisdom' but also as 'wisdom of love' was the theme of his whole life. Reality cannot be understood by only one of Man's faculties or in only one of its dimensions. Philosophy demands total involvement, that is, philosophy as a lifestyle. 'Only when you are yourself, your pure self, will you understand things as they are', as a Zen master had said and which Panikkar reiterates.

As I did not wish to retreat into a world of abstract speculation, I opened myself to the life around me in all its physicality, and I discovered that—far from being profane—it is sacred. This experience gave rise to my interest in the issue of secularity.
(Vol. XI, *Sacred Secularity*)

This is understood as the experience of the intrinsic relationship between the two dimensions of reality in man himself, the point of convergence between Heaven and Earth, overcoming the division between the secular and the religious.
(Vol. XII, *Space, Time and Science*)

We do not live in a time and space: we *are* time and space. Time is not the outer wrapping of beings but a constituent and specific dimension of each being who is inasmuch as he 'persists', and he 'persists' precisely inasmuch as he *is* this specific being and not something else.

Science and technology, born within Western culture, have led to great conquests, but the scientific mentality threatens to impede true knowledge of reality—knowing is more than deciphering a message, it is identifying oneself in the known thing, it is a process of conversion, it implies communion, the loving embrace which puts us in communication with reality and whose interpretative element is only one dimension. Reality is multi-coloured, and the monochrome vision of modern science does not have universal validity.

Panikkar's writings, which cover a period of about seventy years, do not originate from mere idle musings. They are of an autobiographical nature—not in the sense that they recount the events of his life, but that they are a map of his journey, inspired by a life and by a praxis, and only subsequently moulded into writing. The sequence has given prevalence to the topic rather than chronological order, so within the same volume the style can at times appear diverse. His *Opera Omnia* does not want to be a mere collection concerned with philological rigour, but rather the fundamental design, the organisation of what Panikkar wished to propose again to the reader, the work which he offers as the fruit of his mature life, as he explains in the editorial of each volume.

He also adds, 'I did not live for the sake of writing, but I wrote to live in a more conscious way so as to help my brothers with thoughts not only from my own mind but also arising from a superior Source….' For Panikkar, knowledge and experience accompany each other, and are put at the disposal of the reader, who is called to a work which cannot be limited to the intellect but is an incentive to the experience of the fullness of life. It is no accident that Panikkar wanted to begin the publication of his *Opera Omnia* with the volume *Mysticism*.

Allow me now to make some personal observations.

I had the good fortune and privilege to be at Raimon Panikkar's side for the last twenty years of his life, spending long periods together at his house in Tavertet, or at my homes on the Costa Brava and in Milan, as well as in numerous journeys/pilgrimages to Tibet, Peru, and India, his father's native land. Initially, the reason I remained with him was to undertake the translation of his books, which was for me an opportunity to learn because it allowed me to discuss the most salient passages with him, and this often offered him the opportunity to review, clarify or deepen his thinking.

It is well known that Panikkar took ten whole years to draft his magnificent anthology *The Vedic Experience*, but I then needed three more years to translate it into Italian (Rizzoli, 2001). Thanks to that, however, I was able to discover the richness of Indic philosophy and spirituality. Similarly, with the translation and editing of another dozen of his most important books, I could go ever deeper into his thinking. I remember in particular *The Fullness of Man: A Christophany,* written directly in Italian. He spoke and I wrote, the mind (him) and the hand (me) united in love for Christ (whom he knew and I discovered through his words).

Thus, step by step, almost unintentionally, I became his closest assistant and collaborator to whom he in the end chose to assign the very weighty and responsible task of editing the *Opera Omnia* and letting it be known throughout the world.

Why me?

I wondered this myself, and I asked Raimon, who knew well that I preferred to spend my time in contemplation rather than action, and in human relations rather than intellectual work. His reply echoed the one he had given me several years before to my question, 'Why have you chosen me as your disciple?'

I remember he answered me with his ironic smile,

> For three reasons. First and foremost, I did not choose you but I came upon you, not to speak of karma or anything else; second, because it is easy for people to be fond of you and, not having academic ambitions, you will not cause envy; third, 'a nearly empty glass is easier to fill', that is to say, not being weighed down by more or less intellectual models and doctrines you have approached my thinking with more freshness, managing to grasp it in depth, so it will be easier for you to be faithful in the work of pure 'transmission'.

This is the task I try to carry out faithfully.

Nothing is free from criticisms, of course. Yet, I can imagine Panikkar's ironical reaction on hearing that some critics have considered his *Opera Omnia* 'incomplete' because some minor articles have been omitted or because just one article has been chosen among several dealing with the same topic; of course the one in which the topic was better developed or reviewed. Smiling he would ask, 'Why are you surprised? I was constantly criticised when alive (as being too Western-minded for Easterners and too Eastern-minded for Westerners, or too philosophical for spiritual people and too spiritual for philosophers, too Hindu for Christians and too Christian for Hindus),…and now what am I criticised for? For how I decided to organise my 'complete works'? And even for my wish to keep my private life away from gossip? Can one not understand the work of an author without knowing the details of his life? Then what about Aristotle or Heraclitus? Do we know if they were right- or left-handed? Pay no heed to critics; just keep following my guidance.'

I am also often asked the meaning this task has for me; I will try to reply with a metaphor.

For the past twenty years or so I have been immersed, almost submerged, in the writings of Panikkar, yet the putting together of each new volume is always a new experience for me. Each time it is like repeating the *pradakshina*—the pilgrimage we made together around Kailasa, the sacred mountain of Hinduism, in Tibet. As we struggled on at a height of over 5,000 metres, we set our eyes on the snow-capped peak in the centre of the panorama that, for the most part, was shrouded in clouds which, from time to time, opened up to give us glimpses of the breathtakingly beautiful *darsana*. I remember Raimon pointing to it and shouting '*Miralo!*' (look at it!), with the excitement of a child, despite his years. (It was 1994, so he was 76.)

No one has ever had the courage to climb the Kailasa. Metaphorically, its centre cannot be reached by man as long as he remains 'in time and in space'—that is, on its circumference—but it can be glimpsed. In all his writings, on a variety of subjects ranging from pluralism to myth, from Christianity to Buddhism to Hinduism, from sacred secularity to inter-religious dialogue, Raimon always invites us to look to the Source of Life, the sacred Centre, that can only be reached after the death of the ego and the overcoming of our 'mentality', to which we are so bound and attached.

The writings of Raimon represent to me the finger that points towards the Centre. We must not, of course, focus our attention on the finger, but look with our eyes in the direction it is pointing. I will never forget the enthusiasm in his words, 'Look, there it is!' This is the cornerstone of the message that we find in his writings, simple to understand, but not so easy to put into practice.

Now his pilgrimage on earth has ended. His ashes, part of which rest in the cemetery of Tavertet, buried according to Christian rites, and some—after receiving the Hindu and Buddhist blessings during one final pilgrimage to India—were scattered over the sacred Ganges at Varanasi and were carried by the current towards the sea, the symbol of the Source he looked to all his life.

Raimon has shown us the path to the Self; now it is up to us to tread it ourselves.

*

I remember the last Saturday before he died, when, after reading the daily page of the Gospel (Mt. 23: 1–12) where it talks of the scribes and the Pharisees sitting in Moses' seat and Jesus' exhortation to call no man master, for there is only one master, Christ, Raimon commented, 'You see, he does not say "me, Jesus", but *Christ*, that is, the Spirit which speaks within us, whose voice can only be heard in the silence or in a heart that is pure, emptied of its own ego.' Then he added, 'Keep looking with your eyes, listening with your ears, and speaking with your words, without mediation and without compromise; the true Master is within you.'

And with this exhortation addressed to each of us I conclude.

*

Plan of Raimon Panikkar's *Opera Omnia*

Vol. I Mysticism and Spirituality

Part 1 Mysticism, Fullnes of Life

Part 2 *Spiritualita*, the Way of Life

Vol. II Religion and Religions

Vol. III Christianity

Part 1 The Chrisian Tradition

Part 2 A Christophany

Vol. IV Hinduism

Part 1 *The Vedic Experience*: *Mantramanjari*

Part 2 The Dharma of India

Vol. V Buddhism

Vol. VI Cultures and Religions at dialogue

Part 1 Pluralism and Interculture

Part 2 Intercultural and Interreligious Dialogue

Vol. VII Hinduism and Christianity

Vol. VIII Trinitarian and Cosmotheandric Vision

Vol. IX Mistery and Hermeneutics

Part 1 Myth, Symbol and Ritual

Part 2 Faith, Hermeneutics and Word

Vol. X Philosophy and Theology

Part 1 The Rhythm of Being

Part 2 The Philosophical and Theological Thought

Vol. XI Sacred Secularity

Vol. XII Space, Time and Science

Miscellanea (Lectures, Courses, Prologues, Poems, Letters and so on)

Fragments of a Spiritual Diary

Raimundo Panikkar's Trans-religious Theology from the Perspective of the Perennial Philosophy

Côme Carpentier de Gourdon

Panikkar's Approach to Comparative Religion

In the introduction to his *Opera Omnia*, Raimundo Panikkar writes,

> I was attracted to spirituality in my youth and I approached the study of religions, firstly examining in depth the religion I was born into and brought up in, Christianity. I then discovered my father's religion, Hinduism, and later became fascinated by Buddhism while nevertheless remaining faithful to my Christian origins. With this store of experiences and knowledge I spontaneously opened myself to dialogue with the different cultures and religions, having already experienced the opening internally. The fact is that one cannot discover the truth of another religion if one has not "lived" profoundly from within.

This statement describes well Panikkar's experiential and meta-scholarly immersion in the spiritual traditions he studied, from both academic and a 'mystical' standpoints, intended to achieve inner communion with the doctrines and practices he sought to understand on the basis of his personal Indo–Spanish and hence Euro–Asian identity. Just as he distrusted classical 'Western' objective scholastic methods that require the investigator to keep an emotional distance from the object of his inquiry, he avoided the temptation to draw superficial explicit parallels between similar symbols, analogies, rituals, and images across culturally and geographically separate creeds and cultures. Dialogue, he thought, requires its participants to retain their own identities, to be deeply involved in and remain committed to their respective traditions without attempting to absorb, eradicate, or defeat the others nor surrendering to them. Thus true dialogue, according to him, is dialogical and not purely dialectical[1].

He also pointed out that he aimed to 'discover some of the hidden threads that constitute, as in a weaving process, the connecting links within the whole fabric of human experience'[2]. In this, he followed a mainly inductive methodology, starting with a particular observation and then relating it with similar findings in other religious or sacred texts to draw a more general, synthetic interpretation of convergent ideas or revelations denoted by 'homeomorphic equivalences'.

Many aspects of Panikkar's accounts of spiritual notions and principles shared by the religious systems he investigated are consonant with the precepts of the Perennial Philosophy. Therefore it is proper to briefly describe the latter before identifying parallels and perhaps, divergences.

Definition of Perennial Philosophy

As a notion that spiritual and religious systems conceived by human mind in all times and places are pervaded by a single divinely or naturally inspired wisdom or gnosis which reflects eternal truths, perennial philosophy is probably as old as civilisation. It has been defined as 'each of the world's religious traditions (shares) a single, universal truth on which foundation all religious knowledge and doctrine has grown'[3]. We can relate that assertion to the esoteric teachings of many Eastern and Western masters. In ancient Europe, Pythagoras, Plato, the neo-Platonics, and the Orphics, among others, professed a similar creed. In the Christian fold, Augustine of Hippo spoke of the true religion that existed since the beginning of the human race[4] and the Cappadocian Church Fathers wrote about the divine revelation enshrined in nature but it was the Renaissance and the associated Humanistic movement, with its focus on 'liberal theology' that formally laid the basis of 'Prisca Theologia' or Philosophia Perennis, on the basis of comparative studies of Biblical literature, Christian scriptures, Kabbalistic texts and Hellenistic, Egyptian and Persian Zoroastrian philosophical documents. The most famous names in the field are Marsilio Ficino (1433–1499), Giovanni Picco della Mirandola (1463–1494), Agostino Steuco, who wrote an influential work in 1540 titled *Philosophia Perenni* and *Cosmopoeia*, as well as later Giordano Bruno, who sought to reconcile those various gnostic (in the broader meaning of 'knowledge-seeking') traditions with a cosmological system influenced by some of the contemporary discoveries in astronomy and physics. Predecessors of those 16th century thinkers are esoteric Orphic and later Hellenistic authors Iamblichus, Porphyry, Apuleus, and Plutarch, who inspired the artists and scientists of that age. One might also connect Leonardo da Vinci's universalistic philosophy of knowledge to that heritage.

Indeed, Perennial Philosophy evolves out of the encounter or confluence of two or more different spiritual and cultural schools of thought through a synthesis or syncretism of these components. The widening access to non-European and often more ancient civilisations from the 17th to the 19th centuries resulted, in a climate of increasing religious tolerance, in the proliferation of works dedicated to the rediscovery of common origins for or at least parallels between all major religious streams and we ought to mention in particular Leibniz's philosophy of harmony[5] which he explicitly equated with Philosophia Perennis and which laid the grounds for the 'unitarian universalism' of certain, mostly American, Christian churches. Leibniz was powerfully influenced by Chinese spiritual literature since he read *Confucius Sinicus Philosophus* and was also interested in metaphysical and cosmological texts in Sanskrit, though little was available in Europe in his days. In a different vein, some 150 years later William James's *Variety of Religious Experiences* as well as the New England Transcendalists[6] reflected the impact of oriental thought.

By then, both China and India had become much better known in the West and, in spite of the lingering restrictions and taboos enforced by the various Churches, Confucian, Buddhist, and Hindu philosophical systems were being recognised by many scholars and thinkers as precious sources of universal wisdom that could either, in their views, be reconciled with the Christian Revelation or might even supplement it or remedy some of its perceived inadequacies or inconsistencies. The revival of symbolical occultism that took place in the 'Age of Enlightenment' in connection with Free Masonry and the widespread fascination with pre-Christian antiquity were indebted to now mostly forgotten 'illuminist' authors such as Montfaucon de Villars and Fabre d'Olivet who, with his symbolic exegesis of the Bible in the light of neo-Pythagorean esotericism, recalled many aspects of 'pagan' mystery traditions and myths and their survival in Christian icons and ceremonies.

The German Romantic movement was partly fuelled by the 'anamnesis' of 'Indo–European' cultural roots championed by Schlegel, Schelling, Novalis, and Bopp and others and it led later to the advent of what was loosely referred to as 'theosophy', before that name was claimed by Helena P Blavatsky and her colleagues and followers in the society of the same name for a specific 'cosmo-theology' inspired by both Eastern and Western ancient esoteric documents and beliefs. In parallel, however, some students of religion and spiritual traditions formally revived the Perennial Philosophy in a less systematic and 'ideological' vein. A few, such as Saint Yves d'Alveydre, Rudolf Steiner, and Rene Guénon were involved with the Theosophical Society before defining their own independent schools of thought, often in contraposition to the TS's gnosis. In his vast and rich corpus of work, Guénon laid the basis of what is regarded as modern Perennial Philosophy, although he is more often defined as the founder of the Traditionalist School. He inspired several towering figures, the better known ones being Ananda Coomaraswamy, Julius Evola, Henri Corbin, Fritjof Schuon, Mircea Eliade, and Sayyed Hosein Nasr.

Those prolific and erudite authors came from diverse backgrounds and encompassed different disciplines and spiritual lineages in their respective quests. While Guénon started from 'Western' alchemical and Masonic occultism and discovered Indian Vedanta (which he presented in his *Introduction Générale aux Doctrines Hindoues*) and esoteric Buddhism before converting to Islamic *Tasawwuf,* Coomaraswamy, from his own Sinhalese–British mixed background grew at ease with both European and Indic civilisations and was particularly attracted to art history and critique as a way to decode and penetrate the spiritual message of the various cultures of South and East Asia. Baron Evola did research in alchemy, hermeticism, Christian esotericism (the Grail myth) and found equivalencies and 'mirror images' in Buddhist metaphysics, tantric yoga, and other oriental practices. Likewise, Schuon, Corbin, Titus Burckhardt, and Nasr studied various esoteric systems on four continents, including alchemy, astrology, African shamanism and North American native religions in Schuon's case) and followed Sufi *Tariqas* in order to achieve the *Haqiqa* (ultimate truth) that is the goal of all spiritual paths. Eliade too investigated notions and teachings shared by many great traditions from all over the world.

Finally, Aldous Huxley, who perhaps can be more aptly regarded as an exponent of the overall concept of Philosophia Perennis than as a teacher of it, played a seminal role through books like *Means and Ends*, *The Perennial Philosophy* and *The Doors of Perception* in the evolution of 'American' Neo-Vedanta, parapsychology and sophrology and in the subsequent development of 'integral studies' and 'contemplative science', in parallel with the rise and fall of the 'beatnik generation', the hallucinogenic experimentation promoted by Timothy Leary, Allen Ginzburg, the 'Dharma bums', and the hippie counter-culture in general.

In this summary retrospective on the Perennial Philosophy, we should mention that science, in the wake of the relativistic and quantum revolutions, has not been absent from the field of spiritual inquiry either. Many of the leading physicists, chemists, and mathematicians of the last century have been decisively influenced by religious and philosophical notions bordering on mysticism, from Nikola Tesla to George Lemaitre (who lectured on the relations between scientific cosmology and spirituality in England in 1932),

Niels Bohr, Erwin Schrödinger, Werner Heisenberg, Brian Josephson, Ilya Prigogine, George Sudarshan, and Amit Goswamy. Indian and Chinese native philosophies have been particularly present in the thinking of most of those mentioned above. The connection or even merger between the various rivers or oceans of human thought and investigation, according to the beautiful metaphor (*Majma al Bahrain*) used by prince Dara Shikoh to title his comparative study of Vedanta and Sufi wisdom, guided by his spiritual master Sarmad Kashani, has also taken place between the 'soft' disciplines of spiritual inquiry and the 'hard' methods of 'natural philosophy' as physics used to be known.

We can now define in a few lines the main common principles and conclusions etched by 'perennial philosophers'. They all profess to go back to the origins of religion and philosophy, to the source of holy or sapiential texts which speak of the ineffable, transcendent truth or reality, beyond being and non-being, the 'In the Beginning' or rather 'In the Principle', as it is timeless and outside space—*Bereschit* or *Arche* of Genesis, the *Yatha purvam* of the Veda, once and for all, *Idam agr'eka*. Further, from that formless Source, *Tao, Kasmai, Kham, Pleroma,* and *Sunya*, they detect all things emanating through the power of the Logos, Word or Sound, *Aksara, Eta sya, Fiat Lux,* and *Kun* as the self-generation and multiplication of the Primordial Being, the Vedic Prajapati, the Vitruvian Man represented by Leonardo, the *Insan ul Kamil* of esoteric Islam in whom some of them also see the Christos, not as a historical figure born in Galilea at a particular time but, not unlike Teihard de Chardin as the Cosmic filial ontological principle, present in all traditions and cultures. He/she who endlessly sacrifices himself to create the infinite diversity of existence and into whom all things will return in the eternal successions of *prabhava* and *pralaya, proodos,* and *anodos*.

Perennial Philosophy does not reject the recording and pedagogical value of history but it restricts it to a lower level of perception and understanding, as an unessential and unreliable reckoning that must be envisioned and transcended through a meta-historical, symbolic, and anagogical grasp of the timeless metaphysical nature of things. 'Symbols' come from *sumbolein* which means 'bringing together' and the truth of religions lies in their hermetic or gnostic, trans-historical dimension. Reality is meta-chronic and consists in archetypes which duplicate and repeat themselves while diversifying in infinite multiplicity. Hence, as Plato knew, myths are 'truer than (historical) truth because they enshrine the noumenal essence that manifests in the innumerable phenomena of what we call visible reality'.

Therefore, perennial philosophers do not accept the literal interpretation of progress in a Darwinian sense because they hark back to the 'Imaginal' world of the eternal origin, where all things that ever were, are, and will be, are potentially in their seed. They naturally reject the positivist contention that humanity has progressed from the primitive 'theology' of its origins through metaphysics in order to achieve the higher category of scientific rationality which studiously ignores the gnosis accumulated over the past centuries since its origins. We should not, however, infer from this that perennialists shun or disdain rationality. On the contrary, like Leibniz they see reason as the indispensable litmus test needed to understand the ancient wisdom and Schuon for one exposes the paradox of Freud's own rejection of rationality which relies on a rational theory to make its case.

Since, in the wake of the race for material techno-scientific 'development' triggered by various revolutions, mankind is losing its atavistic connection to this metaphysical awareness in the name of 'modernity', it is in fact declining spiritually or at least is wandering away from its genuine mission and losing sight of its inner identity as Rene Guénon points out in *The Crisis of the Modern World* and Evola in his works *Revolt against the Modern World* and *Men amidst the Ruins*. In that sense, those who belong to that family of thought are pessimistic like many essential conservatives and they tend to predict a dire near or medium term future, as Huxley did in his *Brave New World,* but they also light a beacon of wisdom and hope to redirect all people towards the only worthy goal, spiritual liberation and ultimate freedom and inner and outer peace. They emphasise the unity of our species, of all life and of all creation and erase the causes of conflict and animosity between religions and civilisations on whose common ground they have pitched their tents.

There is no fatalism in Perennial Philosophy, given that the truth and the freedom it brings are always accessible to the seeker, and our world may or will anyway, depending upon the individual interpretations, return to the Golden Age—we never left Paradise, for the Kingdom of Heaven is within us, and all signs are given to enable us to find our way back to *Svarga, Dharmakaya, Agarthi, Avalon, K'un lun*, the Green Isle, the Inner Castle, and all the other names given to it over the centuries. Its favourite viatics are the *Upanishads* and the *Bhagavad Gita*, Patanjali's *Yogasutras*, the *I Ch'ing* and the *Tao Teh Ching*, the great Buddhist sutras, John's Gospel, Meister Eckhart and Jakob Boehme, Hermes's *Kybalion* and the *Enneads* of Plotinus, Rumi's *Masnavi*, Ibn Arabi's *Bezels of Wisdom*, and Attar's *Dialogue of the Birds*, read as a few of the innumerable chapters of the One ageless and unending Book.

While for instance, René Guénon in his aforesaid books *La Crise* and *Le Règne de la Quantité et les Signes des Temps* diagnoses the symptoms of our industrial societies' diseases and predicts many of the ills that have become so prevalent in recent years, Coomaraswamy in the remarkable treatise *Hinduism and Buddhism* conducts a parallel summary elucidation of the two great Indian traditions and provides constant and numerous equivalences in the scriptures and classics of Taoism, Christianity, Islam, Norse and Celtic myths, and modern philosophy. Perennial philosophers do not advocate a merger of all creeds and cultures into one global system or an inchoate *multi-kulti* welter, but they have their gaze set on the one point-like summit (*ekagrata*) of the spiritual mountain in which all differences met on the slopes vanish while respecting the variety of the human intellectual and devotional experience that make perennial philosophy possible. Guénon establishes a clear distinction between syncretism of heterogenous systems, which he sees as a feature of Blavatsky's and Besant's theosophy and the synthesis rooted in the 'great primordial tradition' which he professes.

Another important aspect of that discipline is the reconciliation it brings about between theology and cosmology, between the wisdom of the Invisible Causes and the science of visible or physical effects and manifestations since

Nature is born out of mind and mind is born from Consciousness as most ancient metaphysical schools teach in one way or another. Wisdom is cosmic and as such it is ontological, soteriological, psychological, and ecological at the same time. By definition it is a total science that embraces all others. David Frawley calls it 'the internal sense of the Divine, the Universal and the Internal along with an external recognition of the Sacred in Nature'.[7]

From Christology to Cosmotheandry: Panikkar's Journey

Panikkar is generally regarded as a Christian philosopher who transformed and expanded the domain of theology and its affiliated disciplines more than a 'perennial philosopher' as such. He is sometimes compared to Pierre Teilhard de Chardin, Thomas Merton, or Louis Massignon who carried far their respective reinterpretations of the Christic legacy in the light of other influences—evolutionary biology, paleontology, and quantum mechanics in the case of Teilhard; Vedanta and Tibetan and Zen Buddhism for Merton; and Islamic eschatology for Massignon. However, it is fundamental that like Coomaraswamy, Panikkar was born and raised between two cultures, or two 'kosmologies' as he liked to define them, the 'world myths of particular cultures'—the Hinduism of his father and the Catholicism of his mother of which he often reminded his readers. That is a key to understand the logic of his gradual transition from Catholic Thomist Christology and Western philosophy to a universal 'christophany' shaped by oriental metaphysics and mysticism which he called 'cosmotheandry'. In that way, he is one of those great Western intellectuals who assimilated oriental philosophies in order to absorb their universally valid insights to transform the modern (i.e. Euro–American) civilisation. Hermann Kayserling is another outstanding example of such 'bridge builders'. Panikkar noted, in the vein of that Baltic Russian aristocrat, that:

> Modern cosmology…functions with total independence (from God, gods or sacredness). God is a scientifically superfluous hypothesis and the Sacred a hindrance to clear and precise scientific thinking. (The traditional attitude) is at loggerheads with the modern obsession

with production, which is how practically all activity of modern life is measured.[8]

Panikkar wrote that insofar as he was original, it was by 'going back to the origins'[9] and he sought to demonstrate it in his 1961 PhD thesis which his friend Father Bede Griffiths convinced him to title "The Hidden Christ of Hinduism". Therein, he recognises in Christ a meta-historic 'supername' and undertakes a detailed and virtuosic parallel analysis of Sankara's *Brahmasutras* and Thomas Aquinas's theodicy. In that process, as he said later, his initial 'tribal' Christology became ecumenical Christophany while he realised that a Christian did not have to be spiritually Semitic (contrary to what Pope Pius XI had stated in a famous address) or intellectually Greek. In that way, he was reconciling his earlier clerical training with his inborn nature, while detecting common features and attributes ('homeomorphic equivalences' as he was to call them later) between the *Isvara* of Vedanta or Samkhya and the *Christos* principle, between Brahman as defined by Sankara and the *Logos* of the Evangelist ('Brahman is not God but there is a homology,' he suggested).[10]

That was to be the common work of all his writings—the quest for mutual fecundation, cross fertilisation between the Western religious traditions and India's oceanic spiritual heritage; between the 'Vedic Epiphany and the Christian Revelation'[11] leading to 'a higher harmony, a unifying myth, the existential reconciliation between all scriptures.'[12] It is noteworthy that his approach and his methodology are very similar in this venture to Ananda Coomaraswamy's in his 'cross-religious' studies. However, he also cautioned, not unlike the latter, that 'we cannot understand without reducing the known thing to a certain unity but this does not prove that reality should be intelligible'[13].

In his investigations Panikkar distinguished the inherited *traditum*, which he called 'the burden of the past', the need to remain faithful to the original texts from the ongoing *tradendum*, 'the challenge of the future' in his words as he saw any transmission or translation of a tradition as tantamount to a transformation which led to transcending that very tradition. He opposed that spontaneous evolutionary process to the programme of conversion carried out by the Christian Churches. In his view, the inner realisation of Christ's trans-cultural, anagogical dimension was the real conversion, not the often clumsy, arrogant, or brutal endeavour to convert others to one's religion. Religions are not frozen in time, he reflected, they change, grow, and decline like all living things. They are and should be enriched, vivified, and renovated through mutual interactions and exchanges. It is not enough to find out doctrinal parallels or work out a cultural synthesis based on the mix of their superficial elements (the syncretism also decried by Guénon). Rather, there must first be intra-religious dialogue (within the religion itself, so that its followers may fully comprehend their own tradition) followed by genuine inter-religious (dialogical) dialogue and not a mere duologue consisting of alternating monologues between ideologues or dignitaries who need to prove that they alone are right and have the whole truth so that they may convert all others to their way of thinking.

Panikkar's Methodology and His (Non-)Conclusions

As we already noted, Panikkar puts great faith in 'authentic' dialogue which 'forces us to examine contradictions that a monocultural and monolithic vision tends to ignore'[14]. He further reflects that 'we cannot dialogue with another faith if we abandon our own but, if we dialogue from and about faith (which he distinguishes from mere belief that is a socially acquired impression as opposed to the inner conviction that faith manifests), dialogue becomes intra-religious, with religion…as a common fact'[15] between the parties. He makes no false *distingo* here between religion, way of life, and philosophy as those terms are co-terminal and overlapping. Our religion, if it is followed and practiced, determines or guides our way of life and shapes, consciously or not, our philosophy. He suggests that such a dialogue about faith can lead its participants to become one and in many spiritual traditions, to become one is synonymous with simply being. Coomaraswamy had similarly noted that the Greek verb *teleo* means at once to become, to be perfect, and to die. Nevertheless, Panikkar warns against the tendency generated by the 'trap of monistic thinking' resulting in the 'ontological status given to the epistemological *reductio ad unum* as if what is necessary for the intellect were also a necessary axiom for reality.'[16]

His own dialogue within himself and with others as a form of meditation on religious symbols and metaphors led Panikkar to draw some revealing parallels between such fundamental metaphysical notions as the Pleroma (fullness) of Christian theology and the Buddhist *Sunyata* (emptiness) which illustrate the differences of approach between what in India might be called two *sampradayas* but also point to their possible reconciliation through the Upanishadic concept of *Purna* (present in the most important *santimantra* of Hinduism), meaning 'fullness', though derived from *puran*: ancient, original, primeval. The Vedantic *purna*, like the Buddhist *sunya,* encompasses and transcends the ideas of void and plenitude, since it equates ultimate Being with Non-Being and yet surpasses the latter.

Through such a process that could be assimilated to *purvapaksa*, a time-honored dialectical methodology practised in 'Indic' cultures, Panikkar 'overhauls' the familiar Cartesian proposition, 'man is because he thinks'. He adds, in a characteristic Indian vein, 'he is because he thinks to be' and in that he reflects the well-known Hindu–Buddhist proposition, *cittamatra lokam* (this world is a creation of the mind). Like the perennial philosophers, he acknowledges the historical dimension of the human phenomenon but he points to its insufficiency and to its potentially misleading character which can lead to the typically erroneous and discriminatory interpretations enshrined in Western colonial exoticism, academic orientalism, and in much of scholasticism, with its claims to detachment and objectivity.

In view of his own rejection of the Cartesian rule of splitting all questions into smaller fragments, a practice which he calls 'fallacious', Panikkar presumably agreed with Merton's criticism of the Cartesian 'reification of concepts' espoused by contemporary Western Christianity as well as with Guénon's critique of the 'forensic' and rationalistic academic method of analysis of Eastern philosophical and metaphysical systems. He even warns that 'modern techno-science (he could have said "civilisation") is the Trojan horse which will destroy those cultures that unconditionally introduce 'modernity' into their midst'.[17] By that, he clearly meant what Kapila Vatsyayan categorises as the 'trinity of Descartes, Newton, and Darwin, to be followed by Freud and others'.[18]

By recognising the mythical, meta-historical as well as the cosmological dimension of religions in their own terms—for example, by explicitly accepting the reality of Vedic *devas* (deities) and not regarding them as mere symbols or as the figments of 'primitive minds' trying to make sense of reality—Panikkar explains that he seeks to familiarise modern secular man with the wisdom of his ancestors and in that endeavour, he adopts a 'hermeneutics of retrieval' in both the Buddhist Sanskrit dimensions of it, *nitharta* (historically, semantically, and textually accurate) and *niyertha* (allegorical, interpretative, and updated), guided by the recognition that 'traditional cultures have a vitalistic *kosmology*. The universe appears and is experienced as a living organism.'[19] One of his pithy aphorisms is 'one cannot understand a text without participating in it' and another is 'the interpreted must understand itself in the interpretation'. (Gerald Hall) Given that Panikkar equates conviction with conversion, according to the semantics of both words, one might thus infer that his acceptance of another spiritual religious legacy is tantamount to his conversion although he vigorously affirmed he had never left his native faith. Fittingly enough, the formal process of conversion known to Christianity and Islam and even to some extent Buddhism does not exist in Hindu tradition, which is a geo-culturally shared heritage, *sanathana dharma*, and not a 'passport' to meet a specifically defined godhead and achieve salvation according to a single historically recorded divine revelation. He would probably have at least implicitly subscribed to the subtly enlightening distinction made by Lokesh Chandra, 'While in Revelation man is in the image of God, in Realisation gods are in the image of Man.'[20]

In practice, Panikkar advocates going beyond the mandatory methods of scholarship in order to deeply absorb and integrate the religion that is being studied. His orthopraxis is experiential and his work of 'translation' implies an emigration into the world of what is being translated. In that process, comparisons with other spiritual vocabularies and images come to the mind of the student inductively, and indeed the inter-cultural research of this Indo–Spanish man of faith who was also formally a 'man of the cloth' is inductive rather than deduced from a set of initial precepts, as is the case for some of the perennial philosophers who moored themselves on the 'hidden original gnosis'—the *Kitab al Maknun* alluded to by Sufi mystics—in order to study all the spiritual lineages which they believed to have flown out of the former.

It is also significant that Panikkar acknowledged the impact of the contemporary physical scientific discoveries on philosophical thought and their intriguing affinity with the propositions and revelations of traditional Indian *darsanas*. As a man of dialogue and a 'translator-transformer' between various spiritual languages, he could not fail to notice the revolutionary effect of Relativity and Quantum theories on the understanding of nature and mind and he probably found there scientific support for his assertion that 'epistemic plurality does not contradict ontological unity' and that God himself is 'Nothing' until He/She brings forth the created universe. This may be defined as radical relativism—as opposed to the skeptical, agnostic relativism condemned by various traditionalists such as Schuon—and it indeed shocked many Christian theologians who, and not only for this reason, regard Panikkar as someone who broke away from fundamental dogmas of the religion. Yet, it is not much different from the statement of the 9th Century theologian John Scottus Erigena, to the effect that, 'We know not what God is. God himself does not know what He is because He is not anything. Literally God is not because He transcends Being.'

Radical relativism in his perspective is connected with radical trinitarism, or in other words, understanding the Mystery of Trinity as a universal, epistemological reality to be found in all religious traditions. Going further than the thesis of *vestigia trinitatis* whereby some Church fathers like Saint Bernard sought to explain the existence of trinitarian symbols and systems in pre-Christian times as prophetic inklings of a truth yet to be fully revealed in

Christ, Panikkar in his 1970 book *The Trinity in World Religions* identified the three well-known spiritual pathways defined in the *Bhagavad Gita* as equivalent to the three hypostases (persons) of the Spiritual Being. The path of action or *karmamarga* consists in worship of idols (*theos*) and ritual sacrifices as well as in acts performed in compliance with divine commands. It is illustrated in the Biblical Old Testament as what Joachim de Flore in his 'Franciscan' brand of Christianity called 'the Church of the Father'. The *bhaktimarga* or path of mystical devotion is shown in the synoptic gospels of the New Testament which highlights the personality of God as Divine and Human Son (*Anthropos*) and the *jnanamarga* or path of wisdom is inspired by the Holy Spirit or Logos (*kosmos*) invoked in John's Gospel and in his Apocalypse. The Joachimite Third Age is placed under its aegis.

By thus defining 'cosmotheandry', just as the *Bhagavad Gita* shows the complementariness between and inseparability of knowledge, devotion, and action, Panikkar sought to reunite polytheism and monotheism as two sides of one coin, like the wave-particle duality evinced by quantum physics. He was thereby illustrating his precept that 'the real world is the world discovered by total human awareness, not by calculus'.[21] He espoused India's traditional mission, defined by J.C. Kapur as the search for an eternal and universal tradition of truth and not a particular historical revelation. He also implicitly endorsed the cyclical vision of time that Perennial Philosophy enshrined. Eliade, for one, devoted much study to the 'eternal return' and Panikkar points out that there is 'no celebration, no awareness of the rhythms of life without recurrence'.[22]

In that light and through that process, Panikkar found himself 'reaching crossroads outside walls where…(he) put up a tent' so as to 'open himself to others and allow them to remain other'. His resolute rejection of proselytisation resulted from his conviction that the results of a dialogue are unpredictable and that in its highest form it leads to mutual interpenetration in terms that are accessible to both believers of all faiths and agnostics, by 'piercing of the *logos* to attain a truth that transcends it'. In this regard, he makes one of his most profound and eloquent statements when he writes that 'to reveal is not to lift up the veil but to realise the veil covers and conceals. That is revelation.'[23] In that sense, the veil is an inseparable aspect of reality, the Sanskrit *maya-samsara*, and there is nothing perceptible beneath it, though one must discover that the appearance of the veil is not all there is to it but rather is a delusional impression. As Kapila Vatsyayan points out, 'all strivers and seekers have arrived through different routes to a level of knowledge where knowledge, the tool itself, is renounced and transcended'.[24] Therefore no religion truthfully claims to show us 'God', the Ultimate reality as He/She is, but rather suggests images to bring us closer to the ineffable invisible reality.

Those images are very diverse but they are often extremely similar across time and space.

Panikkar drew a number of fascinating equations between the most fundamental icons of the Indian theogony and of the Judeo–Christian tradition. For example, just as he connects *Brahman* or *Paramatman* to the *Logos* and Dharma to Truth (and not merely to religion, as it is usually interpreted) he shows the homology between Agni as both the fiery First Born and Redeemer of the *Rg Veda* and the Christos in his soteriological, eschatological significance. Likewise he does not fail to see the analogies between *Soma* and the Eucharist, between the Vedic *yajna*, as the mediator between the pre-cosmogonic solitude and the eschatological reintegration, and the mystical Crucifixion, the Sanskrit *Hridaya* and the Christian notion of the spiritual or Sacred Heart, the Hindu *tapas* with the Ardor or Passion, *Vac Devi* (the Goddess of the Word) and Our Lady Sophia or Maryam (Mary) called 'Mother of her Father' in the Vedas. In sum, he qualifies the Vedas *in toto* as 'the crystallised culture of man' from the earliest days, thus endowed with intrinsically universal value. André Malraux alluded to the same awareness when he told Nehru that India was what Europe sought, consciously or not, as its Holy Grail.

Clearly, Panikkar was impressed by the capacity of the Hindu *dharma* to retain in its fold even dissidents and agnostics such as the *charvakas* and materialists and, keen to 'speak a language that makes sense to the believers as well as to the agnostics'.[25] He sought to reflect that all encompassing equanimity in his paradoxical definition of 'sacred secularity' best describes the true character of traditional Indian secularism, as opposed to the aggressively materialistic form practised in much of the West under French Jacobine inspiration. Panikkar does not teach or advocate a form of eclecticism which is always tainted with skepticism. He aims to 'rediscover the silent harmony, the Rhythm of Being', as he defined it in his Gifford lecture in which he equates that rhythm to the vedic *Rta*, or the Right (what is right) that shall make all free, together with *tapas* (passion, striving) and *Satya* (truth) in the Vedic message.

The result of this approach is that, instead of attempting to acclimatise Christianity in India as Roberto di Nobili and other Jesuit missionaries did by highlighting formal resemblances and seeking common points with the local practices and beliefs to draw new converts, Panikkar looks for the common ground on which there is no room for estrangement and conflict. 'Only by stepping over present cultural and philosophical boundaries', he concludes, 'can Christian life again become creative and dynamic'.[26] Though this was written several years ago, recent and ongoing developments in most Christian denominations, and especially in the Catholic Church, seem to bear witness to the accuracy of his diagnosis.

By striving to keep its theology separate from non-Christian, and especially from so-called 'polytheistic' ones, Christianity is visibly losing its mass appeal and intellectual relevance and often reduces itself to a social doctrine focused on humanitarian and socio-economic concerns while its metaphysical notions are accused of being outdated and inadequate in the light of modern scientific advances. The 'evangelical' protestant tendency to return to a form of Biblical Judaic archaism bears the risk of ghettoisation for the 'born again' flock in an increasingly secular and poly-religious society. By orienting his inter-religious quest towards the transcendent and immanent unity that underlies phenomenal plurality, Panikkar reconnects religion with the ecological awareness common to all ancient spiritual systems. He essentially subscribes to Aldous Huxley's definition of the Perennial Philosophy through the Upanishadic aphorism *Tat tvam asi* ('that thou art')—the divine self is in all, irrespective of the religious lineage to which they belong.

Conclusion

Through his long, rich, and intellectually fecund life, Raimon Panikkar sought to illustrate in various languages the timeless adage enshrined in the *Nisadiya Sukta* of the *Rg Veda* that 'the wise find the bounds of being in non-being', and he thus followed within himself a process to recover the soul of eternal India. He found that, as J.C. Kapur put it, 'when the mysteries disappeared from the life of the people, the link that existed between the cosmos and the traditional knowledge was broken'. His quest was for the Grail of a holy, holistic, and simple harmony (*samanvaya*), the Vedic *Hrita* or Cosmic Rhythm which determines and regulate the *dharmas* of all things and dispenses the only true freedom. He realised that such a pursuit far exceeds the reach of academic scholarship even though as he said in the epilogue of his aptly titled *The Rhythm of Being*, 'the tree of knowledge again and again tempts one at the costs of neglecting the tree of life'. That uncharacteristically laconic message has been called his spiritual testament. He gave up his initial intent to write a summary of his eschatological conclusion as he probably realised that it would be an ultimately unsatisfying exercise in intellectual virtuosity.

Like Merton, Panikkar as a Christian who remained faithful to his faith and his Church kept a certain restraint in spelling out some of his intuitions and inductions. In consonance with the conclusions of relativistic and quantum physics he advised his contemporaries to 'abandon the claim of man to be a neutral spectator of the world and king of the whole earth'. Instead of the quest for mere 'facts' and 'figures' he points to the *Paravidya* or *Brahmavidya,* the Buddha's *Anuttara Samyak Sambodhi,* for 'who has this knowledge becomes creator with the Creator' in the words of the *Brihadaranyaka Upanishad.*

Was Panikkar, as some conservative Christians still suspect, seeking to bring his native tradition back to the alleged metaphysical Source of religion called the *sanathana dharma* or the *dharmani prasthanani* in Sanskrit? That return to the source would also be, in the light of perennial gnosis, the merger with the shoreless ocean of cosmic spirituality that Rabindranath Tagore so lyrically evoked, 'the lesser moving water has its affinity with the great motionless water of the ocean…and its motion has its finality when it reaches the sea'.

In liberating itself from prejudice and dogma, in breaking free from the golden cage of exceptionalism and self-proclaimed superiority, in renouncing its monistic imperialism, its claims to sole moral and philosophical authority and to the monopoly of truth lie, according to him, in radical pluralism, the viable future for Catholicism and the other Christian denominations. As he perhaps perceived when he wrote one of his rare fictional works, Panikkar brought the remedy to 'Torquemada's virus' within Christianity.

Now that all Churches, including Roman Catholic, are at an existential crossroads in their evolution, his appeal for a cosmological and ecological reintegration of each faith with universal wisdom in all its forms, a cosmotheandry, rings as the very voice of Divine Providence.

Endnotes

1. Panikkar dedicated many writings to the analysis of the nature of dialogue and his concept of it. See for instance Eruption of Truth: An Interview with Ramon Panikkar (www.religion-online.org/showarticle.asp?title=2015).

2. Mantra Manjari: The Vedic Experience (hereafter MM), Motilal Banarsidass, 1977, A3, p. 17.

3. Perennial Philosophy, en.wikipedia.org (checked on 3/1/2014). The article adds that the summum bonum for man, according to the PP is an "experiential union with the supreme being which can only be achieved by undertaking a programme of physical and mental purification".

4. In Retractationes 1.13.3, quoted by A Coomaraswamy in St Augustine and the Perennial Philosophy (H Oldmeadow, "Crossing Religious Frontiers" (2010), p. 78 (World Wisdom).

5. Leibniz was powerfully influenced by the writings of Malebranche, a French philosopher whose theodicy has been compared with both Chinese (neo-Confucian) and Indian (Vedantic) definitions of the ultimate reality. Leibniz himself built a cosmology around

the notion of panpsychitism ("all is consciousness") and he saw, like the Mahayana Buddhists, the universe as made up of nomads that are non-spatial and eternal but reflect the whole and each other as if they were holographic mirrors. As a founding thinker of the rationalist school, though he was faithful to the scholastic tradition in his methods, Leibniz held that religion and philosophy cannot contradict each other. That great German polymath is also regarded as the founder of symbolic logics and he believed in the universality of "true" symbolic characters. For that reason he was fascinated with the hexagrams of the I Ching in which he saw the earliest systematic presentation of binary numbers. His fundamental concern was to grasp the universal truth within the diversity of knowledge systems, whether (interchangeably) theological, logical, mathematical or physical which he expressed in the aphorism: salva veritate.

6. The transcendentalists, mainly Emerson, Thoreau, Margaret Fuller, John Muir, and Walt Whitman, were variously influenced by German romanticism, liberal protestant theology and also by the Swedish mystical philosopher Swedenborg. They admired the Hindu scriptures which they took as the highest spiritual message available to mankind and they drew out of it a universal cosmic and ecological mysticism which, in the Christian tradition could be traced back to the Cappadocian Church Fathers such as Gregory of Nyssa. They provided a major source of inspiration for American intellectualism, poetry and religion throughout the 19th and 20th centuries and they also influenced the Hindu reformer Ram Mohan Roy who founded the Brahmo Samaj in Calcutta on similar premises, at the crossroad of Eastern and Western traditions.

7. In World Affairs, (hereafter, WA) vol. 6, no. 1 (Jan–Mar 2002), "Religious Diversity and Biodiversity", p. 59.

8. Ibid, "The Dharma of India", p 103.

9. Common Patterns to Eastern and Western Scholasticism", Studies in Comparative Religion, vol. 9. No. 3 (summer 1975), www.studiesincomparativereligion.com) and Christophany, the Fullness of Man (Orbis, 2004)

10. MM, A 3, p 24.

11. Edward T Ulrich, "Catholic Theology, Comparative Study and Practice of Hindu Meditation", (Monastic Interreligious Dialogue), www.dimmid.org.

12. MM, A 2, p. 13.

13. WA, ibid,. p. 109.

14. Interreligious Dialogue (www.ramon-panikkar.org)

15. The Intrareligious Dialogue (revised edition, NY: Paulist Press, 1999).

16. WA, ibid., pp 108–09.

17. WA, ibid., p. 102.

18. WA, ibid., "Eternal India-Epilogue", p 200.

19. WA, ibid, p 106.

20. Gerald Hall, "Multi-Faith Dialogue: In Conversation with Ramon Panikkar" (Australian Journal of Religion, 2, February/March).

21. WA, ibid., "The Broken Pitcher of Dogmas", p. 148.

22. MM, A3, p. 62.

23. The 13th century mystic Joachim de Flore defines in his Concordia, God the Father as the root, the Son Jesus as the branch and the Holy Spirit as the bark of the tree of Divinity. In the Exposition in Apocalypsum he relates the three ages or "status" of History to respective orders of mankind, the conjugal, clerical and monastic lifestyles, not unlike the three adult asramas of the Hindu dharmasastras. He attributes to each a specific equation with God; the fear of the Old Testament is replaced by the Faith in the New which will in turn blossom in the Grace of the future Religion of the Holy Spirit which will follow the Eternal Gospel still to be revealed. In the future age, he prophesied, the filial love of man for God which took the place of his primitive servility, will lead to complete freedom born out of spiritual intelligence and resulting from the full manifestation of God to his creatures. Although Joachimite theories were viewed with suspicion by the Dominican inquisitors and dismissed by Thomas Aquinas, they had great influence on Franciscan Christianity until and even after the Renaissance, especially in Portugal.

24. WA, ibid., p. 106.

25. MM, A4. p. 28.

26. MM, A2, p. 13.

27. WA, ibid., p. 202.

28. MM, A2, p 11.

29. The Intrareligious Dialogue (ibid.)

30. WA, ibid., "A Message", p. 8.

31. MM, C, p. 114.

32. R Tagore, "Lecture at Harvard University", 1913 (WA, ibid, p, 217).

33. "The Tragedy of the Grand Inquisitor", Temenos Academy Review Issue 11, Autumn 2002.

Holism and Particularism: Panikkar on Human Rights

Fred Dallmayr

The notion of 'human rights' is a pivotal conception of modern thought, especially of modern democracy. Clearly, given the experiences of autocracy, despotism, and totalitarianism, the importance of human rights is beyond doubt. Yet, despite the obvious significance of the conception, meaning and range of application are not easily determined, which has to do in large part with the elusive character of its terms.

The rights in question are called 'human', which has a certain intuitive appeal. But what is 'human'? Does the term denote a compact entity, with fixed or clearly defined boundaries? Sometimes, or rather most of the time, the rights are called 'individual rights', in conformity with the modern penchant to identify 'human and individual'. But again, does the latter term designate a compact entity with fixed and unalterable contours? And when we turn to the composite expression 'human rights', are rights here somehow humanised (which would yield something like 'humane rights')? Or is it not rather the common assumption that rights are attached to the 'human' like a rightful possession or property? Which means that, in addition to other belongings, human beings also 'own' rights. And when it comes to the notion of 'rights', can we assume that their exercise is always rightful or 'right'? Hence, what is the rightness of 'rights'?

The preceding questions only scratch the surface of the cauldron of issues connected with the conception of human rights. What is clear is that the conception stirs up difficult questions about human nature, justice, and the good life; hence, its discussion can hardly proceed without attention to such fields of inquiry as anthropology, philosophy, and even cosmology. It is commonly acknowledged that the phrase 'human rights' arose basically in Western modernity and hence forms part and parcel of a complex constellation of ideas which circumscribes the meaning of 'modernity'. This constellation differs significantly from the pre-modern nexus of ideas and life-forms prevailing in Western antiquity and the Middle Ages; and it also differs profoundly from many non-Western constellations of thought and conduct. In addition, as many writers have suggested, our contemporary period is marked by a transition between paradigms, bringing into view new horizons of life including new horizons for the understanding of 'human rights'.

Hence, the notion, to the extent it is transferrable, occupies a different places in different cultural constellations and cannot simply be transposed intact. All one can do is to look for 'equivalences', provided the differences are not ignored. Moreover, different cultural contexts are not available for neutral inspection; they are not reified pieces in a cultural museum. If paradigms, especially linguistic paradigms, are also 'forms of life', as Wittgenstein said, then any move beyond a given paradigm involves an existential agony, a wrenching experience challenging ingrained assumptions and habitual modes of conduct. In the following paragraphs, I want to explore some of the 'wrenching' induced by cross-paradigmatic comparison. In particular, I review arguments advanced by the Spanish–Indian thinker Raimon Panikkar about human rights, focusing on his comparison of the modern Western conception with traditional Indian views. By way of conclusion, I explore what character 'human rights' might assume in the dawning post-modern and post-Western era.

'Human Rights' a Western Concept?

Probably the most troubling and frequently debated issue about human rights is whether they are culture-specific or at least potentially universal. As it happens, Raimon Panikkar has discussed this issue in an illuminating way some three decades ago in an essay titled "Is the Notion of Human Rights a Western Concept?" He answers the question ultimately with 'yes' and 'no', but only after having subjected the notion to close cross-historical and cross-cultural scrutiny. Broadly speaking, one might say that the concept of human rights is one way in which human beings generally articulate the desire for a just social order. 'Human rights', Panikkar states, 'are *one* window through which one particular culture envisages a just human order for individuals'. But, of course, there are other possible approaches, and those who live in a given culture 'do not see the window', or do not see it as a window. Other cultures or historical contexts may use different formulations which are what he calls 'homeomorphic equivalents' to, though not identical with, human rights. Yet, this very broad and irenic way of looking at things is not how the concept is predominantly used today. In its distinct contemporary usage, the notion of human rights glances definitely through a particular window, that is, modern Western culture, and bears the earmarks of the genesis and unfolding of Western modernity.[1]

To grasp this modern character, historical comparison is helpful. The so-called modern age emerged through rupture from a preceding and very different paradigm—a pre-modern paradigm in which human beings and all particular entities were subordinated to, and integrated into, a broader social and cosmological fabric. In Panikkar's words, Western societies have been involved in 'a process of transition from more or less mythical *Gemeinschaften* (feudal principalities, self-governing cities, guilds, local communities…) to a 'rationally' and 'contractually' organised 'modernity' as known to the Western industrialised world.' Differently phrased, life in the West passes 'from a corporate belonging in a community based on practically accepted custom and theoretically acknowledged authority, to a society based on impersonal law and ideally free contract, to the modern state,' a passage accompanied by the steady 'growth of individualism'.

Nowhere is the drama of the passage more evident than in the work of Thomas Hobbes (not mentioned by Panikkar). In a radical move,

Hobbes brushed aside the holistic teleology and cosmology of Aristotle and proceeded to disaggregate social wholes into an array of isolated particular individuals struggling for survival in the 'state of nature'. To human beings in this condition he assigned basic human rights, in effect a 'right to everything' (*ius ad omnia*) necessary for their survival. Here the paradigmatic reversal is clear—while previously the 'whole' (*omnia*) embraced particulars, the latter were now entitled to appropriate the whole as a proprietary right. This proprietary character came to overshadow and mark the subsequent course of Western 'liberalism', as is manifest in John Locke's formula 'life, liberty, and property', where the former two are likewise natural possessions.[2]

Panikkar's essay lucidly distils the basic 'assumptions and implications' of the modern Western paradigm. Focusing on the Universal Declaration of Human Rights of 1948, he notes the 'liberal Protestant roots'' of that document. Among the guiding ideas of the Declaration, he singles out chiefly these features—the assumption of a 'universal human nature common to all people' which is knowable through the exercise of reason and which is 'essentially different from the rest of [non-human] reality'; further, the assumption of the basic 'dignity of the individual' irrespective of rank, race, or religion, coupled with the autonomy of that individual vis-à-vis society, nature, and the cosmos; and finally the assumption of an actual or possible 'democratic social order' where all individuals are equal in rights and where society is the aggregate of individual wills and interests.

Summing up these various assumptions, he finds underlying the Declaration the premise, not always consciously embraced by the framers, of 'a certain philosophical anthropology or individualist humanism', often called anthropocentrism and egocentrism. As Panikkar acknowledges, this general premise is contested even within modern Western culture. Thus, we find religious dissenters who challenge the 'naïve optimism' regarding human goodness and autonomy; cultural dissenters who challenge the cogency of the paradigm based on the rise of multiculturalism; and economic, especially Marxist, dissenters who treat human rights as a camouflage for class rights and economic privilege. But even in their critical remonstrations, dissenting voices often share basic features of the contested paradigm.[3]

To illustrate the contours of the modern conception of rights, Panikkar turns to the Indian philosophical and religious tradition, as recorded in the *Dharmashastras*, the *Bhagavad Gita*, and the great epics. As he points out, the term *dharma* is perhaps 'the most fundamental word' in the entire Indian tradition and could conceivably serve as an 'homeomorphic equivalent' to human rights. However, the equivalence is undercut or rendered doubtful by the multivalent character of *dharma*, which can mean, in different contexts, things like law, norm of conduct, right, truth, justice, righteousness, and even religion and cosmic order. To find the common core of these notions, one has to uncover the 'root metaphor' of all these meanings which reveals that the term basically refers to 'what maintains, gives cohesion, and thus strength to any given thing, to reality, and ultimately to the "three worlds" (*triloka*)' or the cosmos.

In every case, the emphasis is on keeping together, keeping intact, maintaining order. Thus, *dharma* in its various shadings is 'not concerned with finding the "right" of one individual against another or of the individual vis-à-vis society'. In Panikkar's words, 'The starting point here is not the individual, but the whole concatenation of the Real'. Differently phrased, *dharma* is 'the order of the entire reality, that which keeps the world whole or together'. To be sure, to maintain this order, individuals and all particular elements have to play their part. Thus, the individual's duty is indeed 'to maintain his "rights"', but the latter here signifies the task 'to find one's place in relation to society, to the cosmos, and to the transcendent world'.[4]

At this point, one needs to guard against holistic extremism. The Indian tradition also has the notion of *svadharma*, that is, a *dharma* which is appropriate for the self or one's own life. However, even here the equivalence is limited, because the notion cannot be abstracted from the holistic order. In confrontation with the Western model, Panikkar notes, the Indian tradition would critically stress that 'human rights should not be absolutised'; it would contest that 'one can speak of human rights as "objective" entities standing on their own in isolation from the rest of the Real'. Proceeding on this critical plane, the essay highlights a number of important distinctions.

First of all, from the Indian vantage, human rights are 'not *individual* rights only'. The reason is that, in that tradition, the individual is seen only as a 'knot' embedded in a 'net' of relationships which form the fabric of reality. Hence, individuality is not a 'substantial category'. Basically the cosmic structure is 'hierarchical', although this does not mean that 'higher echelons have the right to trample upon the rights of lower ones'.

Second, rights are 'not *human* rights only'. They mesh with 'the entire cosmic display of the universe'. Thus, animals, all sentient beings, and even supposedly inanimate beings are all involved in the interaction or correlation of '*dharmic*' rights. Finally, human rights are 'not *rights* only', because they are also duties and both are interdependent. Thus, taking the core right in the Western model, that of survival or self-preservation, one can say that human beings, in the Indian vision, have the right to survive only insofar as they also perform 'the duty of maintaining the world' (*lokasamgraha*). As Panikkar states, 'our right is only a participation in the entire metabolic function of the universe'. From this angle, the Declaration of 1948 would need to be amended or rephrased as a 'Declaration of Universal Rights and Duties in which the whole of Reality is encompassed'.[5]

Panikkar does not claim or pretend that the traditional Indian model can be preserved or reaffirmed intact in our time. He is fully aware of the blemishes and defects of traditional culture as it developed through the centuries, especially the blemishes of untouchability and an increasingly rigid caste structure—defects against which Gandhi, Ambedkar, and many others have struggled so valiantly in recent times. Moreover, he realises that Western modernity has penetrated Indian culture and society on all levels, bringing with it such changes as urbanisation, market economy, and an increasing focus on the rights of individuals and particular groups. As he states clearly, the notion 'that the rights of individuals be conditioned by [or dependent on] their position in the net of Reality can no longer be admitted by the contemporary mentality.'[6]

There is also a further consideration. Under present conditions, clinging to old-style holism can be misleading and even dangerous. In a context steadily marked by Western style individualism and anthropocentrism, holism is in danger of being perverted into an ideological project manipulated by demagogic or extremist political leaders. The controversy about 'Hindutva' and the excesses associated with Ayodhya are vivid reminders of this possible decay. This does not mean that concern for the 'whole' or the 'common good' must be completely abandoned, but it does mean that such terms have to be used with utmost caution as a distant horizon and always with full awareness of prevailing differences of perspectives which are precisely not 'common'.

What emerges from these considerations is the desirability of a mid-way position, of a simultaneous affirmation and critique of the Western model. Panikkar is emphatic on the needed affirmation, especially in view of the immense dangers to human dignity posed by the rise of modern mega-powers, such as mega-states and mega-corporations. In his words, 'For authentic human life to be possible within the *megamachine* of the modern technological world, human rights are imperative.... A technological civilisation without human rights amounts to the most inhuman situation possible.' At the same time, the Western model should not be unduly glorified, for it seems excessive to claim that 'the rights of individuals [or groups] be so absolute as not to depend at all on the particular situation or context'. To make such a claim conjures up the noted perils of anthropocentrism and egocentrism.

For Panikkar, the sensible position involves negotiation, more specifically a mutual learning process between cultural paradigms or constellations, 'A mutual fecundation of cultures is a human imperative of our times.' To make such fecundation possible, an 'intermediary space' needs to be found which allows for mutual learning, criticism, and transformation. This intermediary space is that of dialogue, what he also calls a 'diatopical dialogue', because it involves a movement between different places or contexts (*topoi*). 'No culture, tradition, ideology or religion,' we read, 'can today speak for the whole of humankind, let alone solve its problems. Dialogue and intercourse leading to a mutual fecundation are necessary.' To be fruitful, such dialogue has to rely on mutual interpretation, and hence on the resources of a 'diatopical hermeneutics' which makes it possible 'from the *topos* of one culture to understand the constructs of another'.[7]

Panikkar's essay is most helpful and promising for future developments when he turns from a simple opposition of models to some fruits of inter-cultural fecundation. One such fruit concerns the bearer of human rights. Moving beyond the absolutism of separate individuals (marking the Western model) and the collectivist holism (of tradition), he introduces the notion of the 'person' seen as an ensemble of relations. 'The person', he writes, 'should be distinguished from the individual'. While the latter is an abstraction, 'my person' calls forth all my correlates, 'my parents, children, friends, foes, ancestors and successors', none of whom can be called my property or accessory. Thus, while an individual is an 'isolated knot', a person is 'the entire fabric around that knot, woven from the total fabric of the Real'.

An equally important fruit has to do with a reformulation of the philosophical character of rights, a reformulation intimating a new correlation of 'knot' and 'net' or fabric. 'Basically', he writes, 'traditional cultures have stressed the net (the role of each part in relation to the whole), so that often the knot has been suffocated and not allowed sufficient free space'. On the other hand, 'modernity stresses the knots (individual free will to choose any option), so that often the knot has been lost in loneliness, or else wounded or killed in competition with other more powerful knots.' While traditional culture may be termed 'cosmocentric' and the modern Western model 'anthropocentric', maybe the time has come for a 'cosmotheandric vision of reality', where 'the divine, the human, and the cosmic' are each given their due, functioning in harmonious cooperation and allowing for 'the performance of our truly human rights'.[8]

Rights and Right(ness)

The preceding discussion attests to an impending paradigm shift in the area of human rights—a shift from the exclusive focus on the Western model to a more global and ecumenical model of rights. In their basic thrust, the reviewed arguments seek to modify or at least supplement the Western focus on individual self-interest and anthropocentrism with a greater attentiveness to ethical and religious considerations. However, although valuable, this ethical-religious correction by itself may not be sufficient to satisfy universal aspirations. There are other impediments to the universal functioning of human rights. These obstacles have to do mainly with geopolitical, economic, and technological asymmetries. Here, the question raised by Theodor Adorno becomes relevant—how ethics might function in the general context of a 'damaged life', that is, a context where rights and ethical concerns are systematically marginalised?[9] What emerges here is the realisation that the question of human rights presupposes the cultivation of a broad context of 'rightness' reaching from political to economic and social domains. This might be called the 'rightness' frame of rights.

As it happens, contemporary human rights discourse is aware of this need for a broader frame. It is customary in this discourse to distinguish between three 'generations' of rights. First, civil and political rights (anchored in modern Western individualism); second, social and economic rights (sponsored chiefly by socialist or socially progressive movements); and third, cultural and collective rights (championed mainly by non-Western and indigenous peoples). The three generations are by no means in pre-established harmony or easily reconciled. In fact, the dominant Western rights discourse grants almost exclusive preference to the first generation, while sidelining, and even accepting the infringement on, second and third generation rights. For this reason, East Asia expert Henry Rosemont Jr calls the dominant human rights discourse a 'bill of worries' concealing or papering over underlying conflicts and inequities.

These inequities have been eloquently highlighted by Chandra Muzaffar in his comments on the three generations,

> By equating human rights [solely] with civil and political rights, the rich and powerful people in the North hope to avoid coming to grips with those economic, social, and cultural challenges which could well threaten their privileged position in the existing world order. What the rich and powerful do not want, above all, is a struggle for economic transformation presented as a human rights struggle, a struggle for human dignity.

These comments are ably seconded by the Indian social theorists Smitu Kothari and Harsh Sethi, in their book *Rethinking Human Rights*, when they charge the Western model with hiding from view the plight of the vast majority of humankind, including the majority of people in their native India.[10]

What these critical voices challenge is not so much the importance of civil and political rights per se, as rather their presumed ability to operate in a vacuum separated from social, economic, and cultural aspirations. Viewed from this angle, what the contemporary 'Axial Age' brings into view is a new and integrated human rights paradigm where the 'generations' of rights would be reconciled on a global level. In the words of Kothari and Sethi, what is demanded in our time is a human rights praxis which is also a 'humane' rights praxis inspired by 'rightness', that is, 'a social praxis, rooted in the need of the most oppressed communities, that aims to create shared norms of civilised existence for all.'[11]

As it seems to me, this kind of social praxis was at the heart of the American civil rights struggle led by Martin Luther King Jr, a struggle which aimed not only at securing for African Americans political rights in a narrow sense, but also to foster their economic, social, and cultural freedom and dignity. It was a similar comprehensive vision which guided Mahatma Gandhi in his struggle for Indian independence where the ouster of British rule was only meant as a preamble to the cultivation of India's flourishing in the political, economic, and cultural domains.

To this extent, Martin Luther King, Gandhi, Nelson Mandela, and others have been pioneers in rekindling in our time the integral sense of humaneness (*jen*), rightness (*dharma*), and justice as guiding motifs for the conduct of human and public life. The point today is not to erect monuments to these pioneers, thus reducing them to museum pieces. Rather, the task is to follow their lead by practicing 'rights' in a non-unilateral, but rather interactive and ethically responsible manner oriented toward the 'cosmotheandric' or 'anthropocosmic' flourishing of humankind.[12]

Endnotes

1. See Raimon Panikkar, "Is the Notion of Human Rights a Western Concept?" in *Diogenes*, No. 120 (1982), 77–78. The essay is an expanded and revised version of his presentation at the "Entretiens de Dakar" in Senegal, 1982. The meeting in Senegal was preceded by a UNESCO symposium held in Bangkok, Thailand, in December 1979, under the title "Meeting of Experts on the Place of Human Rights in Cultural and Religious Traditions". See *Final Report*, SS–79/CONF. 607/10 of 6 February 1980.

2. Panikkar, "Is the Notion", 80, 88. For Hobbes's formula see *Leviathan* (London: Dent & Sons, 1953), Part I, Chapter 14, 73; for Locke's formula see *Two Treatises of Civil Government* (London: Dent & Sons, 1953), Book 2, Chapter 2, 119.

3. Panikkar, "Is the Notion", 79–85.

4. Ibid., 95–96.

5. Ibid., 97–99. A similar notion of self-preservation can also be found in the philosophy of Spinoza (in contradistinction from that of Hobbes). See in this context my "Nature and Divine Substance: Spinoza," in *Return to Nature? An Ecological Counterhistory* (Lexington, KY: University of Kentucky Press, 2011), 11–32.

6. Panikkar, "Is the Notion," 100.

7. Ibid., 75, 77, 100–01. Compare in this context Panikkar, *Myth, Faith and Hermeneutics* (New York: Paulist Press, 1979).

8. Panikkar, "Is the Notion", 90, 102. See also his *The Cosmotheandric Experience: Emerging Religious Consciousness*, ed. Scott Eastham (Maryknoll, NY: Orbis Books, 1993). Regarding personhood, he adds ("Is the Notion", 91), 'In drawing the distinction between individual and person I would put much more content in it than a French moral philosophy would do nowadays." The reference is apparently to Emmanuel Mounier, *Personalism*, trans. Philip Mairet (Notre Dame, IN: University of Notre Dame Press, 1970). To be sure, the notion of 'personalism' is associated with numerous other thinkers, such as Max Scheler and Cardinal Karol Wojtyta (the later Pope John Paul II).

9. Compare Theodor W. Adorno, *Minima Moralia: Reflections from the Damaged Life*, trans. E. F. N. Jephott (London: Verso, 1978).

10. Smitu Kothari and Harsh Sethi, eds., *Rethinking Human Rights* (Delhi: Lokayan, 1989), 9–11. See also Muzaffar, *Human Rights and the World Order* (Penang: Just World Trust, 1993), 39; and Henry Rosemont Jr, "Human Rights: A Bill of Worries" in Wm. Theodore de Bary and Tu Weiming (eds), *Confucianism and Human Rights* (New York: Columbia University Press, 1998), 57, 60.

11. Kothari and Sethi, *Rethinking Human Rights*, 9.

12. See Panikkar, *The Cosmotheandric Experience* (cited above, Note 8).

The Intercultural Adventure of the Third Millennium: A Homage to Raimon Panikkar

Oscar Pujol

Can we imagine a man who would want to map the surface of the sea by putting signposts upon the waves? What would be the result of this absurd task? The posts would float on the water and instead of being landmarks to orient the traveller, they would make him further lose his way adding to his confusion about his sense of direction and the horizon. And yet the man would be constantly engaged in signposting the sea of time. The man, be he a Westerner or someone from the East, with or without a sense of history, invents eras in order to fix chronologies and delimit this area of the temporal field that he feels is his own; and then with a sense of urgency he busies himself in following the erratic course of the guideposts and the latter keep up with the tide for a while conserving their relative positions and creating a mirage of precision and exactitude which is known as history.

It can be said that the man has other resources with which to signpost the paths of the sea—he might plunge to its depths, anchor the rope to the bottom and let the buoy float, indicating an immovable point. However, the result is always the same or worse—the shifting position of the surface is fixed by the immutability of the sandy bottom of the same myth. It would be better to float on the surface; at least one flows with time, although one can have the illusion that this flow advances through determinate points and takes us in reality to some place. Or we could also say, limiting the reach of our metaphor, that the sea of time is unfathomable and there is no solid land on which to anchor the obstinate hook of the buoy.

For months we waited expectantly for the moment when we would peg in the sharpest and biggest post, cherishing the idea that we have reached a decisive point—the change of a millennium. Will we really have a change of a millennium? One cannot answer this question with a simple affirmation or a complete denial. Not because we are not sure if a 1000 years end in 2001 or in 2000; it is not just a simple question of arithmetic calculation. The question would still be difficult to answer, even if it were to be formulated in a year's time.

Let us look at some of the difficulties. On the calendar on my table here in Benares, there are five different epochs—three are Hindu, one is Muslim, and one is Christian. Today, the 10th of January of the year 2000, is also the second day of the month of Shabbla of the year 1420 of the Muslim Hegira. Various periods are excluded from the calendar, like the *Kaliyuga*, the oldest era in India that was celebrated last year with the change of century and the passage to the year 5101. Responding in the affirmative to the question would mean excluding all those who continue counting the days with a calendar other than the Gregorian. It is thus evident that the change in millennium is a matter that affects just one era and that although many people might not know, there still exist many different eras in the world. If we pause for a moment and look around we will discover other cultures floating on the surface like shipwrecked companions in the choppy waters of time. In the following months we will celebrate the Buddhist, Tibetan, and the many Hindu New Years, etc. When we look at our shipwrecked friends breathlessly following the course of their respective signposts we will discover that the castaways who follow them are less numerous than those who clash against the imposing signpost of the year 2000. Responding in the negative to this question would also be a lack of consideration towards this majority group. Let us try then to find an answer. There has been a change in millennium according to the Gregorian calendar; which, despite its being that of a dominant culture, is followed by people of diverse cultures. On the other hand, we continue without having changed millennia, the latter do not exist as the post nailed by the man on the surface of the sea of time has left no mark on it. Time does not admit arbitrary breaks that the human mind imposes on it. The millennium has changed but even time ignores this and continues to flow on scandalously as if nothing had happened.

Nailing posts in the passage of time is like imposing imaginary divisions in a reality in constant evolution. It is an absurd task, if you will, but at the same time necessary and wonderful. The beauty of creation is the beauty of the ephemeral. Man acts from the limited point of his body; he speaks from the reduced space of his mouth; he thinks in this dark room that is his mind. However, the closed space of his body brings him in contact with the immensity of space; the reduced space of the mouth connects him through the golden thread of the Word with all the other beings who also speak; all images are revealed in the dark recesses of the mind, both those that can be externally contemplated and those that are only seen in the interior. For this reason it would be erroneous to condemn the celebration of the millennium as a simple human quirk or a mere sign of the cultural colonialism of dynamic Western society. We celebrate the millennium knowing that what we are celebrating is not the millennium, but the spirit of celebration that this entails. It is true that there is an overwhelmingly hegemonic culture that imposes its norms and criteria with the mere weight of economic and military might. It is true that certain cultures become intransigent when they feel threatened. It is also true that the millennium is a handy tool to wipe away the memory of other eras. But we find ourselves at this juncture. We still do not know if the 21st century will mean the real end of the colonial adventure or the culmination of the colonial impetus of the West. It might well be that the last 400 years of this latest millennium have been merely a rough and physical preamble of the empires of the West and the latter will achieve all its aims thanks to the Internet, cable television, genetic engineering, and other inventions of the future. But, I reiterate, here we are. This is the point of departure from which to juggle with the start of the millennium. This is the reality that has been given to us and our task is not to judge it, but to try and understand it in order to wholeheartedly participate in it. The spirit of celebration would have to be one of the keys to the third millennium, because celebration is acceptance and the latter is the only way to fully participate in reality without constraining it with our desires and fears. Acceptance neither waits nor investigates, it only opens wide its arms and stretches them out to embrace and be embraced.

In the five-year calendar that I have on my table, for the 31 days of the month of January, 22 are classified as festivals or religious celebrations. There are 26 such days in the month of March—Hindu, Buddhist, Muslim, Jain, Parsi, Christian, Sikh, and national holidays, festivals from the south and the north, etc. Bypassing the temptation to add frivolous anecdotes on the working days in the Indian calendar (of the 22 days mentioned only three are working days for festivals) what this really indicates, apart from the religious pluralism in India is that every moment is 'potentially sacred', if it is adequately singularised in a celebratory spirit.

It is surely this spirit of celebration that made a civic organisation, with the approval of some religious leaders, celebrate the arrival of the Christian millennium with Vedic chants and Buddhist sermons on the banks of the Ganga in the city of Benares. The Dalai Lama and representatives of other religions were also present. The first sun of the millennium shone its rays in Benares with the first psalm of the songs of the *Rig Veda* that it is worth recalling were sung thousands of years before Christ. It would be inaccurate to think that the celebration of the millennium on the banks of the Ganges is just a symbol of the inexorable cultural expansion of the West. It would also be erroneous to suppose that this expansion comes without unforeseen consequences; but, perhaps, it would be better to interpret these celebrations as a sign of the times that reveals that cultures cannot ignore each other, and that we can neither expel the others nor absorb them. As far as the first option is concerned there is no room on the planet now 'to expel the Other'. Where would we relocate those expelled if modern civilisation is so all-encompassing for which there is nothing now beyond the pale and out of the reach of technological control?

The all-encompassing pretention is an intrinsic imperative of technology; the latter cannot have the luxury of leaving nooks and crannies where 'cobwebs' still hang that would immobilise the functioning of measurement, prevention and control systems, etc. The option of swallowing up the Other is, however, active and present although at times inadvertent.

However, some of the immediate reasons that motivated the organisers of the millennium celebrations on the banks of the Ganges are more prosaic—to attract millennium-end tourists to spend a spiritual and ecumenical year-end on the banks of the Ganges. But, in this case, the immediate causes do not interest us as much as the context in which they were produced. It is significant that there is such a proliferation of 'spiritual tourism', on the banks of the Ganges or even in the deserts of northern Mexico.

On the edge of the millennium, thus, cultures are thrown into the arms of each other often despite themselves. It is, of course, not the first time that this has happened, and history is a faithful witness of this often violent encounter of diverse cultures. The difference, however, lies in the reduction of cultural as well as geographic spaces and the indisputable supremacy today of one civilisation over another.

This is the new context that forces us to write a new text with a different syntax and orthography. It should be emphasised that the desire of invoking a 'new vision' or a 'new mentality' in order to face 'new challenges' that a 'new situation' puts before a man who senses the 'need to renew himself' already belongs to the Western post-Renaissance myth that makes change and novelty one of its principal drives. From the perspective of the traditional myth, one does not feel the need for a new mentality. At the most one can talk of a 'recovery' or of a 'bringing up to date', but often it is not this that preoccupies the person who is well entrenched in his tradition. What traditional man desires is the conservation of inherited knowledge, the lack of rupture of the transmission chord, the initiating chain that is the spinal chord of his culture. But the problem we face at the beginning of the 21st century is, where can we find today the person so well-entrenched in his own tradition? Is there still someone who has not been directly or indirectly 'touched' by the precepts of modern civilisation? For example, the Indian Brahmin, the fount of Sanskrit wisdom in the last four millennia, is the direct witness of this rupture in the transmission of inherited knowledge. His children, with a few exceptions, cannot any more fulfil the requirements of traditional learning that demand a notable investment of effort to internalise what has been learnt and whose teachings can only be externalised when internal assimilation has reached an optimal level of maturity. The modern cultivation of knowledge requires different practices. There is a constant emphasis on the exteriorisation of what has been learnt and in the external production of cultural artefacts—articles, books, reports, paintings, performances. These artefacts have the objective of manifesting as quickly as possible the result of this learning. Shanta Rao, a known representative of Indian classical dance, recounted to us a few years ago in Bangalore, that she refused to give classes because of the pressure put on her by the families of students who wanted her to get them to perform as soon as possible. When this artist dies, more than 2000 *mudras* (the hand gestures made while dancing) bequeathed to her by her teacher and which are almost impossible to pass on due to the change in educational goals, will disappear.

Traditional man is thus faced with a paradox. If he is faithful to his own tradition and resists change, he will become a passive witness to the dismantling of his own traditions. If he gets contaminated by the modern myth of novelty and the need for change, he will lose perhaps a part of his traditional soul, becoming more modern in the process, but unable to face the usurping encroachments of modernity. In modern India there are a number of examples like this one. In the most traditional circles, least touched by modernity, discouragement, perplexity, and lack of motivation prevail. Paradoxically, the diverse neo-Hindu groups (and we could also add neo-Muslim, neo-Buddhist, neo-Christian and neo-animist groups who have been born of the encounter with the West) are the ones who challenge the mono-cultural pretentions of modern civilisation.

All this brings us back to the central point of this piece—on the threshold of the 21st century we find ourselves in the midst of an obligatory encounter of cultures in a reduced human habitat. This encounter of cultures is the end result of the formidable expansion in the last 500 years of Western civilisation. When we talk about 'cultural encounter' we are already under the spell of the Western gaze which has made possible or provoked the encounter. There are neither pure myths nor autonomous cultures. The perfume, the stink, or the odourless breeze of the West—each one chooses the most convincing alternative or a combination of the three options at different times—has permeated everything. The future, as the Senegalese poet Léopold Sedar Senghor citing De Gaulle said, belongs to the *mestizos*. Those who are at the confluence of one or more cultures will have a much richer vision of the 21st century as compared to those who still adhere to some kind of monoculturalism.

At the end of the XXth century a singular *metis* disembarked once more on the shores of the Ganges; not just to stay by the riverside, but in order to get to the centre of the Buddhist Wheel at Sarnath, a little distance from Benares. We must remind ourselves that it was here in Sarnath, that the Buddha 2,500 years ago started the wheel of *dharma* and this wheel is still spinning. The singular *mestizo* was none other than Raimon Panikkar. In Panikkar *metissage* takes full shape—he is a cultural, biological, intellectual, and also a spiritual *mestizo*. Born in Barcelona in 1918 to a Hindu father and Catalan mother he was brought up in Barcelona and learnt Catalan and Spanish. Being Catalan is already a way of being *mestizo*, as a Catalonian always has to juggle with two often conflictual identities—Spanish and Catalan. The characteristics of *metissage* become evident—Indian father, Catalan mother, Spanish nationality. But this cultural mixing does not end there. *Metissage* is not just biological and cultural, but also intellectual. Raimon Panikkar first had a scientific and then philosophical and theological education. He was from the field of chemical sciences and worked in chemistry but he is also a philosopher and a theologian trained in the rigours of scholasticism. In *La filosofia como estilo de vida* (philosophy as a way of life), a brief reflection on his own intellectual autobiography, Raimon Panikkar has succintly described his journey through the different paths of learning,

> Where studies were concerned I began with the study of the subject. For seven years Physics and Chemistry were my most serious occupations. At the same time I began studies of Philosophy not because I was disenchanted with my scientific work but due to a continuity of my interests; my philosophical *pathos* was there right from the beginning. I only needed patience to devote myself fully and systematically to it. Long years of strict philosophical studies and intellectual activity followed.
>
> The consecutive structure of language makes me speak, in 'third place', of my theological studies, but this urgency was also present since the earliest times of my consciousness. There was no rupture nor any brusque change. But even theology began seeming a very restricted word to describe my interest and my consuming need for a total immersion in life, a full communion with reality.[1]

Behind this manner of introduction to his intellectual formation we find some important premises in Panikkar's thought. First, Panikkar's attitude towards the adventure of knowledge is not a dialectical attitude. It is not a dialectical process from which one starts from the thesis of scientific knowledge. Instead, an antithesis is followed, that of philosophical and theological knowledge in order to reach a synthesis—the religious experience of a full communion with reality. There are no deep ruptures with modes of knowledge but a solution of continuity which has to be expressed in a sequential manner by the very consecutive structure of language. We can simply state that this non-confrontational attitude is a typically 'Indian' way of facing reality. There is no rejection of what is apparently discordant but a complementary integration of what is contradictory. There is neither a negation of the essential peculiarity of each mode of thought, just a recognition that these distinct modes of thought are necessary and constitutive factors for a full knowledge of reality. We should think for a moment of the intellectual trajectory as it is lived in the West. Let us propose a hypothetical but also a paradigmatic case. A European thinker liberated from his bourgeois past gets drawn to

Marxism. In his Marxist phase he will renege his earlier convictions with an exemplary vehemence and dedication. He will try at all times to analyse his attitudes and also those of the others with the tools of Marxist analysis in order to discover the unconscious contaminations of capitalist mentality and purify his own thought and manner which have been affected by these infiltrations. What he is doing is putting the whole flow of reality through the sieve of Marxist ideology.

The fluid of the real is thus reduced or filtered till a refined liquid is obtained which becomes his political and intellectual commitment for the world. There are big gestures, great rejections, and an unequivocal taking of positions. There is also great passion that generates a dynamism vis-à-vis existence. The truth is there before our eyes. Not to put it into practice is already a betrayal and a cowardice. The modern history of Europe is full of examples of this kind. A new idea takes hold of all society and this society reneges immediately all earlier ideas and takes on the formidable task of modifying its social praxis in keeping with the new guidelines. But the insufficiency of any ideology in apprehending reality soon leads to disenchantment. And so our hypothetical Marxist thinker reneges once more from his Marxist ideology and embraces neoliberalism in the rationalist mould. He gets enamoured of 'the open society' and its defenders and passionately lashes out once again against 'the enemies of an open society' that he arbitrarily finds amongst the followers of any kind of essentialism not in line with the premises of his critical rationalism. With time a new disillusionment sets in and he could renege again from his liberalism and convert once again, for example, to Islam. Impassioned exclusivism is always a constant in this imaginary case. When the Marxist converts to Islam, other intellectuals who also live in this exclusive atmosphere wring their hands and talk of betrayal or of capitulation. One advances always in fits and starts and each time one has the impression of having achieved everything or almost everything. The conflict thus produced releases a great amount of fabulous energy that has been and is one of the main drivers of the adventures of the West. The destructive potential of this energy freed through ideological passion, be it Western or Eastern, is also tremendous and poses one of the greatest challenges of the 21st century.

The Indian manner of facing reality seems more likely a kind of growth and accumulation rather than a rupture. Before continuing I will make a clarification in order to avoid misunderstandings. When I say that exclusivist ideological passion and the rejection that this implies has been a constant in the modern European history, this does not mean that this attitude was completely absent in India. At the end of the day these are the basic attitudes of human beings in all cultures. Simply put, this is a characteristic of a certain period of European civilisation but not that of Indian civilisation. A principle of Hindu scholasticism states that things can be defined in virtue of the preponderance of their distinctive qualities. If we say that Russia is a cold country and India a hot country, we are not saying that it cannot be cold in India or hot in Russia. Besides, the majority of these 'neo' movements which we have referred to above also tend to be passionate and exclusive.

Panikkar shows, thus, his Indian side when he describes his intellectual trajectory as a continuity without ruptures nor abrupt changes, and he is like so many other Indian scientists who do not see any tension between modern science and religious practices. This attitude creates, as we have earlier said, a certain perplexity in the Western interlocutor accustomed to exclusive modes of thought. For this reason questions like the following often arise, 'How can a man of science affirm that the religious dimension is fundamental to humankind? How can a Christian priest also feel Hindu?', and so on.

While describing his intellectual voyage, Panikkar expounds on the insufficiency of theology and talks to us about this 'pressing need of a total immersion in life, a full communion with reality'. He continues,

> This is the meaning of religious urgency for me, as by religion I understand the different paths that people think lead to plenitude, happiness and liberation. I consider religion not so much as something that reunites as much as something that disunites, that is, as something that offers us the freedom and the happiness of all limitations.[2]

We finally arrive at the spiritual miscegenation which we talked about earlier. India, the land of his ancestors has played an important role in the realisation of this spiritual *metissage*. As he himself has said, 'I started out a Christian, I discovered I was a Hindu and I became a Buddhist without ever having ceased to be a Christian.' His experience of India covers two complementary currents of the Indian being—the Hindu and the Buddhist, of plenitude and of emptiness. He lived beside the Ganges, but also made inland journeys to Sarnath in order to spin the Wheel of *dharma* in the company of his Buddhist companions. The existential risk of interculturality is, however, high. We can easily disintegrate into schizophrenia or barricade ourselves in cultural paranoia to finally crash to the ground like a broken tree with the roots (our origins) in the air and the branches (our life activity) on the ground. But Panikkar says,

> The existential risk is that of a life that is rooted in more than one culture and religion, of an existence given up to orthopraxis rather than to orthodoxy. My personal circumstances (biological, historical and biographical) have made it possible for me to accept the risk of a conversion without alienation, adoption without repudiation, synthesis or symbiosis without being waylaid by a syncretism or eclecticism. Here the Indian doctrine of *karma* is a living symbol for me. I am not voluntarily an Indian and a European, nor do I pretend to be a religious and at the same time a secular person. Rather due to my birth, education, initiation and real life I am a person who lives through the original experiences of the Western tradition: Christian and secular, and that of the Indian tradition: Hindu and Buddhist. I have had to pass three-fourths of life in order to be able to say this with confidence. I am conscious of the risk that this entails. But the challenge remains. Mutual understanding and the fertilisation of different world traditions can only be realised through the sacrifice of one's own life, toleration of existential tensions without becoming schizophrenic and being able to maintain polarities without personal and cultural paranoia. Only then can a serene acceptance produce

> the desired transformations. Intercultural dialogue is not merely a political necessity nor an academic enterprise. It is a personal matter and it has to begin with an intra-religious experience. If I do not feel and suffer in myself painful tensions and the polarities of the real, if I see this as one part from within and another from without, I am not in a capacity to understand, this is what it means to cover two points of view and do justice to both.[3]

Without any doubt, Panikkar's karmic circumstances have played an important role in facilitating his inter-culturality which is theoretical but which has been put into practice and incarnated in life itself. As R. Smet has said,

> We have before us a complete man who lives intensely each moment of his life, a scientist with a rich erudition, a philosopher in the European mould influenced by the Indian currents of thought, a theologian…a man characterised by openness given to dialogue, a man of prayer and silence, a mystic.... On the other hand it is a surprise when one gets to know Raimundo Panikkar to perceive that he lives what he says, he is not just into discourse. As he commented to us once, 'It is not easy for man to know if he is correct or in error, but he should at least try to live coherently.'[4]

The karmic circumstances of Panikkar are really exceptional and their necessity for his genesis cannot be dismissed. But inter-culturality due to the reasons enumerated above seems to be one of the key features of this millennium. There are today thousands of people who search for contact with other cultures as a way of enriching their own life experience. But inter-culturality is not free from risks. The dangers of schizophrenia and paranoia have been mentioned above. Anyone who has lived in another culture different from his own knows that these dangers are not the simple theoretical abstractions of a philosopher, but are rather very palpable realities with which one has to battle in daily life. The most tragic and spectacular dangers of inter-culturality are already evident. There is another risk that, though less spectacular, is perhaps more frequent and threatening. It is more common to find inter-cultural caricatures rather than schizophrenia and paranoia. It is not enough to put on a sari, a dhoti, or a kurta pajama in order to be an Indian. It is not enough to chew betel, eat with one's right hand, and offer incense to the gods to be an Indian. Of course, it is not just a question of wanting to be an Indian, a Tibetan, or an Arab. One ends up parodying oneself and the culture towards which one directs one's affects. One cannot stop being what one is. A tree without roots does not grow—in its static horizontality it will end up being the food for moths. It is true that contact with another culture can change our life and our way of seeing things very radically but this transformation is slow and does not depend on our will. It is like the maturing of a fruit; the interior becomes soft and sweet but the exterior is not an unequivocal sign of change. It is not always possible to know if a fruit is ripe by the colour of its skin. At times it is necessary to feel it and smell it. Of course, if inter-culturality is desirable, trans-culturality seems impossible.

A culture does not possess any other instrument other than its own to come nearer the other. It would be ingenuous to think that trans-culturality could exist. We cannot leap across our shadow. Not only is the ecological medium a part of man; the cultural atmosphere in which we live constitutes our third skin, although there are pores and osmosis of various kinds and sizes. So when we open our mouths to say something we say it in a particular language and we reveal our links to a determinate sub-culture. There is no 'no-man's land' in this every-man's land. 'Even reason is not transcultural. If we don't carry the life jacket of our own culture we would drown if we swam in other waters.'[5]

In fact one suspects that beyond his biological inheritance, one of the keys to the inter-culturality of Panikkar, among other things, is that he wears well the triple life-jacket of his cultural background in the West. This, together with his own reflexive chores, allowed him to equip himself with valuable tools to take on this encounter between cultures—dialogical dialogue, homeomorphic equivalents, ontonomy, diatopic hermeneutics, *tempitemidad*, radical relativity, cosmoteandria, the distinction between faith and belief and a long etcetera of intuitions born from the cross fertilisation of the Orient and the Occident that he has bequeathed to all those who out of choice or necessity plunge into the intercultural adventure of the third millennium.

On the other hand, not everyone in the West agrees that it is necessary to conserve the diversity of cultures if this means putting up with what is considered unjust from the Western viewpoint. But the same notion of 'injustice', 'abuse', or 'affront to human dignity', apart from extreme cases such as assassinations, robbery, rape, flagrant exploitation, etc. seems to greatly vary from one hemisphere to another. This is due, in part, to the current ideas of the individual in society, like for example, the notion that European and Indian societies are very different. An Indian is shocked by the high percentages of divorce in the Western model and he/she interprets it as a manifestation of human selfishness and almost like an affront to the moral integrity of children. For a European, on the other hand, the divorce option is a liberatory and responsible one as it allows for the separate development of individuals who, for any given reason, suffocate each other. A European is horrified at the way an Indian submits to family and caste injunctions and interprets it as a kind of sellout, a surrender to fear and insecurity that inhibits his full flowering as an individual. The Indian, on the other hand, understands that obedience to family norms is not just a way to pay a biological debt to the family, but also a way of integrating his tiny identity into the greater identity of his own community. The submission of one's own identity to the greater community is for him a kind of expansion and a liberation from enslavement and limitation. The cosmovisions are really very different and what in one place is interpreted as honesty and courage seems like madness and selfishness in another. What seems in one context like redemptive renunciation is interpreted elsewhere as cowardice and submission. There is an infinite number of examples that give rise to dilemmas more complicated than we can imagine.

In the final instance the intellectual as well as political divergences of humanity proceed from what I have called a conflict of 'cosmologies'. Cosmovision is not an image of the world because we are already in it. Cosmovision refers rather to an experience of the world itself in which we are immersed. It is the subterranean horizon of reality that each culture assumes. Earlier I called it myth. *Mythos* is narration. We understand by *kosmology* not so much cosmology, i.e. *logos* (doctrine) on the cosmos (which is modern scientific cosmology) but the experience of the *kosmos* (reality) when this is presented to us instinctively. Simply put, we can call it 'cosmovision'. It would then be like the narration of the myth (as we perceive it). In other words, myth is revealed to us in the measure that we give sense to our thought. It is the *life* circle between the *mythos* and the *logos*.

For at least two millennia the West lived within a cosmovision that is not very different from the classical cosmovision of India, admitting differences amongst and within the core of these traditions. From Pythagoras to Dante, the world in which Western Man has lived was a *kosmos* where each thing and each event had a place, a time, and a sense, often mysterious, uncontrollable, diffuse. Despite the tremendous effort of Goethe with his *Faustus*, where he tries to modernise Western cosmovision, the West has tried to deconstruct this *kosmology* without substituting it with another cosmovision. Hence, the fragmentation of human life and the specialisation of knowledge. More recently with the 'advances' in the astronomical and physiochemical sciences, a scientific cosmology is being constructed that is inscribed in evolutionary thought.[6]

Panikkar's words lay emphasis on the cosmovisions of the West and India in a space of at least two millennia. A phenomenon is being referred to here that has been observed by thinkers of different affiliations, but that in my view has never received the treatment that it deserves (and neither will it be in these pages). The question can be formulated in the following manner: What is the nature of the European culture that was born with the Renaissance and then exported to the whole world? There are two clear answers, each situated at one end of the ideological spectrum. The first one would say that the culture born of the Renaissance is the culture of reason, of Enlightenment, of progress; the humanist culture of man for man; egalitarian culture that does not allow man to invoke the gods in order to exploit other men; a culture of personal effort and hope that aspires to stop this world from becoming 'the valley of tears' bequeathed to us by medieval obscurantism. The other answer would be that of the musty traditionalists who would unequivocally affirm that modern civilisation is evil and has to be contained at all cost.

Inter-culturality refuses to accept either of these two answers. It resists the temptation of simplifying the problem and of situating oneself on one side or another of the divide. The positioning is not intercultural. Going to the other side is also not just a change of position as it signifies. Whoever wants to practise inter-culturality will have to get used to advancing, possibly on tiptoe, through the line of fire, even at the risk of receiving blows from either side. In fact the practice of inter-culturality is an exercise in equilibrium that is not very common, like walking on the edge of a sword if we take an Upanishadic simile. This is, in fact, the dialogical knowledge proposed by Panikkar that requires constant attention in order not to fall in the abyss of extremes; it is a divine and at the same time human knowledge.

We are saying that we must overcome the fragmentation of life without falling into an indiscriminate blinding light or into the confusion of shadows. We cannot leave the destiny of man in the hands of the Gods. They have failed us. We cannot only depend on man alone. He is being lost to us.

> But we also cannot let our destiny be driven into an abyss. It is true that the winds blow in a cycle and perhaps the spirit is divine. It is true that our boat is perhaps floating on the waves of a sea that we have not created. But the rudder is in our hands and the wind is in our favour. We lack a human and divine knowledge at the same time. Humanity has seen this from the beginning; but harmony has rarely been achieved. The equilibrium has been displaced towards dehumanising theocentrisms or degrading anthropocentrisms. The

> relation between oppositions is not dialectic but dialogic—neither monism nor dualism.[7]

We are always just about to enter a conflict. Perhaps one of the most important tasks reserved for philosophy is this invitation to dialogue in order to avoid the breakdown of relations and the recourse to violent solutions. We do not know if confrontation is inevitable; the space offered by doubt invites us to try and avoid this through words. Panikkar, who worked much to strengthen the concept of peace, has made it known on many occasions that if men cannot avoid war, they should at least fight with the instrument that is characteristic of the species—speech. Although dialogue might degenerate into a war of words, the casualties will always be less and the outcome will be bloodless. This is possibly one of the tasks that contemporary philosophy has before it.

> But this invitation [to the philosophical experience of India] is not the frivolous invitation to know a more or less exotic and interesting culture. It is an invitation to the most important task, and which is now becoming one of the most urgent in our epoch: a radical even anthropological change in civilisation as I have repeated time and again. The historical time of man has reached its end, and it is up to us to try and see that it not be as traumatic as announced. This is a completely philosophical imperative.[8]

It is said that in the middle of the 20th century a philosopher strolled along the beach delighting in his hypothesis, when he saw a child filling a hole in the sand with the water from the sea. The philosopher went closer to the child and asked him what he was doing. The child replied unblinkingly. 'I want to put all the sea water into this hole!' The philosopher guffawed and said, 'Son, can't you see that all the water will return to the sea?' The child replied, 'Oh, that means that the hole is already full.'

It is said that the philosopher was so moved by the child's reply that he immediately began to help him in a task that had already been realised. They say that the philosopher understood that the hole and the sea were not radically distinct, nor were they completely one, and that the child's activity was the golden thread that joined the eternity of the sea with the temporality of the hole. It is said that the philosopher was Raimon Panikkar; the child was the philosophical experience of India; and the change of buckets was orthopraxis, life as adoration and constant celebration of reality. And the water?

Endnotes

1. R. Panikkar, "La filosofia como esfilo de vida', *Antropos*, No. 53–54, 1985, p. 13.

2. Ibid.

3. Ibid., pp. 13, 14.

4 R. Smet, *Raimundo Panikkar: un profeta para nuestro tiempo*, op. cit. pp. 73, 76.

5. R. Panikkar, *La experiencia filasofica de la India*, Trotta, Madrid, 1997, pp. 13, 14.

6. Ibid., pp. 83–84.

7. Ibid., p. 15.

8. Ibid., p. 22.

Concepts of Space: Ancient and Modern – There is No Outer without Inner Space

R. Panikkar

Jesus saw children that were being suckled. He said to his disciples, 'These children being suckled are like those who enter the kingdom.' They said to him, 'If we are children, shall we enter the kingdom?'Jesus said to them, 'When you make the two one, and make the inside like the outside, and the outside like the inside, and the upper side like the underside, and when you make the male and the female into a single one, so that the male will not be male and the female will (not) be female, when you make eyes in place of an eye, and a hand in place of a hand, and a foot in place of a foot, an image in place of an image, then you shall enter (the kingdom).'

This paper has nine heads with their corresponding 18 arms. It is an icon, a *murti*. The spoken discourse has nine gates. They are the nine *gopurams* (CP. II 2), of this study as a temple. Each entrance represents a direction in space. They are biunivocally related—open-closed, right-left, rear-front, up-down, respectively, except the ninth which is 'beyond', the ungraspable turiya, and towers over the others. Each door represents a perspective, a method of approaching the mystery of space. But we shall dispense with an explanation of this spatial symbolism and proceed more academically. Yet, every intellectual creation should be also a work of art. Space, after all, is an ultimate canvas of human life.

A further disclaimer has to be voiced at the outset. The more the author meditates upon and studies the nature of space, the more powerful and mysterious it appears, the less certain one's own convictions become, and all the more humble the approach. A coefficient of uncertainty accompanies the assertions that follow. This, on the other hand, should not be considered as a negative feature, but as a positive symbol of the immanent-transcendent, hidden and revealed nature of Reality. We are only be-ing. Space makes possible this pilgrimage into Be. We shape our Space through Space. A meditation on this configuration are the pages that follow. We shall enter by the open gate of the very field where we are.

1. Space:The Fundamental Symbol of Potentiality, Universal Receptacle: An Open Gate (CP. II 3)

For practically all traditions Space is a fundamental symbol. The psychological experience of Space begins probably with the awareness of external distances. But the child's awareness of distance goes together with the distinction between itself and the other, or others.

For the undivided, i.e. non-reflexive consciousness of a child (spatial), separation means also (intellectual) distinction. Only two different things can be distant. Distances would 'constitute' the outer space. Distinctions would 'make' the inner space. 'Two' spatially inseparable entities would be indistinguishable and therefore not two.

In a word, inner space and outer space are the two faces of one and the same Reality. Inner space is not a metaphor taken from the outer space. This primacy given to exteriority is a feature of some cultures, but represents already a split in human consciousness if not balanced with interiority. Any extreme would be equally lopsided and unconvincing.

It is characteristic of modern Western culture to have reduced Space practically to physical extension. Any extreme would be equally lopsided and unconvincing. And this is also the experience of Western Man. The West is reacting strongly against monolithic 'scientist' conceptions. In short, Space is more than just only a 'physical' entity. 'For who could otherwise breathe, who could live (breathe forth) if (this) Space were not bliss?' says one Upanishad.

This fact of one single word symbolising a reality both spiritual and material, is not an exception. On the contrary, the sacramental conception of the universe is the prevalent one. In this view each material reality is imbued with a spiritual component, each thing is at the same time carrier of physical and psychical forces. In point of fact, most traditional languages do not make the rather modern dichotomy epitomised in the Cartesian dualism of *res extensa* and *res cogitans*. *Kahod* (*kahed*) in Hebrew means both heavy, precious, and holy, *pneuma* in Greek means wind, breath, and spirit, and even in many texts of St Paul we cannot make out whether he refers to the human or divine spirit. *Atman* in Sanskrit means also body, soul, and self *Salus* in Latin means health and salvation, just to give a sample. In most of the old traditions when they refer to the primordial elements they mean a Reality which is at the same time material, spiritual, and even divine. The Vedic *agni* (fire) would be a point in case. The same could be said of the elements of the Presocratics. The *hydor* (water) of Thales, for instance, is certainly not H_2O.

In brief, the separation between inner and outer space, identified respectively with spiritual and material, is a rather modern conception. Space may be conceived as the continent that makes any contents possible because it is as much container as content. Space is 'that' within which 'things' happen and are because Space is equally within 'things'.

'All is within it', says the *Chandogya Upanishad.* All (*sarvam*), that is the outside and the inside. Or according to the same Upanishad, 'As far as there is *akasa*, so far also there is *akasa* within the heart.' The text goes on to say, 'Within it, indeed, are contained both heaven and earth, both fire and wind, both sun and moon, lightning and the stars, both what one possesses here and what one does not possess; everything is contained within it.'

The *Brahadaranyaka Upanishad* says, 'Space is the honey of all beings and all beings are honey for space. That radiant, immortal Person who is the space within the heart, is indeed that very Self. This is the Immortal, this Brahma, this the All.

The *Chandogya Upanishad* answers to the question of 'what is the goal of this world?' (*asya lokasya kagatih*?), 'Space is the final goal.' The Upanishadic tradition equates *akasa* to *atman*.

Plato says, Space (*chora*) 'provides a habitat for all created things'.

At any rate the correlation between continent and content is constitutive. Space can be the universal continent because it is equally the universal content. Not only are things in Space, Space is also in things. This is the case because Space is a primordial reality which defies our categorisation in inner and outer, subjective and objective, material and spiritual, created and divine. It is both, and yet without confusion or separation. It is important to distinguish between the objectifiable (scientific) approach to an aspect of Reality by means of accepted categories (like asking what is the atomic composition of the molecule of sulphuric acid (H_2SO_4), and the method required to approach ultimate notions (like that of Space). In the latter case we can neither reduce those notions to previous ones (which do not exist), nor can we presume that we 'know' them without any categories or *pramanas*. Hence the difficulty of such investigations.

We may begin with a truism—Space is everywhere. It is the where and also the situation of things. Everything is somewhere because it is situated, because it is in relationship. Being is being-with (*co-esse*) but also being-in (*in-esse*). This amounts to recognising that Space is everything, but not 'all of everything'. Space coexists with everything. Space surrounded by Space is unconceivable, could we say paraphrasing Aristotle? But how could it be otherwise without destroying all intelligibility to Space?

For this reason our first approach is that of an open gate. Properly speaking we cannot enter an open gate. It is not a gate at all. We are already in—and equally out. This means that in spite of all our holistic and intuitive methods we need the rigour and effort of partial approaches. It is here that we find all gates closed and that we will have to force our entrance through specialisation, that is, one gate or another. The harm begins when we forget that our entrance was only a hole we made in the complete building but leads us outside it, since the temple we are considering does not stand 'over there', but encompasses us. We are part of it.

2. The Modern Fragmentation of Knowledge: A Closed Gate (CP. II 4)

Both individual development and cultural 'evolution' preceed by means of distinctions. The child grows by discriminating more and more. Cultures refine and deepen knowledge by means of specialisation. The human mind works *componendo et dividendo,* says Thomas Aquinas. So we begin distinguishing between spaces; right and left, up and down, East and West, physical and psychic, terrestrial and astronomical, inner and outer. But distinctions should not lead to separation.

In some cultures Space has become mainly a physical notion and only by extension a spiritual one. Yet Space is an all-encompassing category as African cultures still remind us. But modern Man is mostly under the influence of the dominant scientific culture which has succeeded in fragmenting knowledge up to the extent of disintegration. It has cracked the nut, although now it does not know how to 'remake it', like a child having disassembled a watch. Now 'we' are so imbued with the modern so-called scientific ideology that we tend to overlook that the fragmentation of knowledge is not just fragmentation of the known object, about which we may grasp only a portion. It rather entails fragmentation of the knowing subject, Man himself. There is nothing wrong with specialised skills (*Erkenninisse*, *conocimientos*) and particular methods of research (investigation). The problem is that authentic knowledge (scientia, *gnosis*, *jnana*) cannot be fragmented without affecting the knower. This is the modern predicament.

Space follows the same destiny of being converted into an objectifiable or specialised notion and finally it is reduced to a sort of Newtonian space, and even deprived of Newton's theological moorings. It is no longer a *sensorium Dei*, but a kind of empty box where the movement of bodies 'takes places'. Space is conceived just as exteriority. This would oblige us to speak of inner space only metaphorically. The modern scientific attitude is to consider space as a Kantian or non-Kantian category, but at any rate as something which allows us to perceive (and measure) distances as something related to physical bodies in their external relations. No 'place' here for the inner space. Not even for distinctions between space and space in different places. All physical space is homogeneous and generally isomorphous.

It is important and encouraging to recall that contemporary physical science, specially after Einstein and Heisenberg, opens a scientific way to overcome the pure objectivity of Space. After all, 'objective space' has no deep roots in human history. Not only is Space inseparable from time and cannot be severed from the observer, it also presents characteristics which defy pure exteriority.

We have here an unavoidably political problem. Should we pay tribute to a certain scientific Modernity and call 'space', properly speaking, only the external space of physical bodies, or should we keep to a more traditional and wholistic use of the word? It is certainly semantics. But our languages are languages spoken by Man, a political animal, and they shape the world we live in. I suggest that it is an unnecessary tribute to Modernity to restrict the use of the word 'space' to the physical sense. It would amount to another defeat of traditional cultures in front of the all invading technological complex.

One example may suffice. Practically all traditional cultures live both in contemporaneity and coexistence with the ancestors. The three Churches (triumphant, purgant, and pilgrim) are one Church, says Christian ecclesiology; the ancestors are around us, say most of the classical religions. It is obvious that they cannot coexist in a Newtonian space. There is no place for the dead there. The *Svargaloka* (heaven) of the Hindu tradition requires a Hindu cosmology. The same from the corresponding Christian notion. Heaven and hell have to be spatial if they have to be real, but it would be absurd to ascribe them to some physical localisation in the sense of modern science. We cannot conceive them as being located in an astronomical outer space, nor in a merely subjective, and metaphorical, inner space. Either heaven or hell do not exist or we need another notion of Space altogether;

another where, another conception of existence. As I have often elaborated, there is no theology without cosmology and vice-versa.

Whatever this may be, the fact is that we have to reckon with the modern predominance, in the Western languages at least, of the naively (pseudo) scientific conception of space. In a word, the notion of Space has also been fragmented. If we want to rediscover a more complete notion of Space we will have to reconstruct it. Modern space is closed. We will have to turn to the right and enter through the philosophical gate. It lies on our right, as this direction usually indicates the locus of tradition.

3. Three Different Philosophical Viewpoints: The Gate at the Right (CP. II 5)

We shall limit ourselves to studying the relationship between those 'two spaces'. What makes those spaces to be Space? If inner space is only space by analogy with the outer space, what is the *primum analogatum* which allows such a linguistic treat?

Here it all depends on our implicit philosophical assumptions. We shall only sketch them.

Reality is open to us, I submit, by a set of corresponding organ or organs. These organs are, of course, intertwined, although we may give predominance to a set or another and even deny the existence of some of the organs. Our notion of Reality will accordingly vary. We distinguish three spheres of the Real because our pramanas or means of valid knowledge are ultimately three. Plato, representing the West, would call them the sensible (*ta aistheta*), the intelligible (*ta noeta*) and the mystical (*ta mystika*). Madhva summing up a great part of the indic philosophical speculation calls them the five senses which perceive (*indriyas*), the mind which infers (*manas*), and the spirit which intuits (*saksin*).

a. If our viewpoint begins and ends with the sensual data, Space will be considered fundamentally as physical distance between bodies, and, by extrapolation and metaphorically, space will refer also to spiritual space as the 'place' which allows for the human unfolding of life.

b. If our emphasis lies on the intelligible reality, Space will refer primarily to the very foundation which makes distinctions possible. Space will here be the symbol for the underlying basis of all multiplicity.
c. If our view is directed the experience of the ineffable, the mystery, that which 'lies' above and beyond (again a spatial metaphor) the sensible and the intelligible, Space will then be the very invisible 'container', potentiality, emptiness in which diversity of beings is possible. It will be the empty bosom enclosing everything. Space will them be directly related to kenon (*to kevov*) sunyata, *asat*, emptiness, non-being, as so many traditions have affirmed.

A philosophy of Space would have to consider these three different viewpoints, a task which we cannot do here and now. We will, instead, assume a mature development of the three philosophical options and proceed towards a certain integration of those views. For this we will have to leave the temple and enter it from the left; the left being in our times the symbol for newness and a certain non-conformism.

4. An Effort at Integration: The Gate at the Left (CP. II 6)

We recall that we concentrate on the question of the nature of an inner and an outer Space. Our thesis defends the advaitic or non-dualistic relationship between the two. This means that we neither identify inner and outer space, nor differentiate the two in such a way so as to make only one of them the real space and the other a subordinate concept. This implies that we recognise an underlying and fundamental experience of Space of which the inner and the outer are two qualified modes, without entering now into the epistemic nature of those modes. We did call them aspects.

Trying to overcome dualism without falling into monism we shall try to defend a more wholistic view. By analysis, i.e., division and differentiation, we distinguish, for instance, between *locus*, *situs* and *ubi*, between physical and spiritual spaces and the like. But Space, we said, is an all-encompassing notion.

The dichotomy between inner and outer space corresponds to the opposition between subject and object. The outer space is considered to be 'over there' it is 'objective', even if all objectivity were to be a projection of the mind. For Kant, for instance, space may be a category of the mind, but it still refers to objects. The inner space, on the contrary, is supposed to be within us, it is 'subjective', it belongs to the inner structure of the knower, the human being.

Outer space means specially the 'physical' distances considered mainly in Physics, Astronomy not excluded, and many of the Arts. Inner Space seems to refer fundamentally to the awareness of distinctions. Psychology, Epistemology, and Philosophy are supposed to deal with inner spaces; the natural Sciences with outer spaces. The twins have been for a long time on no-speaking terms.

One 'scientific' bridge between 'Sciences' and 'Humanities' is the commonality of time. Both cannot dispense with time. Physical space, after Einstein, is not conceivable without time. Nor has inner space any meaning if the temporal experience is excluded. Thus, the space–time scheme seems to be common to all human disciplines. But this time–space is still far from the wholistic experience of Space we are looking for. We shall have to look elsewhere to find a synthesis.

We need to look at what most traditions have been trying to investigate—how to combine unity and diversity. We cannot let all multiplicity be lumped into an undiscriminated whole. Nor is it convincing to renounce all intelligibility and let chaos prevail.

We shall have to leave our temple again and enter through the rear—the rear being the more humble and realistic way to go into any building.

5. Scientia Architechtonica: The Rear Entrance (CP. II 7)

We shall now focus on one old and central discipline which is both a science and an art and which in Western languages carries the ambitious name of architecture. Archi-tecton—art of the principles, the chief of the crafts, the most important techne, the primordial builder.... *Scientia architectonica* amounts still in XVIII century Europe to *philosophia prima* or ontology

(Christian Wolff). God, after all, is the architect of the Universe (Leibniz). Even for Kant architecture has the connotation of wholeness. It is a system. And until Schleiermacher architecture suggests the systematic gathering of a multiplicity under a whole. The architect is not the engineer, the Man with wit (ingenium), but the head of the artists, the imitator of the Creator.

The traditional architect became the builder of houses for God and Men. A house is neither a box, nor a hole, and much less a garage. A house was, is, the main symbol for being in the world, and the proper Space to live and handle things. Agriculture was the culture of the fields, while architecture was there to make possible the cultivation of things within the human Space, that of the human habitat, the field of humaneness. The house represents the cultural world, and architecture the art and science of building a cultural system, i.e. a coherent whole.

The old jewish sapiential tradition knew it well. A house is not a haphazard construction according to the whims of man. 'A house is built by wisdom.' And wisdom, we know, is the first born of God, the creative power of Yahweh, the model of all his works and the maker of the entire creation. The house is the continuation of the creative power of God with the collaboration of Man. The most lofty notions of the Old Testament are used in this connection. In the Christian tradition St Paul uses this double metaphor, 'You are God's 'agriculture', husbandry tillage; you are God's building.' Three currents of thought run through the wisdom of the etymology,

1. The house, *domus* (cf. dome) is the family, the basic human group (the husband is bound to the house, the spouse is *casado*, *casada* (from *casa*, house; in Spanish) i.e. the *human element*.
2. The house is the building, the construction, the shaped space, the timber used for it, i.e. the natural element.
3. The house, domus is the enclosed circle where one is tamed and also protected (cf. Sanskrit *damayati*, Greek and Latin *domare*), to tame and also to constrain, and doing a certain force, i.e. the technical or artificial element.

Architecture here amounts to the human and cosmic order, *rta* and *dharma* combined. The panorama changes Modernity. The house ceases to be a habitat, a habit of a particular family to become a piece of protected enclosure.

The modern architect would be mainly the artist of the outer space, the engineer being the scientist of the same. What we call the artist would then be the shaper of the inner space, the philosopher being the thinker of the same.

Our thesis defends that this dichotomy is culturally bound and it should be overcome. In fact, any authentic architect, even today, will agree that true architecture is more than just a manipulation of outer space with technological means, that architecture is intimately linked with anthropology because anthropology is not independent of cosmology. The architect does not construct holes for privacy and comfort; the architect shapes Space as an unfolding of human life in the cosmos.

The function of the architect is not that of exclusively creating an outer space, nor is the task of the artist that of merely describing an inner space. Both belong together. This is why the good architect is an artist like the authentic poet is much more than a versifier. Further, those actions are not individualistic performances. To build houses for the exclusive sake of monetary profit, or to do verses, paintings or pots only for sale is a human and cosmic aberration. The craftsman is a shaper of Space where people can breathe, live, and enjoy. This Space is an expression of the genius of a person, a generation or a culture. It does not imply conformism or mere repetition. It requires creativity. True tradition never repeats the old. It makes, often remakes, the old things new. But it does not pretend to start anew from zero.

The architect senses the Space of his time. While the poet rhymes the times of his space, the architect 'expresses' what 'impresses' the people of a particular cultural period. We could continue the paradox and add that the creative architect, as any creative person, lets Space emerge from a non-place, from a *utopia*. The creative genius lets the thing that has not (yet) found its *locus*, be incarnated in Space, become Space.

When classical traditions tell us that the artist has to undergo purification, contemplate, and / or follow some rituals, they are telling us that there is no real outer space without an inner space, that nothing will influence the outer if it does not come from the inner space, that the arrow will not hit the target if the target is not in our heart. But, equally vice versa, the outer shells somebody else creates—and we all are interrelated—will also condition our interior. Our acts are not private. As we shape the outer space so will the inner space reverberate and vice versa.

I am speaking of something much more primordial than the psychological influence of a building on the tenant or visitor. I am also having in mind something much deeper than the aesthetic taste of the architect to choose places, forms, and shapes pleasing to the eyes or comfortable to the senses and the aesthetic influence on the beholder or user. The true architect deals with Space and not just with forms. I am referring to something much more primordial than psychology, aesthetics, or even ethics (the influence of goodness). I am referring to this intrinsic link within the inner and the outer, the spiritual and the material, the cosmic and the human, and also the divine. Link may be a misleading word and 'relation' will not convey the meaning either if we interpret the relation as a result of the things related and not vice versa. It is rather the relationship which lets the 'related' things emerge—like in the Buddhist *pratitryasamutpada*, the Christian Trinity, and the philosophical transcendental relation. I have called this insight the radical relativity of reality, the cosmotheandric experience.

It is my 'inner space', my sense of distinction, of discrimination (*viveka*) which will open up for me the sense of place, distance and orientation, i.e., the 'outer space'. We live in a Space that we ourselves help to create. But vice versa, it is the Space in which we find ourselves living which will shape our lives, taste, style, and feelings. The artist is the person who breaks by a vital circle this logically vicious circle. The traditional *ars architectonica* lets us at once breathe in a Space that cannot be 'located' just within or without. Body and soul are not separable.

Artistic here means the poetic activity of shaping a new world out of the very world in which we are already living. We create our own Space as much as Space creates us. Spatiality is a human existential. But this spatiality, which is constitutive of Man, is not an exclusively inner world of thoughts, dreams, and actions where we live. It is not either the external places, buildings, or cities in which we exist. Both are compenetrated so that the one is impossible without the other. This spatiality is more than a vestment we wear. The architect is not the engineer. This spatiality is part of ourselves. The architect is the first technician, the co-shaper of that Space which we are or shall become. Living enough time in any environment shapes both the environment and ourselves. Not only do shoes take the shape of our feet or old couples resemble each other, also Space is an active and passive anthropological configuration. Thus the inherent limitations of the architectural activity. It is for the concrete human being, culture-bound and living in a particular time and Space. Nobody produces universal works of art (the dream of a colonial mentality), although some very concrete and culture-bound artistic creations may overstep the boundaries of a particular time or culture. A really multipurpose building is an aberration, as much as a construction without any concrete purpose, be it that of realising beauty.

All this has very practical effects. To live in a rented house is like wearing somebody else's clothes and even borrowing a foreign body, it is like having an artificial limb. To have lost this sensitivity is one of the results of the technocratic civilisation. A prefabricated house is like a prefabricated (transplanted) kidney—an emergency solution. Most modern apartments in a big city are no longer natural habitats or cultural places. They are prefabricated prostheses—to get along. The ancient builders of cities, temples, and even houses knew the anthropological factor of Space. Not every building is for everybody and everything. The interdiction to non-Hindus to enter Hindu temples, the ancient *disciplina* arcane of the Christian liturgy down to the privacy of nuptial chambers and private quarters may have degenerated today into intolerant bigotry and often social injustice, but have a much deeper meaning than defending religious intolerance or private property. You do not have indiscriminate intimate relations with any one whom you happen to meet, you do not share the skin of your own time and space without having the required intimacy. Time and Space are not neutral and objective values. They are not commodities for sale—as unfortunately they have become in the technocratic complex of modern civilisation. It is against human dignity to sell one's own time and one's own Space—as it is to sell one's own body. Creative work is not dehumanising labour. In a word, the outer cannot exist without the inner, as well as vice versa. The indwelling in a place is not occupying a certain number of square metres on neutral grounds. The tragic expropriations of Papua New Guinea, the no less tragic Israeli and Palestinian war, the gypsies and poor people evicted from suburbs where they have lived for generations furnish us with dramatic examples of the conflict of cosmologies I am describing. For them Space is part of their being, for others just a geometrical area everywhere the same, a market value.

Having approached our building by the indirect way of architecture, from the rear as it were, we should face it now straight from the front gate, that is, from the anthropological viewpoint: Space as a constitutive element of the human being.

6. Space as Human Landscape:The Front Gate (CP. II 8)

There is an English word *country* which in the expression *countryside* vaguely reminds of the Latin *contra,* as found in the Romance Languages, French *contrée* (from which the English word came), Italian and Spanish *contrada*, Portuguese and Catalan *encontrada*. The German *Gegend* has also the same meaning, and the same origin. The accepted etymology may not be correct,[1] yet historically it has conveyed the suggestion of a land, earth, or place situated in front of us, facing us, a region which we have before us, opposite, against us. Objects are objects because they are situated in front of us in a land or domain which is our country. We are in dialectical relation with objects. They have been thrown in front of us (*ob-jecta*). They form our country. The country is objective, it stands over against us. Peoples wage war to conquer another country, a new territory.

The 'conquistadores' went, like the astronauts go, towards the discovery of new frontiers, to the conquest of the other, the aliud, with the consequent danger of alienation, as history shows.

Something very different is the landscape. Landscape is not sheer objectivity. Landscape is part of us. We are not without landscape. Landscape is not without us. Landscape is not in front of us as an objective datum. Landscape is not just 'inscape', a merely subjective mood either. The landscape is that piece of land, lawn, lane, enclosure and / or free space; all meanings suggested by the word. It is our native or natural region, i.e., that which 'regents' guides, us, which is neither a mere 'instance' nor a sheer 'circumstance' of our being. It is neither exclusively interior to nor merely around us. It is our spatiality.

We live in a country but we are not in a landscape. We are landscape, although not only landscape. This landscape is part of our spatiality. This spatiality can neither be equated with the topos or locus of the Aristotelian and Western-Scholastic tradition nor with the *χώρα* or general habitat of all things in the Platonic sense, nor is it identical to the Sanskrit *akasa*. This spatiality is that concrete landscape which we are and which allows us to move. We are landscape and we move within it, not as tourists going to foreign places, but as pilgrims reaching our real centres. We are not limited to our physiological bodies. But the landscape is neither like a bigger or subtler body nor like a clothing we wear. We are spatiality in the described sense that we are it being within it. Space would then be the general abstract noun for the spatiality, an existential proper to the human being, as we already advanced. Animals occupy a place, and this place also constitutes them. Animals live in a territory, and their territory is vital to them. Man is spatiality, not because the human being merely needs a territory, but because Man knowing himself to be spatial and corporal knows at the same time that Space belongs to him. This Space is the landscape. Spatiality is not primarily what makes distance possible, but what makes nearness possible. Spatiality makes us to stand in tension to one another, i.e., neighbours. We are sharers in Space as we are sharers of the Word. *Homo loquens* is *homo spatialis*. We share in Word and Space. The relation is intimate. The experience of language may help us to realise the space that we are. We have two forms of speaking. The one is to chatter, to gossip, to go on repeating learned things and already conceived opinions, generally by others, to utter phrases on the level of the mental. The other is when we inhabit the words we say, when language is the very house of our being, when we live in the very words we utter, when we create each phrase out of a concrete experience in time and place, experience which we allow to crystallise, as it were, in the very words which flow spontaneously out of our whole being. We do not think beforehand such words, we do not calculate them, nor do we arrange them trying to make an impression on our heaters, nor even reflecting on the meaning of what we say. We simply say it, we inhabit those very words, they are a revelation of what we truly are and not the result of what we 'want' to say. Those words are truly sacraments. They create the proper space into which they draw the listeners as a whirlwind engulfs those near it. These authentic words themselves create a space which encompasses both us and the true listeners. For this reason it has been written that we shall have to give account of every idle word, i.e., of every word which does not work, which does not effect what it says, because it is deprived of inner energy; without power. Most of the Indo–European languages have practically lost the chanting and the tones as integrant part of language itself and not just as an accompanying phenomenon. However, singing together often produces this space, as any real liturgy will easily show.

Landscape is the Space that we are. It is not just outer space, it is not the surroundings. Contemporary ecology goes in the right direction, but it has still a long way to go in order to overcome its dualistic assumptions. The house is not just a comfortable platform or a pragmatic shelter, as we already said. But landscape is not the inner space either. It is not the product of the imagination. Landscape is not our shell either, because generally we do not have the inner experience of the shell as a living being or do not consider the shell a placenta. Landscape transcends our individuality, but is part of our personhood. Modern individualism is the great obstacle to even understanding spatiality. In fact spatiality is something which cannot be so easily individualised and privaticised. Spatiality belongs to the person, not to the ego.

The implications are far reaching. We humans are not foreigners of this planet earth; we belong together. The so-called time-lag, i.e., the human uneasiness after a long jet journey, because it has disturbed within us the temporal rhythms of the earth, is well-known. Less studied is the 'spatial-lag' due to the same phenomenon, generally less felt because modern habitats (from airports to hotels) are monotonously homogeneous.

In a word Man is not only soul, nor even soul and body. Man is also society and cosmos. The animals, plants, and the earth are not just useful or dangerous creatures. They are linked with us more ultimately, like Space itself. Humans are not to be confused with any other being and yet there is in Man something of all beings. Man is a microcosm, says traditional Hellenism. The correspondences between the inner and the outer, the here and the yonder are the warp and woof of Reality, say the Upanishads. Our spatiality is a human feature. 'Outside' landscape we could not be. The flight into astronomical space may betray a flight of modern Man from himself. And yet we cannot escape naked to our outer planetary flights. We have to take also our earthly Space, our atmosphere and our space-ships when we try to escape. There is something shamanistic in our interplanetary feats. And yet, the fictional Man of the technocratic universe carries with him the most distressing anthropological uniformity as practically all futuristic and interplanetary description of popular and non-popular science-fiction show. Man is incapable of actually leaving the landscape that he is. The Space where the futuristic astronaut lives is still an earthly Space—even if without gravitation.

The ecological consequences lie also at hand. We are Space and not only dwell in it. We cannot be without landscape. We would stifle. Man is not only a corporeal being, he is also 'inscape' and landscape.

Landscape not only forms, but also informs the human being. A person without a proper landscape becomes dehumanised. This is one of the causes of the erosion of humanness in the agglomerated and over-congested apartments and slums of many big cities. Dehumanisation occurs when humans lack the vital Space which constitutes part of their lives. The difficult adaptation of horses, for instance, to new environments is a well-known example. Many of the problems of immigrants have to do with the surroundings. The reason is deeper than lack of familiarity. It has to do with the 'inscape' of each individual which is linked to the landscape. This is also the case with modern urbanism. Modern technological megalopolis force people into straightjackets which change their very constitution. A telling example is the contemporary discussion in India around the Correa Commission on urbanism.

We are saying that Space belongs to man as language does, and that the relation is reciprocal. Man speaks language and language speaks Man. Space constitutes Man and Man constitutes Space. Spatiality is an anthropological existential, we said.

But Man is not the whole of Reality, nor is Space the whole of Man. Man is more than spatiality and Space is also more than just Man or a human feature. This is why our front-door analysis is not enough. We shall have to climb to the heights of the temple and try to have a look from the top. We shall have to break the roof of the house in order to discover the divine dimension.

7. Sacred Space, Real Space:The Upper Gate (CP. II 9)

We may simply mention now what historians of religions, with more or less exotic connotations, have described as sacred Space. Sacred Space is simply Space, real Space, and not a geometrical or physical abstraction.

Sacred Space is real Space, i.e., it is that encompassing 'structure' of distances, distinctions, and diversity. Profane space is partial space, i.e., specialised space. Physical space is thus profane space and an exclusively inner space would equally be profane. There is Space when our existence is open (spacious). We suffocate when we narcissistically shut ourselves within our individualistic capsules. The landscape which permits us to fully be is created by a sacred action.

We may recall that many a liturgy, from the Amerindian to the Christian worship, begin by creating a proper space where fellowship with one another and with the Divine may occur. To sacrifice is the means to organise the

Space, says Vedic wisdom. Indic music does the same. It begins by creating a Space where the singing, playing, and worshipping can take place. This Space is neither exclusively exterior nor interior; it is both, it is us who have an 'interior' and an 'exterior' at the same time.

Let us remember that the word Space, from Latin *spatium* (from *patere*), means to lie open, patent (cf. Spanish *patio*, an open courtyard). This sense of openness and freedom seems to be common to the Indo–European words. *Chora* (*χώρα*) is the word Plato uses. The word means empty, free space, or open land, although also a finite region, an inhabited land, but not fenced.

Also in Sanskrit *akasa* means free or open space, vacuity, ether. It comes from *a* and *kasate*, to appear, shine, be brilliant. It suggests that which lets things be seen and thus to see, to know—*a-kas*. *Akasa* would then be that which allows things to appear, to be known, and ultimately to be. *Akasa* is that which makes possible that things manifest themselves. It is the 'place' of revelation, as it were. Things are in so far as they are spatial.

Those who affirm that sacred Space is objective space do so in polemics against those who would dismiss it as merely subjective. Sacred Space as real Space is neither subjective nor objective. Space is prior to those categories. The *Vastupurusamandala* of indic architecture could offer us a perfect example. It is the ritual diagram (*mandala*) which describes the concrete descent of *purusa*, the primal Man or primordial Reality, into a localised thing, entity, *vastu*.

Space is that which makes possible the manifestation of Reality. All Reality, inasmuch as it is manifested, is spatial, although Space is not the whole of Reality.

Space as *makom* and *me onab* is one of the names of God in Judaism. Properly speaking *makom* is the habitat of wild animals, then habitat in the sense of house and more specifically God's house, i.e., the temple, which as refuge can be applied to *Jhwh* himself. As in most old traditions here it is also difficult to separate the temple on earth from the temple in heaven. In sacred Space both meet.

This is so much so that St Paul will say that heaven is the proper Space of Man, the genuine and everlasting house, not as an external dwelling place, as if Space were an empty box within which we move, but as the proper 'place', 'body', i.e., Space of Man. 'Our House is (made) of heaven.'This 'eternal house in the heavens is not made by hands'. 'We have a building from God.'Once we lose our Space we lose our heaven. We are Space. This Space is the divine 'place' where we truly are. It is obvious that all this has no meaning in a Galilean–Newtonian–Einsteinian cosmology. It is also obvious that the idea of heaven as a lofty parking place for the deceased souls has dwindled away.

Astrology also studies the spatial connections between astral bodies and human being and ultimately finds, or searches, the proper hearth of Man. The West is prone now to speak of inner space as the set of human potentialities. But this inner space is also the astrological Space. The astrological connections are not casual connections as if being born under one constellation were the cause of our character. They are spatial relationships of a Space, of course, which is both inner and outer. The stars did nourish themselves of the Earth's exhalation, said Heraclitus. The stars of the firmament, says Origen, are the bodies of those angels which have condescended to remain in the physical universe in order to serve the cosmos and collaborate to the universal restoration of all being.

The inner and the outer Space is the Space that constitutes us. It requires a sense of orientation. This sense of orientation is inbuilt in our own existence. We are not solipsistic entities, but humans-in-the world. We are our world and not just along with our world or in it. All prepositions are superfluous here. We are our world, although the fact of being the world does not exhaust us.

Perhaps music is the proper introduction to the experience of Space. Music is rhythm, is number. Music is movement. Music is sound. The word music comes from the Greek which in and through rhythm unites language, verse, music, and dance. Not without reason the *Nyaya-Vaisesika* philosophy considers sound, *sabda*, the specific quality (*guna*) of *akasa*. It consistently affirms that 'the ear is the only condition (*upadhi*) imposed upon *akasa* which is one and infinite'. The experience of music is the main door to the experience of Space which is at the same time inner and outer. Without outer space there is no music. Music is not sound-hallucination. Without inner space, music is only physiological noise. Rhythm is the movement of inner and outer Space at the same time. Would music be the true measurement of time in Space? We would then unify two classical definitions of music—the science of numbers and the art of melody. 'Heaven and Earth do not exist without music', is supposed to have been said by the legendary Pythagoras.

Having now soared up to the music of the spheres we should come down to the depths of the human being and enter that gate underneath which leads us to an analysis of human existence.

8. Space as the Extension of Existence:The Inferior Gate (CP. II 10)

If Augustine did describe time as a certain distension of our existence, we could, in a non-Coartesian way, recover the word extension and call Space the corresponding extension (dilatation, *Ausdebnung*) of our being. We are, we exist, distended in time, and extended in Space. Existence is both (temporal) distension and (spatial) extension. There is a specifically human time which we may call temporality. There is, similarly, a specifically human Space which we may call spatiality. In what follows, however, we shall not insist on the specific human feature over against the generic nature of Space, not to complicate unnecessarily the issue. Space, I have suggested elsewhere, presents a cosmotheandric character.

The temporal character of our *Dasein* has been often studied. From Augustine to Heidegger, Western tradition has profusely reflected upon human temporality. The Vedas and indic philosophy are equally full of wisdom about the nature of time. So are other cultures. Human fullness implies the synthesis of the three times and/or the overcoming of time. Salvation, karma, death, birth are all basic notions having to do with time. Human existence is a temporal pilgrimage. Or, as we said, human existence is distended temporally and so is any existence. Time pervades everything and is the coefficient of our fragmentation and the symbol of our contingency. The Absolute, the Divine is considered to be eternal, timeless or perhaps even timeful.

Much less attention has been paid to Space, although implicitly it has been subsumed into the temporal considerations. The only major exception being perhaps the modern scientific thought on the nature of physical space. And this may be the reason why moderns are prone to take Space as meaning only physical Space. The situation is slowly changing, as we said in the beginning.

The spatial extension of human existence, as understood here, has little to do with the Cartesian dualism of matter as *res extensa* and spirit as *res cogitans*. It is our entire existence that is extended. Our extension is rather correlated to the temporal distension of our being, although not reducible to it. The fact that our beings are distended in time and extended in space means that they exist not all at once or as a whole but extended and distended along Space and time. Putting it the other way round, time and Space are both constitutive of existence and not extrinsic to it. Now, this extension is both inner and outer and makes for distances, distinctions and diversities.

There is a tension in each being which unfolds in temporal distension and spatial extension. We cannot describe it much more because any explanation of primordial intuitions has always to fall on its own feet. We cannot reduce primordial categories to previous notions.

Precisely because every human being is extended, because it shows a tension spreading in space (similar to its tension unfolding in time), it shows an inner and an outer face, it has not filled the whole Space, as it were. This extension allows for growth, movement and change, in Space. Space is that feature of existence, ultimately of Being, which makes 'room' for movement. Movement is inherent to Being because Space belongs to Being. Things do not move in an empty Space; things themselves are spatial, Space being of the very essence of Reality. The ultimate tension is not between Spirit and Matter, but between Freedom and Bondage. Space is neither material nor immaterial, but it can be the 'locus' of freedom or the 'place' of constraint.

But Freedom cannot be put into logical propositions. They freeze the moment they are uttered, and limit freedom. The ninth gate of our building does not lie in any of the eight indicated directions. Is it the *guha*, the *cidakasa*? It may lie in the very centre of the temple. But how can we penetrate the centre?

It would cease to be the centre and become a dimensionless point. That is, how can we describe the undescribable? Truth, says the *Brhadaranyaka Upanishad*, is threefold. In the middle there is falsehood. But it is only through this middle link of approximate and symbolical language that truth can be hinted at. We enter thus into the *garbhagriha* of our edifice. Space is the *yoni* from which life emerges, says one Upanishad.

9. The Advaitic Experience of Space: Turīya (CP. II 11)

It would amount to misunderstanding the advaitic experience of Space were we to imagine this experience as a construct based on the synthesis between inner and outer spaces. It is rather the opposite, although, for the cultural reasons we mentioned, we have had to proceed the other way of re-integrating the 'two spaces' into Space. The advaitic experience grasps immediately the 'two' as 'one', or rather as 'non-two', and is aware of 'their' mutual and constitutive dynamism –the one space is not without the other, because the very nature of Space is constituted by the primordial relationship between the two. We say 'primordial relationship' because it is neither as if the 'two' spaces would make the 'one' Space nor the opposite, as if the 'one' Space manifests itself in the 'two'. We should rather speak of the radical non-duality of the 'two' without neither of them losing their relative reality. The relation is not one, the poles are needed, it is not two either, the relation is not the poles. The 'two' do not make the 'one'. There is neither one nor two. Advaita is neither monism nor dualism. There is a dynamic and constitutive relationship so that each of the poles of the relationship is the whole, because we can in no way isolate the poles without destroying them. They would cease to be poles. If we were to suppress the one pole, the other would automatically disappear. The polarity itself is the primordial reality. Where is the wind when it does not blow? Where is Man when he does not live? There is no wind without blowing, there is no Man without living, there is no Outer without Inner, nor Inner without Outer. It is the Inner that makes the Outer and vice versa.

The advaitic experience has a formidable difficulty, especially for our times. Formidable means that it elicits fear, the terror of losing control, the panic of uncertainty, the obsession for security which is a characteristic of modern times. The advaitic experience implies the abandonment of the sovereign leadership of the *logos*, of the *manas*, without for that matter falling into irrationality. The dilemma between rational–irrational is an ultimate dilemma from a rationalistic point of view. The non-rational does not need to be irrational. I insist that there is no question of transgressing the strictures of thought. The moment that the advaitic intuition has to express itself in intelligible words it has to speak about polarity and thus use a somewhat dualistic language, for the two poles are not graspable at the same time. Reality is not reducible to intelligibility. We stutter, we suggest, we symbolise, speak by approximations, innuendos, *dhvani*, use parables and metaphors as feeble devices. The poet tries, the *rsi* sings, but the song is only in the singing and neither in its notation nor in the thinking or speaking about it.

The advaitic experience of Space is thus neither that of inner, nor that of outer space, but that of the one in the other, as it were. In the inner we discover the outer, and in the outer the inner.

You close your eyes and the outer space flashes; before there were only distances. You open your eyes and the inner space materialises; before there were only illusions, dreams, hallucinations. Many traditions have said it when they referred to the experience of the void, of emptiness of non-being, as we have already alluded to. But properly speaking there is no experience of Nothingness. That is why we can only speak improperly. Nothingness is true nothingness when it also annihilates the alleged experience of it. There is no *it* to be experienced.

Should we say that the true architect is the shaper of Silence (CP. II 12)?'And the brethren remained silent' after the Lord had spoken, says the Buddhist sacred text. 'Brahman is Silence', says a lost Upanishad. Out of Silence the Word came, repeats the Christian tradition. '*Wu wei*' murmurs the Chinese sage.

Concepts of Time: Ancient and Modern – Kalasakti: The Power of Time

Raimon Panikkar

The Awareness of Time

Time is the revealer of all things—*Gaudapada, Karika (1, 6, 8).*[1]

Time is something which concerns all of us. We are all under the power of time. It is inseparable from human self-consciousness. Man lives 'in' time. He is aware 'of' time. He reckons 'with' time. Time is all-pervading. There is no human being without time-consciousness. Man lives time.

We are all in its grips. We, humans, and also matter, the universe, non-sentient, and intelligent beings alike. Everything suffers the bite of time. Time is 'the matrix of all differentiation', says Bhartrhari.

On the other hand, salvation, liberation, enlightenment, divinisation, glorification, *nirvana*, *mukti*…consists in escaping, being free from, standing above, passing beyond time, realising it, bringing it to its fullness, transcending, or annihilating it.

'Time is the Supreme Power in the universe, the great *deva*' (AV XIX, 54, 6), 'Upon time all the worlds repose' (AV XIX, 54, 4). 'From time all beings emerge' (Mait U VI, 14). 'I am time' (*kalo smi*)', says Krsna Vasudeva (BG XI, 32).

One of the results of modern specialisation is that it makes real things difficult to grasp—for who can embrace all details of a single thing?

Modern culture has succeeded in convincing most of our contemporaries that time is so elusive, so difficult, that only exceptional minds like Newton, Einstein, or Pregogine know what time really is. Or, for the more conservatives, that only the vedic rishis, the biblical writers, Sankara or Aristotle, or for those philosophically oriented, Wittgenstein, Nishida or Heidegger, had an idea of what the essence of time is.

It seems that we are quite resigned to leave to some special people to tell us what time is; just as we put all our lives in the hands of technological experts, be they medical doctors, economic advisers, politicians, engineers, or computers. It all seems as if we were condemned to be surrounded by and have daily intercourse with life-decisive factors without knowing what they really are.

The dilemma is clear, either we need borrowed knowledge for something so ultimately essential to our life, or its knowledge is after all not so important.

It we accept the first horn of the dilemma most of us would have to live relying on the knowledge of some privileged creatures. This attitude denigrates immediate experience, asks us to believe in the expertise of others and, ultimately, undermines our personal dignity and self-confidence. While religious belief of this type of alienation is on the wane, this scientific belief is still rampant, although beginning to decline. Contemporary consciousness somehow revolts against this kind of life by proxy. And a sane reflection tells us that authentic faith cannot rely on the belief in the belief of others. If time is so important it cannot be something whose meaning escapes most of us.

Or, after all, the knowledge of time would be only a luxus for idle people and we would not need to know something with which we are having constant dealings. The knowledge of time would then be not so necessary for life, for human life. Do we only need to handle clocks and watches so as to march at the compass of the megamachine? Should we simply 'work' and not worry?

If the acceptance of the first horn condemns us to more or less blind belief and inauthentic existence, accepting the second plunges us into a merely instinctive and irrational life. We would not need to know the fundamental 'factors' of human life. Is there any way out? Time is important and inescapable. We cannot renounce the consciousness of time without renouncing our human status. We can live without knowledge of the law of gravitation or the existence of quasars and fractals, but we cannot have a full and even normal human life without reckoning with the time factor in all our human affairs. Knowledge is an irrenounceable human gift, and reflective knowledge belongs to our human dignity.

The only way out from the dilemma is to discover that there is another type of knowledge different from the fragmented and specialised information which characterises a great part of the scientific and philosophical notions of our predominant culture.

What is, then, this knowledge, or, in our case, what is this awareness of time?

The so often quoted sentence of Augustine, 'If no one asks me, I know; if I want to explain it to someone who does ask me, I do not know' (Confessions, XI, 14, no. 7) indicates that the question–answer–knowledge is not the immediate and most primordial awareness. Any answer to a question, would a certain Vedanta say, is already second-hand knowledge. It is not primal knowledge. It is not saving knowledge. Primal knowledge does not give an answer but solves, dissolves the very question; it makes it transparent. The philosophical and pedagogical consequences are revolutionary. We should be alerted to the intrinsic violence of the questions (including the questionnaire of the polls).

We touch here a truly formidable problem, because the awareness of this dilemma upsets our belief in rationality. The rhetoric of Augustine, incidentally, applies to any ultimate issue. All ultimate issues are qualified tautologies. They can only be tautologies, otherwise they are not ultimate, and any further explanation would have to proceed *ad infinitum*. But we qualify them somewhat by letting the ultimate insight of such tautologies unfold in our awareness without breaking the intuition as-under into further (unexisting) components.

In our human existence we have to deal not only with time, but also with space, matter, spirit, self, soul, love, and the like, without really having a specialised 'knowledge' of what they are. But what is knowledge?

There are at least two types of knowledge; the one proceeds by 'cogitation' in the traditional sense of co-agitate, to stir, analyse, interfere. The other proceeds by 'intellection' in the traditional sense of *intus-legere* up to becoming identified with the thing known. We should recover the importance of this latter acception of knowledge, without neglecting specialised cognitions.

In other words, any knowledge which has to proceed by abstractions is not primordial knowledge. Scientific knowledge needs abstractions. Modern science extracts (abstracts) the quantifiable kernel of things and deals with it. It has hardly ever claimed to be saving wisdom, integral knowledge. It is *aldjbr*, algebra. There is no confusion when it utilises letters, that is, formal signs. But often it uses the same language that people use in their daily lives. Time is a case in point, and sometimes this confuses people and scientists (Stephen Hawking, for instance). The reality of time—whatever this may be—is not identical to a scientific parameter. Philosophical knowledge should know better, but a certain type of philosophy has also forgotten its primary character by simply dealing with abstracted aspects of the real, abandoning the whole.

We have too often forgotten that the thing from which the abstraction abstracts the quantitative parameters or even the qualitative features is the real thing. There is a predominant diffused platonic presupposition in the West, and an idealistic assumption in the East that the magma, that is, the original and complete thing, from which the abstraction has abstracted the thoughts, is negligible, unimportant, and ultimately non-real; only essences, and immutable essences at that, are taken to be real. Nature may be written in mathematical characters, as it has been said, but reality is not script alone. And, besides, 'the letter killeth' as it has also been said. Of course, those philosophical systems will reverse the order and claim that things are mere appearances of the real essence(s).

The second type of knowledge, *gnosis jnan*, wisdom, does not proceed by abstractions, nor by inferences, inductive, or deductive. It proceeds by intellectual intuition and integral experience. This holistic and thoroughly loving knowledge easily degenerates into false mysticism when it specialises and cuts its constitutive links with the intellect and the senses, with the *noeta* and the *aistheta*. Let the knower of the whole (*krtsna-vin*) not interfere with those who do not know the whole, warns us the *Gita* (III, 29. Cf. XVIII, 20) echoed by St Paul (I Cor., XIII, 12) and so many others.

Perhaps the conscious *will* to knowledge has spoiled the pristine character of pure *sophia*, experiential awareness. It has introduced a will to power which has substituted the love of knowledge by the desire of dominion. We have to ask whether it is possible to have a new innocent reflection. The pre-critical thinking is a reflection which reflects on the thing but not on itself. We know that we know something, but we leave it at that; we have confidence in our knowledge. The post-critical innocent reflection includes the subject in the very reflection. We know that, knowing something, this knowledge of the thing belongs also to our knowledge; we involve the knower. This is the crux of contemporary philosophy; the subject–object split.

If reflection were only an epistemological act this new innocent reflection would not be possible. It would have to go back to the epistemic subject. Epistemologically, I only 'know x' when 'I know that I know x'. This epistemology is critical when it asks also about the nature (conditions of possibility and what not) of my 'knowing x'. But if reflection is more than just epistemologically knowing that I (the subject) have grasped something (an object), if it is an awareness in which object and subject are fused together, then there may be a knowledge which is not solely an epistemological activity, i.e. an object-directed cognition, which then needs to go back to retrieve the neglected subject. This is precisely the new innocent reflection which does not harm (*nocere*) the object in the act of knowledge, because it equally involves the subject. To know is, then not just to bring an object to a subject (a chasing, called apprehending, grasping of the object), but a growth of consciousness which includes the knower as much as the known in the very act of knowledge.

This type of knowledge is not a purely objective cognition, which would then be a trophy of what I call a hunter-epistemology. Nor is it a merely subjective knowledge, a result of keeping the knowing conquest for the benefit of the psychological ego (gatherer's epistemology). It is rather an awareness of the existing links which constitute Reality, and a creation of new ones. We can know only because we can (old *cunnan*) be conscious of what is, disclosing it to our triple experience (aesthetic, noetic, mystical) which itself forms part of Reality.

Now, this holistic, and thus saving, knowledge is itself under the power of time. It is not absolute or immutable knowledge. It is integral knowledge within a particular horizon, within a particular *mythos*. The holistic knowledge of a Pythagoras or Vyasa is neither immutable nor absolute. The holistic knowledge that we should attempt to attain must certainly well be from a so-called *philosophia perennis*, but cannot be reduced to a retrieval or repetition of an immutable past. We cannot ignore the innovations of specialised science. We should, on the contrary, try to integrate them into a new experience of Reality. But all is under the power of time. *Kalasakti* is here equally at work.

Coming now to our case, we ask whether there is an immediate awareness of time which is not an abstraction, i.e., a picking up of the element 'time' from the rest of the given reality. But is time itself not already an abstraction? Here is the heart of the matter.

An abstraction of what? It should be, obviously, of events, of what we call temporal things. We would then abstract the concept of time from temporal events, substantiate time, and make it a concept, a sort of an intellectual substance.

It may be that we need abstractions in order to reach a certain intellectual understanding of things. But we should then never forget that there are abstractions of something more primordial and keep constantly remembering the link between the abstracted idea and the thing from which we sublated the idea.

If the concept of time is an abstraction it should be an abstraction of temporal things, we said. And here we discover two astonishing facts. We discover that we have to previously detect the temporality of things in order to abstract from them the concept of time. And we discover that everything is temporal, for we do not know anything intemporal. Time seems to stick to everything. Time and Being, some philosophers would say, belong together. Every being is temporal; although this does not mean that it is only temporal.

We should, then, say that time is an aspect of the real rather than an abstraction. It is a perspective under which we envision all things rather than a sublation of an ingredient of reality which we succeeded in isolating as in a chemical experiment.

Under which aspect do we envisage things when we speak of their temporal dimension?

Here again, we detect a startling fact. In order to detect the temporality of objects we have to detect as well the temporality of the subject. Time implies a certain persistence of the objects past and a certain duration of the subject while the future arrives. We may call it memory or the mere awareness that we also need to be temporal in order to have the awareness of time.

Time is neither merely objective (time does not belong to objects only) nor purely subjective (time does not belong to subjects exclusively). Time 'in itself' is as meaningless as time 'for us' exclusively. The very concept of real time is not possible within a dualistic epistemology which starts from the split between a knowing subject and a known object. If we put ourselves out of the picture we cannot obtain the concept of time, which entails a link with the past (or the future) still lingering (or glimmering) in the present. Time implies change, duration, succession, a certain 'passing' which still perdures when it has already gone—or when it is still to come.

Space can be somehow objectified. The subject is, at least, more easily left out of the picture. This does not occur with time. This may be the reason why modern science has reduced time to another dimension of space. We can then measure time. But time is more than a mere measurement of space by means of speed. It is more that *ds/dv*.

'*Kala* (time) is not manifested by *adhva* (space, distance, course, orbit, way, journey) but by *kriya* (action, work, doing)', says Vatsyayana in his *Nyaya Bhasa* (II, 39). We should not reduce time to space, he warns us.

In other words, the awareness of temporal things requires and implies temporal human consciousness. Not only does something have to change at a different speed in order to experience change, something has to remember the 'previous' state as well. But this memory is not only in us. It is also in the things which carry in them the 'passing' of time.

Summing up, we cannot abstract time from anything because everything, including our consciousness, is already temporal. If we were to abstract time from Being, we would abstract the whole of Being. Nothing would remain. It remains Nothingness, Emptiness, sunyata, *asat*, Non-being, the timeless. Many a tradition would say that by the sublation of time we reach the Divine, utter Nothingness, Silence…. As we shall indicate later, the path to realisation, the way to Reality, consists in overcoming, not in suppressing, time. This is what I call tempiternity over against temporality on the one hand and timelessness (eternity), on the other.

A simple reflection will show us the intimate connection between time and nothingness. The experience of time requires the consciousness of past, present and future; it requires a certain flow, change, movement. But our experience as a direct touch with reality can only be in and of the present.

The past is-not. The future is-not-yet. The past *qua* past is annihilated when we bring it to our consciousness. The future ceases to be future when it is, when it has come to be. The events of the past have passed, they are not, they were. And yet we may remember them, i.e., they become again present in our mind. Something similar can be said about the future events. In both cases we cannot skip the non-being. Both, past and future, are at least tinged with non-being. Time has been traditionally linked with the experience of contingency, of limitation of nothingness.

This long preface has been needed in order to prevent the misunderstanding that the reflection on time has to be a specialised subject-matter of some particular discipline. What is, then, time?

We may quote any number of acute definitions and adduce a useful amount of types of time—psychological, musical, physical, mathematical, rhythmic, cyclical, linear…. But the prior question is about what of which we want to give a definition or offer a classification. What is that 'thing'? Who is she? How shall we recognise that lady when she is introduced to us?

We have already said that we cannot understand the nature of time if we forget the understander. Time is so pervasive that it permeates equally the questioner and the question, let alone the answer. We are thus obliged to affirm that everything open to a conscious human experience is temporal, although this does not allow us to say that everything is only temporal.

In sum, prior to the divisions in physical and psychological times, before the talk about time in the arts or time in the different human traditions, is there any justification in applying the same word 'time' when approaching all those and other similar questions? Contemporary philosophy would ask whether there is any phenomenology of time. Is there anything appearing in human consciousness which we may describe as time? We turn now to this question before trying to overcome the dilemma we posed at the beginning.

'Phenomenology' of Time

Ut ergo tu sis, transcende tempus—Augustinus, in Joannem

We cannot escape time, we said. Out conscious life is embedded in time. We have an immediate consciousness of something we may call temporality. But can we think Time? We can certainly think about things and discover that they present a temporal nature. This means that we experience things whose entity is not exhausted in a moment because they perdure. We experience ek-sistence. Existence amounts to the temporal character of things.

The word *existential*, in fact, was introduced (by Marcus Victorinus) in order to distinguish the 'following' of beings from *substantia* and *subsistentia*. Playing both with etymology and the history of the word we could say that the 'sister extra causea' of ek-sistence, which already suggests that we are aware of beings by becoming conscious of their existence, ie. their beginning to be, their emerging from the bottom of nothingness into the presenciality of reality. In a word, existence is already a temporal intuition.

We experience ourselves, too, as not finished beings, i.e. as beings perduring, continuing in our own existence. Our temporal life is *distentio animi*, says Augustine (Conf. XI, 29). We experience ourselves as unfinished in the sense of not-yet-finished, i.e., in the making, living, growing, becoming.

All this implies memory which is the 'faculty' or power which allows the past to re-appear (i.e. to make it manifest) in the now. Alongside with memory (of the past) we have also expectation (of the future) which allows us to think about the future also, i.e. to re-present (now) ourselves or things in a later state.

From the now we jump backwards towards the past and forward towards the future. We may ponder this double fact of past and future. We may easily, although inadequately, objectify the past by materialising it, converting time into a dumping ground of past actions. We similarly may objectify the future by 'spatialising' it, converting time into a dimension of a field of four dimensions. But we cannot objectify the present because, even if we were to consider it as the intersection between past and future, the 'place' (moment) of the intersection depends exclusively on the subject (observer, spectator). We experience the temporal character of things because we (the experiencers) are temporal—our consciousness, as it were, stretches (along time) so as to embrace the (temporal) flow of events. In a word, we discover temporality in things because we are temporal.

But this entails a very serious consequence—there can be no pure phenomenology of time. Time cannot be a pure *noema*. We need at least a lingering of a prior state of consciousness while aware of the second one.

This is, after all, not startling because we well know that there is no such thing as time. Time is not a 'thing in itself' (*Ding an sich*). It exists nowhere. We may have a notion of time, but not a *noema*. For the notion of time we need not one but two particular phenomena plus an awareness of their link. Let us analyse this.

We become aware of time when we perceive change. We speak of change when we perceive situation A, another situation B, and N, our awareness of AB.

Now, what is the kind of relationship between this trinity which constitutes time? For the sake of brevity, I shall reduce the analysis to its bare elements.

There is a situation. A–the birth of a child, the death of a friend, the last solar eclipse, the promise of selling a property, the dropping of the atom bomb, the fall of a stone, the movement of a molecule, the thought of leaving one's spouse....

There is a change from A to B which can be as varied as the examples indicate–that child has been born, the friend is no more, the particular eclipse has gone, that promise has been held or broken, the same place has changed, the very thought has persisted....

There is an awareness of A, an awareness of B, and an awareness of their relationship N. It is A that has changed into B. The perceptions of A and B are not simultaneous, and yet the perception of the relationship between A and B has to be somewhat simultaneous. Otherwise we would have two unrelated states of consciousness. And here begins the difficulty, or rather the encounter with the irreducibility of the temporal experience to one single act of consciousness. There are two observations, two different acts of consciousness. But their relationship is only one. This relationship touches the core of time.

What is this relationship? It is at least an awareness of the difference between A and B. Yet, we could not be aware of any difference if not over against a background of identity. But we would not be aware of any identity if there were not a difference at some point. In a word, identity and difference are correlative. The 'two' different observations are not one, they are consciousness of A and consciousness of B. But they are not 'two' absolutely disconnected observations. Two means 1 + 1, where the second observation is precisely another homogenous (second) 1, which we could add to the first 1. But this is not our case. The second observation or act of consciousness is not independent from the first; it is the very awareness of the mutation of A into B. In other words, the awareness of the difference is a non-dualistic consciousness, an observation which is neither a single nor two single observations, as it were, but a non-second observation which is precisely non-second because it is still connected with the first, without being it. So it is negating the second, as an independent observation, how we relate them. It is neither one nor two. It is non-dualistic, *advaitic*, says indic wisdom.

The observer becomes aware of N, that is of the change of A into B. This awareness is non-dualistic. The relation A–B–N is the specific interplay of this triune event in a field of consciousness. This interplay is what we call time.

Time is not in the things alone. An observer must be there. 'If there would no soul there would no time', said *Aristotle* (*Physics* IV, 14: 223 a26). Without an observer we could not speak of time. Without an observer we could not speak of beauty either. But there is a fundamental difference. The beholder of beauty is needed to discover beauty in things because the relation with the beholder is essential. Beauty is a relation. But the observer of time must, above and beyond, discover a *sui generis* relationship between two 'moments' in the event itself. The relationship is also between those moments of the thing and not with the observer alone.

This means that time is not in the observer alone either. Without things changing from situation A to B there would be no time. If there were just one thing, one absolutely unchanging thing, there would be no time. If there were one single unchanging observer in the universe and one single thing there would be no time. The observer can only observe time if there is change in the observation. In simpler words, one observation of one thing does not yield the notion of time. There must be change in both the observer and the thing, i.e. in the subject and the object. The observer has 'two' observations corresponding to the moments A and B of the thing. The link between the 'two' observations, which negates their duality without letting them coalesce into one, yields the consciousness of time.

In sum, we need 'three' elements to have the notion of time—'two' different situations in mutual relationship and a consciousness of that state of affairs. Time has a triadic structure.

Kant is right; time lies at the basis of all intuitions, but is an intuition which reflects a change both inside and outside our intuition. The very experience of time demands both a subjective and an objective factor; it entails a link between things or events and the consciousness of it. Time, being neither subjective nor objective, is prior to the epistemological split between subject and object. If things and consciousness were not already temporal there could be no reflective consciousness of anything because consciousness is already a temporal process. Time seems to be inherent to Reality itself. A pure consciousness without objects (of that consciousness) would not be conscious of anything and thus would not be consciousness of time. Consciousness of time needs at least one change in the object of consciousness. It needs at least a consciousness of A which is followed by a consciousness of B. Otherwise it would not be conscious of anything, not even of A. A real consciousness of time requires that there be (1) consciousness of A, (2) a reflective consciousness of A and (3) a consciousness of ceasing to be consciousness of A, that is, of the distinction between (1) and (2).

Phenomenology, in the sense of Husserl, is not applicable to understanding the temporal phenomenon, because time, i.e., the very temporal structure of our consciousness and of the phenomena appearing there, is already a presupposition of the phenomenological analysis. On the one hand, time, as the temporal–spatial–material 'reality' of things, enters into the famous; it should be put into brackets. Phenomenology does not deal with the nature or behavior of things. On the other hand, time belongs to the nature of both all our objects of consciousness and our consciousness itself. We are presupposing time all along the phenomenological analysis. This is something more than the so well studied 'epistemological circle', in order to know an object we have to know (already) that it is an object. It is a very special case of the 'methodological circle'; the method we follow derives from the nature of the studied phenomenon, which appears precisely as such because we follow the applied method.

But the impossibility of a phenomenology of time is due to a more important reason than the fact that time does not appear in the pure phenomenological analysis. The main impossibility is not due to the fact that there is not a permanent *noema* in a single act of consciousness. This timeless act, assuming it is possible, would not give us the experience of time. The deeper reason manifests itself in the fact that the experience of time is already presupposed in any reflective act. We cannot define time because time is already presupposed in any definition. We have to circumambulate (define) the *definiendum*; and this requires time already.

This circle means that the concept of time lies in the very concept of a concept, because any concept presupposes precisely the factor time; the concept of time is presupposed in any concept. This is what a certain philosophical language calls transcendental, i.e. a something which transcends all its manifestations without being separable from them. Time is, like Being, a 'something' which we carry along all our conceptions, including the very conception of time.

This means that thinking is not only a temporal process because it happens 'in' time. It is also intrinsically temporal in as much as the very principles of identity and non-contradiction required for thinking have the factor time inherently built in them. A is A only if the predicate A perdures being A. A cannot be A and non-A, only if they have to be it at the same time.

But we are now concerned only with the phenomenology of time. And we assert that, strictly speaking, it is not possible, because the temporal structure of both consciousness and things is the very condition of possibility of phenomenology. Time in this sense is a given, a gift, and before analysing it, we must become aware of it by receiving it. It is the feminine aspect of awareness, different, but not separable from the more masculine function of the same intellect. We can only grasp reality, if we are also aware that we are 'grasped' by it. We understand when we stand-under.

Time is the Life of Being—Hesychius

If our introductory remarks are correct, our conclusion must be very simple—the very experience of time amounts to the experience of reality. We experience time as we experience reality to be. Our experience of time depends on our own awareness of life, of our life. Time is just the word for something which does not belong to us, but that is us. We are temporal beings. We may be more than just temporal beings, but we are certainly not less than temporal beings, and if we eliminate temporality we destroy ourselves. In this sense I have inverted the Greek intuition purely for heuristic reasons. It comes ultimately to the same. Plotinus in fact describes, 'Time as the Life of the Soul' (ennead. III, 7, 11) and Bhartrhari calls time 'the soul of the universe' (*Vakyapadiya,* III, 9, 12) and the '*svatantryasakti* of *Brahman*'. Both life and time are ultimate.

We should ponder that the Greek word is *zoe* and not *bios* (*βios*). The expression *xpoώos Tou Biou*, 'time of life', as in II Clemens I, 6, has precisely the other meaning of a limited duration of our individual lives. The Greeks when wanting to speak about the limited period of time of a life from which we but live only a portion used to speak of the period (time) of life of (enjoyed by) someone; although these academic differences, like the distinction between *Kaιpos* and *χpovos*, were often blurred and not held. Zoe is life as such, life indestructible, life 'eternal', as the Gospels say. 'Life does not die' (*na jivo mriyata*), says one *Upanishad* (CU, VI, II, 3). *Bios*, on the other hand, is private life, individualised life, as it were, finite life, '*Praŋa* is *Brahma*", says another *Upanishad* (Kaus U, II, 1) and specifies further, 'He (Indra) said, "I am life [*prano smi*], rever me as life immortal" [or as (temporal) life (and as) immortality-literally' as life, as immortality, *ayur amrtam*]. Life is *praŋa*, *prāŋa* is life (*ayuh praŋah, praŋo va ayuh*); it is immortality' (Kaus U, III, 2). My personal interpretation here is that the *Upanishad* correlates temporal life, *ayus* (*αιω,* eon, age) with immortal life (*praŋa*).

All this amounts to saying that the conception of time is simply dependent on our conception of reality, that the basic experience of life (reality, Being, the world) will condition our notion of time. We project on time, as it were, our basic *lebensgefihl.* For some, time will be an image of eternity; for others, the power of *Brahman*, the God Supreme or the supreme magician, the measure of all things or the soul of the universe, etc. In a word, the problem is of time, not the question of thing called time. It is the issue of Reality, the issue of Being, 'Time is aptly described as a mimic of eternity, says Plotinus echoing Plato (*Tim.* 37 D), that seeks to break up in its fragmentary flight the permanence of its exemplar' (*Ennead.* 1, 5, 7; MacKenna translation).

If we believe that this world is non-real, like some *mayavadins*, time will be non-real. If we believe in two worlds, like some Greeks, time will be the image of the other world. If we believe this world is evil, time will be the contradiction to the eternal, as some Gnostics affirm. If we believe that this world is here to deserve another one, time will be the passage to the eternal, as most Christians and Muslims say. If we believe that the world is a measurable entity, time will be the specific ratio between space and speed, and so on.

At any rate, the power of time cannot be denied. The main problem consists in the relationship between time (be it illusory or real) with what could be called Being, *Brahman*, Reality, the universe. Time is the link, as it were, with the other side of time. Time relates to temporal beings, but these beings are in and of the world; they are the world, they have something to do with Being.

A new dilemma appears here. It is a dilemma which has almost tortured the indic mind for centuries; either time is real or it is not. If it is real, Reality is temporal, all is in flux, all changes, all is empirical, *vyavaharika*, *samsarika*. If time is not real, the entire world is an illusion, life on earth without ultimate relevance, the real thing is transcendent, invisible, *paramarthika*.

My contention, which tries to continue and deepen an almost perennial human insight, is that time is real and that Reality itself presents a non-dualistic polarity which 'includes' the eternal without excluding the temporal. We should overcome the spatial connotations of these two words in order to avoid contradiction.

In order to maintain the formal parallelism we shall examine this problem under the light of the correlative to time, i.e. eternity, to use only this name, in spite of its etymo (*aeternus* from *aevum*, *aetas*, *αιων,* Sanskrit *ayus*, age; and also Gothic *aiw*, always). In other words, the difficulty with time does not lie with it, but with what it 'reveals', 'points to ', implies', namely that which has sometimes been called eternity. *Nityanitya-vastu-viveka*, 'discernment between the eternal and temporal things', says Vedantic wisdom (*nitya*—continual, perpetual (related to *ni-ja*; innate, in-born) is essential in order to know what we really are, what Reality truly is. 'Time is difficult to overcome', says the *Ramāyana (kalo hi dur atimkramah*, III, 72, 16).

Let us introduce the question trying to show how a reflection on time leads to its other side. Thinking about time, there is something we cannot get rid of; our present point of reference, our temporal stand of the present. We may be able to think eternity, future, past, Being, Nothingness, and what not. It all may be problematic. But one standpoint we cannot eliminate—the present as the point of reference, of departure or arrival, as the point from which and on which we stand for whatever operation of our consciousness. We may remember the past and even foresee the future, but it is always from the platform of the 'now'.

But this 'now' seems to reveal something 'else' or 'more'. On the one hand, the now seems to be the temporal revelation, something more than a past that has come to be, and a passage to a future that will be. It appears as the intersection of something vertical as well. There is a novelty in the present that does not come from the past and which does not determine the future exhaustively. We experience it as freedom. It is neither fully conditioned by the past, nor does it determine completely the future. (Otherwise, when the future becomes the present it would be a fully conditioned present). This freedom, which is only in the now, is somewhat untouched by them. It is the 'gate' to eternity. But on the other hand, eternity reveals itself temporally in the now. The moment is temporal, it is a crossing of the past and the future. But 'at the same time' it manifests in itself (for us and 'now') something of another nature. It is not an indefinite past or a never ending future. Nor is it the integration of all those 'realms'. It is something of another order which appears in the temporal moment. It is the tempitemal moment of the now, the present, the *nunc stans* and not the *nunc fluens*. We could refer here to the human experience of the zenith and the solstice since the neolithic period. The sun must somewhat stop when it changes direction. The stone must somewhat stop when, thrown vertically into the air, 'begins' to fall again. 'The *now* is the link of time…and it is a limit of time', said Aristotle (*Physics* IV, 13 (222 a; Cf. also VIII, 8 (261 b sq.) A similar argument could be found in the famous introduction to the *tat tvam asi* (CU VI, 12, for instance; the nothingness is the eternal).

We may continue our philosophical reflection on the intrinsic relationship between time and eternity by considering the apparent paradox that the most immediate awareness of nothingness of non-being is linked with our thought about me. The very thought of nothingness, which is so central in most oriental philosophies, and not only in them, is the immediate result of our temporal awareness.

In fact, what is the past from the only point where we can have a direct experience of it, namely, the present? What is the past if not something which is not, which has disappeared? What is the future if not something which is equally not existent? We may not have an experience of nothingness in the strict sense of an immediate awareness of non-being. But we are conscious of nothingness by our temporal awareness of something which is no longer or not yet the present. The past is our tomb of, and future our monument to, nothingness—from our only possible present stand. Time is (also) the revealer of nothingness, we could say complementing Gaudapada.

In sum, we have in the present the doorway both to nothingness and to eternity. If we link the two we shall almost automatically overcome the loose and improper, although popular meaning of eternity as a never ending—and never begotten—time, an indefinite time. While this is a legitimate notion, although it leads to pitiful appraisal of eternity and Big Bang, creation and evolution, etc., it is not what we, following a long tradition adumbrated by Plato and developed by Plotinus, understand by eternity.

Eternity is not an infinite time; nor is it the negation of time, like the nothingness of the past or the future, in our present experience, is not the negation of the past or the future.

We cannot eliminate the temporal present where we stand, even if we may experience in it something of another nature. The *nunc stans et permanens* has been given as a description of eternity. The *nunc* (now) is not just the perduration of the instant, the temporality of the present, the freezing of the moment. It is rather the radically *novum* (new) in-stant, as the etymology suggests (including the English; 'now' akin also to 'new'). The Indo–European root *nu* is related both to *nunc* and *novus*, now and new.

In the present now both the past/future and the eternal meet. If we are too obsessed with the past or too worried about the future we may overlook the eternal of each instant.

In spite of the fact that we may be only indirectly conscious of that timelessness, no self-consciousness of it can discard the temporal moment in which the act happens. Reflective consciousness is always temporal consciousness. We cannot shed off temporality. It is not only that we are always situated in time and space. It is that time itself is inherent in the very act of consciousness, although we may remember (thus rescue from the past) that the foundation of that act of consciousness was somehow 'outside' the temporal flow. The now, in a word, is inherently inserted in any act of which we can be aware.

We are saying that not only the moment is the temporal revelation of eternity, but that eternity is the eternal revelation of time. What does it mean?

It means that we cannot separate the two. The moment is moment, not only because it stands at the crossing between past and future, but also because it simply stands, although it does not stop (temporally). It is immediately followed (temporally) by the subsequent moment. But it has a consistency of its own. A con-sis-tency (not a mere dis-tension or ex-tension) which gives each moment its message, its personality as it were—its eternity.

The present is not a mere crossing of past and future; it is rather the encounter of time and eternity. The present would be nothing if eternity were not already 'in' it. The present is not a short time, not even an infinitesimally short time. We should know this since Zeno of Elea. The passage from past to future, happening in the present, reveals to us the eternal. Otherwise there would be not present.

The *citta-vrtti-nirodha* of *Yoga-sutra*, 1, 2 (appeasing of the processes of the mind) may be interpreted in this way, the door to the awareness of eternity.

Now this eternity is not something temporal. Between the moment A and the immediate subsequent moment B, there is nothing. There is not a third moment C. If it were a C we could then always intercalate shorter moments. There are infinite intermediate numbers between 2 and 3. But eternity is not an infinitely small time. It is of another order. Between A and B there 'is' nothing. This nothingness is eternity.

Time belongs to Being. Being is precisely be-ing. Being is temporal. Being is a verb. Being and Time belong together. A timeless Being would be 'dead'. It would stifle itself. It could not breathe, it could not be. Being has to be-ing. And this act implies activity, dynamism, life. This movement may not be an actualisation of a dormant potentiality, it may be pure act, pure activity. It may not be a linear temporal unfolding going somewhere where it has not previously been. But it has to be novelty, a throbbing, a rhythm. Be-ing is more than becoming. Becoming is a transient state. It is a coming-to-be. But when the becoming has come to be, this 'be' itself is not static, but is be-ing.

Nothingness 'is' another name for the eternal. Nothingness is-not. We cannot say, therefore, that it is static. It is not a substance, an under-being. Eternity is not the substantial platform, the 'stand' of time, an ontic *pratistha*. Time does not repose on eternity, not more than eternity decomposes itself in the flow of time. 'In time all things disappear' (Mait U VI, 14). But this going to rest, stopping to go, disappearing (*niyacchanti*) is more, not less, than time. Time has yielded its fruit, as it were.

Nothingness is not the basis of being, not more than eternity is the ground of time. Neither nothingness nor eternity, are capable of offering a basis, a ground, a substance. The relationship is of another order. Neither nothingness nor eternity have consistency of their won. Nothingness is not and eternity does not ek-sist. It has neither ex-tension nor dis-tension. All these tensions and 'sistences' belong to space and time as attributes to Being.

Now, what does it mean that the 'two' belong together? What is their glue? There is no glue because they are not two. Time and eternity, like Being and Nothingness are neither two nor one. They belong together. What is this togetherness? Who or what brings them together? Nobody or nothing! This is what allows us to say that in spite of not being one and the same thing they are not two things.

Here is the proper place of the *advaitic* intuition. Or rather of the trinitarian insight, for the 'relation' between the 'two' is a 'third' that maintains the constitutive polarity which eliminates any oneness without falling into any dualness.

When I say *advaita* I do not mean monism. Monism states that there is one single degree of reality. What is not the real, *satyasya sat*, is unreal. All the rest is appearance, which only appears to the unenlightened one; thus not a real appearance.

When I say *advaita* I do not mean dualism either. Dualism claims that there are at least two incommunicable types of reality. The universe is a two-, or multi-storey building with no ultimate communion with each other, two or more irreducible orders of reality.

When I say *advaita* I mean that the subject and the object are not two, without being one, that the Divine and the Cosmic and/or the Human are not two, without being the same. And this without falling into contradiction because the very nature of Reality is polar, each pole being constitutive of the whole. And without falling into irrationalism either, because all the rights of reason are respected and acknowledged without absolutising reason. Each rational statement is relative, in the sense of relativity and not relativism, to a particular context, and emerges out of a particular *mythos* or horizon of intelligibility which is taken for granted.

Long ago I introduced the notion of *tempiternity* to express this advaitic relationship. I have also attempted to describe the cosmotheandric or the anthropocosmic or *adhi–daivika–atmika–bhautika* insight as the holistic knowledge of the divine, the human and the cosmic. Time, along with space, with matter and energy, are definitive and constitutive dimensions of Reality. All is temporal. But the All is not only temporal.

Time and Being show this *advaitic* character. They are not one. We should not confuse them. Eternity is another attribute of Being. But they are not two either. There is no intemporal Being besides a temporal one. It would be a contradiction if time and eternity were on the same level.

But *advaita* means not only denying. It is not mere negative attitude. It means also affirming non-duality. And this affirmation is worth considering. The positive aspect of *advaita* is not synthesis, i.e., bringing together, as if the original state were separateness. We do not identify Being with time or time with eternity. We do not synthetise them or bring them together. We simply do not separate them. *Advaita* is a primordial intuition. Time and Being (in our example) are not composed. We do not need to put them together affirming that they are not two, that the separateness is only a 'weakness' or an 'imperative' of our awareness. (We do not discuss advaita now, but try to apply the *advaitic* intuition to our case).

Precisely because *advaita* is a primordial intuition it affirms non-duality. If it would affirm unity it would become monism—the identification of Time and Being in our case, or of time and eternity. *Advaita* affirms the radical and constitutive polarity of the real. At the same time it recognises both the power of reason—Time and Being appear as two—and the overcoming of it—they are not two. *Advaita* is rational, but not rationalistic. Our experience of time is a point in case.

My contention is that this holistic vision was often indiscriminate, uncritical, and blurred. Distinctions were needed. But these distinctions led to specialisations, and the latter to the present day fragmentation. It is important and urgent to integrate the fragments into a more holistic union without abandoning the insight of our specialised disciplines.

Attempting to sum up in a cross-cultural way the human experience regarding Time as the symbol of the Real we could distinguish three kairological moments after the holistic but indiscriminate human awareness of Time and Reality.

1. Calendar Time

Since the pre-historic period of humanity man has experienced time in connection with the cyclical periods within himself and in the outside world—periods of rest and activity, hunger and fullness, youth and old age, day and night, summer and winter, etc.

We may say that the first temporal experience of man is the rhythm of life. Time is rhythm; but rhythm is not repetition. Consciousness of repetition enters with the institution of calendar. It has been called the Neolithic metamorphosis. It is the first temporal revolution. The heterogeneity of time, the incomparability of the now and the uniqueness of each day was complete (cf. still Match,VI, 34). Calendar time introduces the uniformity of the second day, the third winter, and the like. Quantity enters into the human consciousness of time. Time begins to be considered as having parts and, except mainly for the present, the past and the future will be projected into a more or less uniform canvas; the unique shape of the past fifth year will begin to blur and be hardly distinguishable from the sixth year, except for the number separating the years. Time is seen as unlimited, 'cyclical'.

2. Chronological Time

When many calendars conflict with each other we need a new degree of abstraction, a new and more thorough quantification. The still rhythmic and qualitative calendar is substituted by a pragmatic and often arbitrary chronology. It offers an allegedly neutral and universal point of reference. The fact that the Christian Era is called by some as Common Era is an example of both; the pretension of being universal (to call this era 'Common' is the acme of colonialistic culture-centrism). To begin a time reckoning with the Big Bang would not be less ideologically loaded.

What interests us here, however, is the move towards quantification and abstraction. Time is then seen as a chronological parameter, a quantitative factor and most expeditiously linked to space and movement as an anonymous fourth dimension. It is the time of modern science.

The possibility of another realm is not defined by modern science. It would be the field of timelessness. Time would then be one thing and timelessness another. This apparent tolerance is easily misleading. The introduction of dualism (time is one separate thing and timelessness another totally different entity) kills reality like the child of the famous Solomon's judgment. And here begins modern cultural schizophrenia in which the fragmentation of knowledge leads to the fragmentation of the knower.

3. Ontological Time

If the first vision of reality could be called monistic—time and eternity coalesce—and the second dualistic—time has nothing to do with eternity—this vision may be named non-dualistic or *advaitic*—time and eternity are distinct but not separable). The notion of eternity will, therefore, be not one of timelessness as a second level of reality or a second story of a non-temporal reality with no connection with the temporal whatsoever, but rather one of *tempiternity*.

'Above time is set the brimful vessel,' sings the *Atharva Veda* (XIX, 53, 3). Eternity is not just the absence of time but its fullness. '*Aeternitas includet omne tempus*,' says Thomas Aquinas (Sum. Theol. 1, q. 13, a1, and 1) and he insists '*omnia tempora*' (ib. 1. q. 10, a. 2), '*totum tempus*' (ib. 1, q. 14, a. 13) not to leave any doubt. Eternity is neither separated from, nor juxtaposed to, time. It is coterminous with it, they embrace mutually. The word *tempiternity* expresses this *advaitic* relationship. It is the *intemporale tempus* of Nicholas of Cusa (*De aequalitate*, ed. Leo Gabriel III, 374), the *niskala kala* of Sankara (*Vivekacudamani* 497). 'Beginningless time and the present moment are the same,' said Huang Po (*Chin Chou,* 31, Blofeld translation).

In point of fact, eternity is neither indefinite time, nor timelessness, nor even timefulness, if we interpret this last word as a sort of integer between –oo and +oo time. The fullness is not of 'all times' but of the present (for, the past and the future are-not), as we indicated already. We may reach fullness of the present by experiencing the *trikalabadhyatva* of the indic tradition, 'The unsublatableness of the three times', that which can never be removed once we eliminate the past, the present, and the future. The *traikalikabadhyatva* as that which can never be contradicted at any time (past, present, future) is a criterion for truth for some vedantins. The full passage of the quoted text by Cusanus says, 'the soul, which is intemporal time, sees in its essence the past, the present, and the future (and) calls the past memory, the present intellect (and) the future will.'

'Ontological time' is only a philosophical and, for many ears, a secularised expression of probably one of the oldest and most universal experiences of humanity. This primordial human experience was at the basis of calendar time since the Babylonians, Egyptians, and Mesoamericans. Time is one aspect of Reality, I have been saying. Time is one revelation of the Deity; or rather, the temporal display of things reveals the many Deities which are at work (alive) in Reality, they were saying. This old and traditional language, well understood, may perhaps help us to better describe the human experience of 'the mystery of time'.

Time is the door to eternity, we find it said almost everywhere. But this threshold is not only the 'last time', death. It is not the future time (of death, of which hardly anybody has the experience), but the real time, ie, the present time. Time is a deity. In time our destiny and that of the gods coalesce. We have here the basis of what later on was called astrology; the facets (measures) or time are manifestations (measures) of gods, men, and the cosmos alike; they are the Divinities, not just hidden (as for many moderns), but patent for man. It is and through time, living it, and not just sliding on it, how, we become what we truly 'are', whereby this 'are' is not a fleeting present, but it is neither 'as we were' nor 'as we shall be'. This 'are' is not only the crossroad of past and future, but a deity. Every day has its divinity; each event is a divine, a human, and a cosmic happening; each happening is a 'moment' in Life. Earth, Sun, Moon, Stars (as also Matter, Fire, Water, Winds) are divine precisely because they move, and they move because they are aspects of Life, 'measures' of time. They reveal time to us. Any Aztec or Maya child would understand it, let alone a Babylonian or Egyptian. Time is the Life of Being, we said, in a more philosophical vein.

Now the circle comes to a full. Time, like Being, is most immediately 'given' to us, and, therefore, also most mysterious when we deal with it as an object, and most deceiving if we handle it as an adjective of the subject. We are it. We cannot speak of it without somewhat splitting it. We should rather let time speak through us, be in us, 'time' us.

Time is the Life of Being. Time is the very life of our own being. We experience time in the same measure as we experience life. Our life is distended. We call time her distension. Our life is fragmented. We call time her fragmentation. Reality, as much as it is fragmented, is temporal. The experience and measurement of the different fragmentations will give us different notions of different times. The *kalasakti*, the power of time, reveals herself as the sakti of the Divine, of Siva, one tradition will say, of Reality we may translate in a more general way.

Reference

1. The entire Karika 3 reads:
   adhyahitakalam yasya Kalasaktim upasritah
   janmadayo vikarah sad bhavabhedasya yonayah

Translated by K. A. Subramania Iyer thus, 'Depending on whose Time-power to which (though one) differentiation is attributed the six transformations, birth, etc., become the cause of all variety in Being." The *Vakyapadiya* of *Bhartrhari* with *Vrtti* (Deccan College, Poona, 1965), p. 5.

The Dharma of India

Raimon Panikkar

There are already a number of perceptive books and articles on the Indic situation, and we should profit from them. The author deals with the metapolitical aspect of the problem. India represents an urgent and important challenge not only for itself but for the world at large. This malaise that characterises the Indian scene is also an expression of the world situation. Today's crisis is the culmination of at least the last half millennium of Western civilisation. It extends over the whole planet because this civilisation has spread all over the world, even more than during the era of Western colonisation. A contact with other cultures has produced what could be termed *a conflict of kosmologies*.

We are assisting the End of History (Cf. Panikkar, 1983/XXXIII, Raimon Panikkar, 79–133), using this phrase with a different meaning than later popularised by Francis Fukuyama (cf. *The End of History and the Last Man*, London, Penguin, 1992). By this is meant the end of historical Man, the end of the dominion of historical consciousness, the end of the temporal future as a paradigm for human life on earth. What is at stake is no less than the last 6,000 years of human adventure. It is important to distinguish between two levels—Modernity and Historicity. I shall concentrate on the first level, while remaining conscious of the background of the second level.

The Indic adventure is a major event in the History of Being. Either Indic Man is swallowed by the 'forgetfulness of the Whole' (Being?)—and he increases the ranks of the soldiers defending Modernity—or he allows for a new disclosure of the Whole (Reality?) opening a new avenue for human life, or rather for Life as such. Although the Indic problem cannot be isolated from the world situation. I shall abstain from general considerations and limit myself to the concrete Indic problematic.

An underlying assumption behind 'scientific and technological modernisation' is the belief in the linear cultural evolutionism of humanity. India today is modernising in the direction of science and technology not because she consciously condemns her three millennia of Indic culture, but because she tacitly assumes that this very culture, well steered, leads to the adoption and recognition of the 'universal values' of the technological society.

My submission, on the contrary, in agreement with an increasing number of voices, is that if we take Indic culture seriously, and do not reduce it to mere folklore and window dressing, it will disappear from the continent once human life becomes computerised. A corollary of this is the prediction of increasing discontent, resistance and bloodshed all over the world. '[S]ince 1958, 87 per cent of the very poor nations, 69 per cent of the poor nations, and 48 per cent of the middle income nations suffered serious violence. Out of 120 armed conflicts which took place after the Second World War, not less than 115 occurred in the developing Third World.' (Poulose, 1986, p. 23). This is particularly acute in India. Here we have to underline that in an increasing number of regions of the subcontinent revolts and violence are the outcome of an acute identity crisis. (Cf. Vidyadharan, 1988, pp. 8–17).

The author maintains that the destiny of Indic culture has a paradigmatic function to perform in the world scene, because many other nations who have already succumbed to that type of modernisation are too small to resist the avalanche of technocratic colonialism or do not have our strong cultural roots. Of course, I am not minimising the role and importance of other world cultures such as Chinese, African, Amerindian, etc. They have an important part to play, but there is a special feature to take into account regarding the

Indic vocation. The redemption, transformation, or even peaceful, though painful, dismantlement of the System can be lastingly effective only if it is an endogenous movement, although perhaps triggered from outside, capable of forging a new style of life for human conviviality. Otherwise, there would only be the victory of one ideology, and victory never leads to lasting peace. India is certainly a mosaic of cultures and religions. Her two oldest strata, however, are the Aryan or Indo–European and the autochthonous or Dravidian, without entering into the necessary qualifications that modern scholarship and present-day political awareness have introduced. In spite of her partial Indo–European roots, India has remained conspicuously outside Western cultural history. (I would substantially qualify the late Nirad Chaudhuri's thesis that India is Europe, although corrupted by the tropical environment, Cf. Chaudhuri, 1978). It is enough to recall her many languages. But she did not undergo the European process of the technological revolution of four centuries ago. By remaining outside this process, she has retained in her myths and traditions which in the industrial West has almost been swept away. This fact makes the Indic culture both more liable to fall into temptation and better prepared to overcome it than many other world cultures. The Indic world has a medial position between the 'Far-west' and the 'Far-east'.

Incompatible Kosmologies

Under the name *kosmology*, I do not understand what is generally understood under the spelling cosmology. This latter word stands for a reflection of our *logos* about the *cosmos*, for a worldview according to the paradigm of the modern 'scientific' cosmology. *Kosmology*, on the other hand, is not a cosmology in the scientific objectifiable sense of the word, but a *kosmos-legein*, a reading of the cosmos as the cosmos manifests itself to us, more passive onlookers and hearers than active calculators and 'experimentors'. *Kosmology* is the world-myth of a particular culture, not a doctrine of a rationally articulated vision of the universe.

In our particular case, I detect the radical incapacity of technological civilisation to satisfy the aspirations of the Indic *psyche*. This is not the place to elaborate on a general critique of *techniculture* (*Techniculture* suggests the cultivation of the machine, which, being inanimate, can only be the object of human exploitation for human benefit or rather profit. While *homo faber (techne)* is the first sign of *homo sapiens, homo technologicus* is a hybrid between reason and machine. Cf. Panikkar, 1964/1). I shall limit myself to the Indic context.

Perhaps I could put it like this—India's *karma* is not in harmony with the genius of the technological vision of the world. Technology is far from being as universal as the new elites claim ('So many of us fail to realise that—whatever its origins, and they are spread over many continents and centuries—the modern industrial culture is a world culture', Moddie (1968), 3).

It is not difficult to realise why Western-born techno-civilisation does not fit every culture. There is certainly enough intelligence among the races of the world to understand the 'know-how' of mechanical processes. It is not a question of non-Western peoples being too stupid to master modern technologies. The question is whether there is a basic incompatibility between the *kosmology* of traditional India (including all *dharmas* which have flourished in the subcontinent) and the *kosmology* underlying technological civilisation. Modern techno-science is the Trojan horse which will destroy those cultures that uncritically introduce 'modernity' into their midst.

Traditional Man considers the world as an holistic, though hierarchical and living, reality. All is interconnected—the realm of the Gods with the world of Man and the field of Nature. Everything is alive. There is a cosmotheandric solidarity. Nothing is purely objective, nor exclusively subjective. This entails a fundamentally different attitude from the one in which modern scientific civilisation can thrive.

I would call it a *transcendental attitude*, which does not necessarily mean an explicit belief in transcendence. It means an awareness accompanying every action, that life on earth is only a kind of 'comedy', 'divine' or not, a sort of l×l (play), a re-enactment of something bigger than ourselves and yet taking place within ourselves. Rebirth and transmigration, heaven and moral responsibility, whatever religious underpinnings they may have, entail a firm sentiment that we are not private proprietors of our life, but actors and spectators of it. We live as if we were performing a role which is greater than us, transmitting a little worse or a little better of the life which we have received.

The most common way of explaining this transcendental attitude is by pointing out that the Sacred—in whatever form—is an essential ingredient not only of the World, but of Man and all human actions. In contrast, modern cosmology, while respecting private beliefs in God, Gods, or Sacredness, functions with total independence of such convictions. God is a scientifically superfluous hypothesis, and the Sacred a hindrance to clear and precise scientific thinking. It is not the place to criticise either modern science or the old conception of the sacred. Probably both require transformation, and to some degree, therefore, the scientific interlude may be a healthy *intermezzo*, although if we get stuck in it the result could be lethal to the human species.

The traditional implicit *kosmology* of India reveals itself in many ways, of which I will mention only three. First, a certain indifference, lack of seriousness, playfulness, carelessness, diminished sense of responsibility, even a childishness, regarding the world of labour and machines. (It is enough to hear typical comments on Indian workers in the world of industry, commerce and politics from a Western perspective to realise how uncongenial the Indic genius is to the technological world. Writers like Naipaul (1977), N. C. Chaudhuri (1978) and others betray their bias adopting unconsciously Western cosmology as the normative paradigm). Traditional Man does not want to dedicate his most important creative forces to the pursuit of earthly comforts, especially in a proleptic fashion. The danger of a future atomic disaster is a powerful deterrent for a Western mentality, but is not specially frightening for a typically Indic mind—making allowances for the over-generalisation of 'Eastern' and 'Western'. What counts for Indians is mainly the present. 'For it is another person who dies / and another that will be reborn'. The linear temporal future is not a main concern.

This leads to a *second* aspect of this attitude. Real human activity is experienced not so much as a means to produce something but as an *end* in itself inasmuch as any single action is directly related to moka (Moksa) through the modification of karma. In this way, any human activity has a repercussion on the ultimate meaning of life, in whatever sense one interprets it. This attitude is at loggerheads with the modern obsession with production, which is how practically all activity of modern life is measured. Traditional Man, on the other hand, is not 'efficient', not obsessed with making the future better than the past. He thinks the modern fad of progress and production causes the fateful neglect of the present, and thus the incapacity of actually enjoying anything. This also explains the often heard complaint that modern 'Indian goods' are not well finished, in sharp contrast with the classical *silpasastra.* The moment that a 'product' is considered only a means, it no longer matters much how well it is finished.

It is matter of a *techne* mentality versus a technological one. Technology is conceived in view of production. This is why quantity, efficiency, and acceleration matter. The more and the quicker the better, the effort and toil will be taken care of by means of machinery. On the other hand, *techne* aims at the harmonic relation between the doer, the doing, and the done. Otherwise, it is not worth the effort.

Techne or art, wit, *ingenium*, ingeniosity, craft, manufacture is not technology. The difference is specific, not just of degree. Technology intends the most efficient way to reach the end product, the multiplication of the items produced and the acceleration of the process, because time is an economic commodity. *Techne*, on the other hand, is concerned with immediate use, inherent beauty, and the intrinsic relationship between Man and the thing made. One cannot separate the ends from the means. No total objectification is possible.

On the other hand, only one culture has developed technology as the application of a measuring, deductive reason in order to accelerate and multiply products and thereby control events, that is, the future. This demands a very specific mentality, which after a long period of gestation, was born in 16th century Europe. Without Galileo, Descartes is unthinkable, and without Descartes there could have been no Newton or modern science.

Just as there is a fundamental distinction between *techne* and technology, I would like to stress the difference between technology and technocracy. Technology, in fact, has two main meanings. The first, and more literal one, is the science about those human constructs which we call technological achievements. This already leads to the second meaning, technological civilisation, connoting the set of values manifested by the dominion of technology over people's minds and lives. To avoid this ambiguity, I propose to use the word technocracy as indicating the actual 'power' of the technological worldview. (Interestingly enough the Greek *kratos* has a double meaning—power and hardness—software and hardware?) And even more symptomatically the Sanskrit *kratuh* besides meaning power and force, also denotes understanding, judgement, will, and shrewdness. Technocracy, therefore, would suggest the hard power acquired by the will to power triggered by the force of a certain type of shrewd skillfulness.

A *third* difference could be expressed in the telling simile of *Santideva*, 'Where would I possibly find enough leather with which to cover the surface of the earth? But (wearing) leather just on the soles of my shoes is equivalent to covering the earth with it.'

Likewise, he goes on to say, we cannot change the external course of things, but we can control our minds, and in doing this perhaps we can be more capable of contributing to the world's welfare, not just because of inwardness but also because we will have eliminated all fear and cowardice.

The technocratic mentality dreams of covering the whole earth with roads, frigidaires, air-conditioners, videos and travelling waves on satellites and otherwise. (The launching of the Indian Remote Sensing Satellite, from a Soviet cosmodrome, on 17 March 1988 has generated much legitimate pride and the hope that this 'new eye in space' will contribute to a better 'development', Cf. e. g. R. Ramachandran (1988), 13–14; Sachitanand (1988), 17–18. It is easy to flatter national pride). It is bound up with objectivity, and will search for 'objective' solutions to any problem. The traditional mind is bound to subjectivity and will first look inside and realistically consider ways to dissolve the problem that lies in our power. This look outward and inward is not only methodological, but corresponds to an altogether different kosmology. The real world is the world discovered by a total human awareness, not by calculus. Modern cosmology looks at the world as a great mechanism, and the human task then consists of oiling it when rusty, and in devising new machineries which may be more comfortably used by human beings. Technological civilisation has an underlying mechanistic cosmology. The universe appears and is experienced as a sophisticated organisation.

Traditional cultures have a vitalistic *kosmology*. The universe appears and is experienced as a living organism. Of course, the traditional universe does not need to be 'animistic' in the pejorative sense, any more than the scientific world needs to be atheistic in the pejorative sense, but they certainly are basically different ways of experiencing reality and thus of being in the world. Can the two be combined?

Let it be conceded that one attitude may be as religious as the other. Both have an ultimate concern, both present a set of rituals, use a world of symbols and have a system of beliefs which allow them to be called religions. The difference is not one of being more or less religious. Both are religious in their own ways. The difference lies in a radically different experience of reality. It could be formulated as a different temporal experience of the real. The experience of time is paramount.

Modernity, in the Western-current sense of the word, represents a mutation in human consciousness. However, no mutation appears as such until a few generations have elapsed, because it is a change of *mythos*, and *mythos* defy the dialectic of the *logos*. It comes about imperceptibly in the very effort at making sense of human existence. The importance of modern science should not be minimised. The consequence is that it has changed the entire symbolic fabric of modern civilisation and, therefore, we force a momentous dilemma. *Progressism*, in spite of its good intentions, will lead India and the world to a disaster. The experience of half a century prove that the possibilities for peace, justice, and well-being diminish with the technocratic progress. Patch-work and half-measures will not do.

Conservatism, on the other hand, will create greater harm if they dismantle the dominant system creating chaos and suffering besides not having the power to do so. We are on a way of no return. If we proceed in this way, there is no place for traditional cultures and religions. The fabric of the last 3000 years, and, if we reckon the *adivasis and adidravidians*, 6000 years, are being called into question and forced to collapse. We see here once again the decisive importance of a theoretical worldview on immediate political decisions.

To advocate compatibility may show good intentions, but implies a very superficial idea of both traditional and technocratic cultures. There are not just two ways of doing things—they represent different worlds, different basic experiences of reality, and different ways of thinking, feeling, and living. Is there any way out?

Alternatives

To ask for an alternative amounts to falling into the same technocratic mentality. There is not one alternative, but there may be alternatives. Yet, most alleged alternatives, however, are only reforms. They are different modes of solving a particular problem, accepting by and large the vision of the technocratic world, forming part of it or idealistic dreams. The real question is not the solution of the problem, but the problem itself. On the other hand, a radical alternative would be incomprehensible within the parameters of the very system of which it purports to be an alternative. It would be immediately discarded, since it would destroy the very foundations of a possible change as seen from the point of view of the *status quo*. Democracy, for instance, may accept a democratic change but does not tolerate a modification of its ground rules. The problem is delicate.

I repeat, to accept *one* possible alternative is already to fall into the trap of the technocratic view of monistic thinking. Sheer dialectical opposition and much less violence are not solutions. Even if the other party could overpower technocracy, the remedy could turn worse than the malady. After all, not everything in technocracy is negative; indeed, it has already pursued a process of adjustment to human conditions. The roots of technocracy are much deeper. It is not a question of right or left, socialism or capitalism.

There could be *alternatives*. And the reason for this is deeper than the obvious strategic observation that, since we cannot solve everything, it is better that some groups tackle the ecological problems, some the political, while others the economic ones. This is to believe that cutting the problem into smaller portions, following the well-known (and fallacious) cartesian rule, we may come to a solution. To want to make things easy, so as not to discourage people, is wrong in itself as well as a bad policy. The human predicament today can neither be minimised nor compartmentalised. Reality is not the great machine that a mechanicist worldview would have us believe. Reality is a whole, and as a whole not equal to the sum of its parts. In this way there are no alternatives either, precisely because there is no alternative. There may be *options* which pave the way for a transformation by means of a provisional emphasis on another side, not of the problem (which does not need to be the same) but of the overall state of affairs. Any alternative which is not capable of discovering the other side is not an alternative.

Using the word alternatives in the plural, we understand that the *alter* may have many sides of which our option is only one side. This is another name for *pluralism*, that is, the recognised co-existence of mutually exclusive styles of life, views of the real, opinions about things and systems of thought. Not *aliud* (in the sense of the other), but *alter* (in the proper meaning of the alterity inherent in any experience of otherness, which is reciprocal). Ultimately what is at stake here is the ontological status given to the epistemological *reductio ad unum*, as if what is necessary for the intellect were also a necessary axiom for reality. We cannot understand without reducing the known thing to a certain unity, but this does not prove that reality should be intelligible.

Cultural Innovation

The question of modernisation has been a slogan in India and abroad. Most studies, however, accept the 'realistic' position that 'there is no way back' and try to find solutions within the technocratic complex of the prevailing socio–politico–economic system of qualified capitalism and reformed socialism. The only voices many hear that speak against the *status quo* are revivalist fundamentalisms of all sorts.

I would like to look deeper into both tradition and modernity in order to discover a middle way, and perhaps find the roots of the problematic. I should mention here the recently reintroduced *Hindutva* ideology which we tackle without its political implications.

It has been rightly pointed out by many sociologists that 'the dichotomous nature of tradition and modernity is really untenable in the light of reality' (Damle, 1983, 7. The author quotes M. Singer, E. Shils, the Rudolfs, P. N. Mittal, and, of course, Max Weber, among others). For the sake of linguistic clarity, I propose to introduce the notion of *innovation*. One could then claim both that every living tradition contains a thrust towards *innovation*, and that all forms of *modernisation* have *traditional* roots. Furthermore, each tradition, inasmuch as it is not stagnant, tends to innovate itself not only from within but also by accepting inspiration from outside. At the same time, modernisation has an exogenous element which is successful only inasmuch as it finds resonance and acceptance in the heart of the very situation it attempts to modernise.

For India, however, Modernity instead of representing innovation, has mostly meant imitating the model of Western technocratic society. The official 'modernisation' of India does not follow a symbiotic pattern, but rather the model of an electronic civilisation.

What Indic culture needs is a conversion into the deep recesses of her soul, while simultaneously turning towards the spirit of the new situation of humanity. India is proud of having achieved its political independence without a formal war with the colonial power, which speaks highly for both sides. But this accomplishment also has its dark side. Partition produced lakhs of victims and other unsolved plagues, such as, communalism, the appalling predicament of the dalits, and the dire poverty of the masses. Besides, in the absence of a founding 'revolution', a native government became the successor of the colonial ruler. Practically everything that makes India a modern nation was inherited from Britain. The rajas, ranas, and maharajas, for all their anachronism and perhaps corruption, represented a certain autochthonous way. Unfortunately, they were stripped not only of their power, but also of their authority and symbolism. This did not happen, however, with the symbols of the British Raj. Architecture offers an interesting illustration. Most of the palaces of the 'princes' of India are now in ruins, others became private mansions or, more tellingly, hotels for tourism. Yet most of the buildings of the Raj are now government mansions. Our parliamentary democracy, legislature, judiciary, and military, administration, economy, commerce, industry, and education—the entire machinery of the modern state, is a replica of the Western or rather the Anglo–Saxon paradigm. (The present writer, in collaboration with the ambassadors of two Spanish speaking countries, developed a project for an Indo–Latin Institute of Culture to be established in Goa, drawing on the Portuguese heritage of that State, when Pandit Nehru was still the Prime Minister. Apart from technical problems, Nehru could not see any point in having any other cultural bridge with the West than the British–American one. Apart from some literary achievements, what else we were given to understand, has the rest of the West contributed to world civilisation?)

This has had a rather important consequence. The 'natives' of India, mainly the villagers, the overwhelming majority of the people, feel strangers in their own country. When the British Raj was in power, the Indian peasant knew that it was a foreign domination. Once the 'colonialists' left, however, their successors behaved in a similar way as the former rulers.

In other words, the majority of our people feel estranged, almost out of place, since they are unfamiliar with the official language, manners and customs.

In a word, our native culture has become the tolerated culture. The culture of independent India was the imported one. The English-speaking elite dictated the rules, and imposed the 'democracy' to be followed (R. Kothari (1976) points out that immediately after Independence India developed a 'typically Indian response' to handle political issues which had been prepared during the struggle for Independence. But he also describes how 'an imported institutional framework' which he calls 'the Westminster model of Government and politics' took the upper hand, and especially after 1967 developed the 'administrative state' according to the 'Anglo-Saxon model'). The Parliament, allegedly representing the people, speaks mainly a language which the majority does not understand. Of course, it does not matter much in a technocratic system, because technocracy also speaks a language that the majority cannot grasp.

This state of affairs is prevalent not only in the political field; education, too, shows an amazing forgetfulness of traditional schemes. In spite of a few token symbols here and there, indigenous values have been consistently downgraded. The elite have become more and more westernised, while most people feel more and more displaced.

In general, the Indic indigenous cultures are strangers, often cajoled guests at television and when elections are approaching, but nevertheless strangers in their own land; grafted, as it were, on the main culture of the future—technocracy. The ordinary people unconfessed but patent inferiority complex, when told that they are uneducated, illiterate, and uncultured; they internalise this judgement of a foreign culture.

Native values, when acknowledged at all, are justified because they are at the service of the 'national goals' which are measured in terms of the modern Western set of values. Indigenous culture is valued inasmuch as it is at the service of the technological scale of values. Except for some private recent initiatives, Ayurvedic and Unani medicines, for instance, are revalued because allotropic science now affirms that they may help in certain cases and complement its weak points. India is proud of her engineers and medical doctors who are present all over the world, but not in her villages! Since they earn too little in the villages, they prefer to emigrate.

By and large, India is officially following the model of the Western civilisation, presented as a universal paradigm, thus creating the myth that 'progress' means to get rid of the 'backwardness' of traditional ways, while modernisation calls for the 'hard labour' of a modern (technocratic) society.

Culture is reduced to arts and crafts, cosmetic aids, harmless anachronistic customs, folklore and amusement; culture as entertainment. This is the prevailing myth that pervades the entire world, and not just India. To change the present state of affairs does not mean substituting one system for another, but something much more radical. We are in need of cultural innovation, not aesthetic surgery.

The Tragedy of the Grand Inquisitor[1]

Raimon Panikkar

'We are in Seville, at the time when the power of the Spanish Inquisition is at its height. The day after an *auto-da-fe* in the cathedral square, 'He' appears before a large crowd.'

So begins Dostoyevsky's extraordinary story of the Grand Inquisitor, which falls within his great novel, *The Brothers Karamazov*. People recognise him; 'He' blesses the crowd and there even issue from him a few miracles which fill the people with enthusiasm. Drawn by the gathering, the Cardinal Grand Inquisitor appears, dressed no longer in the resplendent attire of the day before, but only in his coarse friar's cassock. Behind him follow officials of the Holy Office and a surly guard. Grasping at once what is happening, the cardinal orders the man arrested. The crowd, pliant, falls back, tremblingly obedient, to let the guards through.

After dark the Grand Inquisitor enters the gloomy dungeon where 'He' has been locked up, and the famous dialogue begins in which the ninety-year-old cardinal seeks to justify himself by an attack on the Captive's idealism and elitism. The Captive, says the cardinal, respected men's freedom and promised them bread from heaven, but he did not give them even the bread of the earth, nor did he subject them to disciplined organisation. Those who came after him have had to correct that idealism, but now, it seems, he wants to come back and stir them up again. This cannot be allowed to happen.

The cardinal puts up an intelligent, rational defence of the Church's policy, as a result of which there are still Christians in the world. As well as being utopian and ignorant of human nature, the message which the Captive preached fifteen centuries before was also counter-productive. Subject to severe punishments and constant invigilation, the people might now be afraid, but they at least have food in their stomachs and are able to enjoy life, in the way of the animal contentment of the masses.

The long monologue finishes with the judgment with which the cardinal had begun.

'You may as well know that I am not afraid of you. You may as well know that I too was in the wilderness, that I too nourished myself on roots and locusts, that I too blessed the freedom with which you have blessed human beings, I too prepared myself to join the number of your chosen ones, the number of the strong and the mighty, with a yearning to 'fulfil the number'. But I came to my senses again and was unwilling to serve madness. I returned and adhered to the crowd of those who have corrected your great deed. I left the proud and returned to the humble for the sake of their happiness. What I say to you will come to pass, and our kingdom shall be accomplished. I tell you again, 'Tomorrow you will see that obedient flock, which at the first nod of my head will rush to rake up the hot embers to the bonfire on which I am going to burn you for having come to get in our way. For if there ever was one who deserved our bonfire more than anyone else, it is you. Tomorrow I am going to burn you, *Dixi'*.[2]

When the Inquisitor had finished speaking, he waited a few moments for the Captive to respond. The latter's silence weighed heavily on him. The old man wanted him to say something, however bitter and terrible, in his own defence. Suddenly, the Captive comes towards the Inquisitor and sweetly kisses his pallid lips. This was his reply. The old man shook. He went towards the door, opened it, and whispered, 'Go. Don't come back. Don't ever come back, ever!' And he let him go off into the city's dark streets.

That is how Fyodor Mikhailovich Dostoyevsky ends the charming interpolation of his extraordinary novel, *The Brothers Karamazov*.

*

Another five centuries have gone by. Much has changed, but history has its inertia and legend its staying power, dusted off now by an inept amanuensis who has stumbled on the words in the recesses of his reptilian memory. He dares now to write it down without stopping to interpret or evaluate it.

'He' set off down the city's dark streets without stopping to look back, walking at a pace that was steady but not weary. The cardinal followed him with his eyes as if stupefied, his mind gone blank. When he reached the first corner, he who was no longer his captive turned round. The nascent dawn spilled enough light for the cardinal to perceive the gesture, but not enough for him to see his face. But his eyes shone, reflecting the pallid light from the clouds. That reflection from on high struck the Inquisitor's heart. He fell into the chair in which he had sought to judge the Captive, who throughout the interrogation had remained standing as well as silent.

He wiped his eyes, but they were dry. He put his hands on his lips, which still burned, he let his arms fall, gritted his teeth, and closed his eyes.

Unusually for Seville, where the skies are almost always open, the sun was hidden by clouds when the guard discreetly approached the Inquisitor. That same morning he was to sign the order against another heretic. He sent the guard away, the way the powerful do, with instructions to leave him in peace. But he was not at peace, nor did he show it, and the guard left him alone.

He remembered having dreamed. He had dreamed the silent part of the dialogue that never took place. The Captive did not move his lips. It was as if he were inspired by the other side of his same monologue. It was as if he had told them that he had not come to restore paradise lost but to awaken some other (divine?) depth in human beings which showed itself in their longing for peace and happiness, a longing which was quite different from the desire for external success, which was generally attained only at the expense of others.

He still wanted to defend himself from the one who had never, even with his eyes, accused him. Had he been able to bring contentment to those massed ranks of the unhappy?

Surely not. They were dominated by fear and they lived in terror. The masses obeyed and followed. They shouted and even sang when it suited them, but bartering freedom in exchange for contentment had profited no one. They were neither free nor happy.

The nightmare drew from him a sigh. He realised that he too—he who had renounced happiness in order to take up the burden of attaining it for those millions for whom he felt responsible—lacked freedom. He was a slave of duty, his own duty. He began to realise that if some thread of freedom still remained, it was in his recognition that he was not free to turn back. In a few seconds (or maybe more) he recalled how he had believed he had attained spiritual maturity the moment he had abandoned the puerile images and naive idealism of the Gospel. Fifteen centuries of experience showed him that the world could be saved only by power and force. Order had to be imposed from above. The fear of God was very biblical, but that God was very far away and someone had to represent Him. There had to be respect, and for that reason it was essential that they should fear authority. Punishment awakens fear.

And indeed, he was awoken by a murmuring outside which frightened him more than it would usually have done. Normally he slept soundly, a fact he attributed to his domesticated clear conscience. He heard soft voices outside. The guards were waiting just beyond the door for him to sign the order for the next burning at the stake. He banged shut the door of the dungeon and remained as if nailed to the chair in which, before, he had felt himself judge.

He carried on remembering the dream. He had dreamed that centuries had gone by, that they no longer sent people to the stake but continued to condemn them in other ways. He imagined that they sat him on a papal throne and that finally he had the chance to be free. But how now could he declare infallibly that he was not infallible? He dreamed that he asked forgiveness for the past, yet was not free to alter the present. He could only soften the words of documents which the experts passed him to sign.

He carried on dreaming and saw that those crowds he condescendingly looked down upon were neither docile nor pilgrims but tourists and curious passers-by. His churches were empty of true believers; those who surrounded him in the administration of the legacy of the One Who Had Risen Again were motivated by ambition alone and by a faith which lacked both hope and love. His eyes misted over; his lips were dry. He twisted fitfully in his chair without rising from it, but rather remained dreaming or in a dreamy light sleep—he did not know which.

He could not rid himself of those eyes which had so quickly vanished as the former Captive had turned the corner. They did not speak to him of God, or Justice, or even of Freedom, but of Love. His years of penitence and austerity in the desert had required of him exercises in force of will, and of pride that he could attain something which he then knew as self-mastery. He wanted to reach that same One in order to dominate the world, for he knew more psychology and history than He whom he had sought to imitate. Unconsciously, he felt that the Tempter had been right. It would have taken only a little bending of the knee for him to be king of the world, yet he had resisted. Now 'they' had to recover the lost chance. And he shivered when he thought that a feast of Christ the King would one day be established. How ambiguous history seemed to him! The one whom Pilate had presented as the Man did not, in fact, know men—which is why his life had come to an end. They were ignorant of the fact that when the end is truly good the means are always justified. And they had created a theology around this—God the Father using abhorrent and immoral means in order that his Son could redeem humanity.

Almost sleepwalking he tried to lift himself out of his chair. He was overcome by a terrible doubt. But he let himself fall back into the chair, this time dreaming with his eyes open. It was all he could manage.

The doubt was awful. In front of Jesus he felt strong in his knowledge of Man, a strength confirmed in the speech he had made standing before the Captive. But what had not crossed his mind was that he could or should revise his idea of God. He had been told that Jesus was a Jew; and that his brother James was head of the nascent community which had failed to approve the Council of Jerusalem that had broken the Pact with Yahweh. Perhaps He whom Jesus called his Father was not the God of the Jews, and for that reason they condemned him. He was not the Messiah; if had been, he would have saved the world.

He believed in God the creator of heaven and earth, but not in a Someone who did not dare to be called God for fear of blaspheming and who lived in the heart of Man. He believed in a Lord of the Universe, but not in a guest of the soul, in an immanent God whom that Captive incarnated not with his words—he had said nothing—but by his presence, his flesh; perhaps it was because he himself was the Incarnate, not the Spoken, Word. The Captive's silence, which up until now he had taken for weakness, even fear, now began to disturb him.

The guard, nervous now, banged respectfully on the reinforced door. From outside they told him it was time to sign, to say either yes or no. Where was his freedom?

Overwhelmed by the nightmare, he told them to take him to the condemned man's cell. The man's eyes were filled with hate. He was making as if to spit when the blow from a guard knocked him to the ground, his hands still tied to the wall.

The Grand Inquisitor stood up, went to his sumptuous office and signed the condemnation order. Then he locked himself in his room and said he would not be attending the *auto-da-fe*. He could not get rid of those two gazes, that of the condemned man on whom he had violently closed the door and that of the Captive for whom he had opened it without thinking.

History remembers little else of the Grand Inquisitor. It is known only that he fell ill, which was to be expected at his advanced age, and that shortly afterwards he died.

Among his papers was found a sealed folder, apparently the last of his voluminous legacy, with a note in his handwriting which read, 'To be opened only after fifteen generations by the competent authorities.'

The time seemed to have arrived, although the experts did not agree on precisely how to calculate fifteen generations. The more serious question was who constituted a competent authority. A commission was named. There was little agreement among its members, and the folder was passed from hand to hand. It appeared to contain only a few pages.

Without actually opening it, one of the experts had the document x-rayed. He could make out only some incomplete phrases, because the folios lay one on top of the other. For an immodest sum and the promise of indulgences he allowed some copies to reach trusted hands. These are some of the phrases,

'We have made a mistake.... He made a mistake.... We cannot (put it right?).... It would be [worse?].... Perhaps [to ask?] forgiveness.... I do not [presume?] to judge...to give advice.... Nor to [write? show?] my doubts... tragic...humanity...*Nec cum te nec [sine te]...The problem...God.*'

Because he felt guilt at his curiosity, the expert summoned the commission to decide once and for all what was to be done. Most experts did not attach much importance to what they supposed to be the more or less pious and spiritual testimony of an old cardinal. But those who thought it was likely to contain something more important asked for the document to be handed over to the highest authority. After all, the document belonged to a cardinal. This was done.

During a fairly formal audience in which many other issues were aired, when the commission president reached the allotted two minutes he explained the matter to the Holy Father. The Pope received the folder with great interest and gentleness, and handed it to his camerlengo, who carefully filed it along with the hundreds, if not thousands, of other folders which were waiting to be looked over by the Pope. The Fisherman's successor could not speak directly with his audience as Peter had done.

The years went by and the note which accompanied the folder received neither reply nor acknowledgement. Driven by his researcher's eagerness, and because he could not recover the document, the expert travelled to Seville to inquire whether the Grand Inquisitor had left any trace of it. He told the archdiocesan office in Seville that the document was important, that its author was one of the highest authorities of the age.

After he brought a number of influential authorities to bear, and not without the odd other kind of incentive, he stumbled on a document that seemed quite unfitting for a cardinal that was lying dustily in the bishop's palace. The dates matched, and the handwriting was the cardinal's. The pages were already smudged, and were apparently a brief outline of the document. They contained what looked like notes.

Among what could be read were the following phrases,

'We did not understand him. He fascinated us, but fascination has betrayed us before. We believed him to be the Messiah which is why we wanted to learn from his mistake and improve on it. He failed, but so did we.... Call no one 'father', nor 'rabbi'.... Whoever would be the first...(Do not reform from a position of power).... "If you are asked for your cloak...." Power to loose and unloose.... (only to loose? Just us? And the power of forgiveness?). But then, what must we do? But He said, forgive them for they know not what they do. Maybe we can say the same when the centuries pass...We do know what we are doing. Can we be forgiven? Or are we too ignorant of what we do? I remain a diplomat, but sincerely, and for the edification of the masses....

'Major doubt: is the father of Jesus Christ the God of the Old Testament?

'Practically,...write to the Pope. But what can I realistically propose? The reform of institutions? But without them we cannot govern....

'I am discovering something which I had always criticised (because it can be criticised): that the kingdom is inside us. Is that the Church? We have had the bitter experience of the "pure ones" and the puritans who accused us of wanting to serve two masters. We defended ourselves by saying that one of the masters was the greater. But it seems that the Pope is losing power to the Gold from overseas, which does not need an emperor to administer it. Is there some halfway point? But God vomits forth the timid. What God?

'I must think more. But I have no time. Nor can I ask forgiveness. How can I ask forgiveness for what I did in God's name? Did Pope Leo X not issue his *Bulla Exurge Domine*? [This was probably a reference to a proposition in defence of the idea that the burning of heretics is not contrary to the will of the Holy Spirit.] To ask the Pope to repent in this way seems almost a heresy to me—and unrealistic. Perhaps history is not everything....

'I feel ill and tired. Is that an excuse? Is it perchance not Him but we who have failed? He has not said a word to me. Am I to be Herod? Have I lost my life? *Maranatha*!"

A number of unreadable sentences follow, and it appears as if a tear had also fallen on the page. It might equally have been the damp.

On his return to Rome, our expert requested an audience with the Pope, but he Holy Father was ill, and soon afterwards died.

When he later asked the Curia for the whereabouts of the previous Pope's papers, they told him that out of respect for consciences the papers had been burned. To avoid falling into despair, our expert thought that perhaps a Mikhailovich Dostoevsky would help us learn the lesson. But he reckoned it would be taken for an old wives' tale. To console himself, he thought that maybe some unknown saint would put into practice the teachings.

That night he had a dream in which someone told him, 'If they did not listen to Moses and the Prophets, nor will they listen to any wise man, however holy.' When he woke up he thought, 'nor perhaps will they listen to the grand inquisitors, let alone the little ones.'

Many more years went by. The expert too passed away. In his will was a codicil, which read as follows,

'As a Professor of Ecclesiastical History I have seen the Church's demoniac side, and it is precisely this which has led me to value more highly its divine dimension. I read in a 1661 Latin work by Kepler that one should not throw out the baby with the bath water. The dirty waters of history (of the Church) are not the living child (of the sacrament). I believe the child is still alive. I know of the tradition of the Jubilee which the Jews no longer practise and the Christians only celebrate occasionally as if Jubilees were for the powerful alone, without feeling the need to free slaves nor forgive debts. I had an important document in my hands which was burned, but whose embers remain. Perhaps some future Jubilee might declare Constantine and all those who believed in him to be forgiven. I know that the wheat and the chaff must be left to grow together, but almost 1700 years is a long time. Perhaps a change in the millennium could be an occasion for a change of heart. I do not ask for justice; I ask for forgiveness; that we may forgive, and be forgiven.

'But forgiveness demands repentance. For me, who have never had much power, and who am already at the end of my life, this is easy. I am not in a position to judge.

'As a history professor I have seen that the mystery of mankind—and of the Church—is not just an enigma of history. I know that hope is invisible, but as the Epistle to the Hebrews says, out of the invisible comes the visible.

'This codicil does not claim to contain any message. It is an effusion of my conscience.'

The signature is illegible and the date erased.

Translated by Austen Ivereigh

Endnotes

1. From: *Temenos Academy Review*, 5 (2002).

2. Taken from the Penguin Classics edition of *The Brothers Karamazov*, translated with an introduction and notes by David McDuff (1993).

Contributors

Anand Amaladass S.J. is Emeritus Professor of Philosophy at Satya Nilayam, part of Loyola College (Autonomous), Chennai, India.

Bettina Bauemer is Professor of Religious Studies and National Fellow, Indian Institute of Advanced Study, Shimla, India.

Maciej Bielawski is a writer and painter. He teaches literature at the University of Verona, Italy.

Milena Carrara Pavan is President, International Cultural Centre Vivarium Panikkar, Tavertet, Spain.

Fred Dallmayr is Packey J. Dee Professor Emeritus in the departments of Philosophy and Political Science at the University of Notre Dame, USA.

Francis X. D'Sa is Director of the Institute for the Study of Religion, Pune, India.

George Gispert-Sauch SJ is Professor of Theology (Rtd), Vidyajyoti, New Delhi, India.

Grevel Lindop is a freelance writer and teaches Buddhist meditation under the auspices of the Samatha Trust. He is Fellow and Chairman of the Academic Board, Temenos Academy, London, UK.

Clemens Mendonca is Executive Director of the Institute for the Study of Religion, Pune, India.

Joseph Prabhu is Professor of Philosophy and Religion, California State University, Los Angeles (USA) and Member of the Executive Committee, Parliament of the World's Religions.

Oscar Pujol is Director, Instituto Cervantes, Rio de Janeiro, Brazil.